Great Minds of the Eastern Intellectual Tradition

Grant Hardy, Ph.D.

THE GREAT COURSES®

PUBLISHED BY:

THE GREAT COURSES
Corporate Headquarters
4840 Westfields Boulevard, Suite 500
Chantilly, Virginia 20151-2299
Phone: 1-800-832-2412
Fax: 703-378-3819
www.thegreatcourses.com

Copyright © The Teaching Company, 2011

Printed in the United States of America

This book is in copyright. All rights reserved.

Without limiting the rights under copyright reserved above,
no part of this publication may be reproduced, stored in
or introduced into a retrieval system, or transmitted,
in any form, or by any means
(electronic, mechanical, photocopying, recording, or otherwise),
without the prior written permission of
The Teaching Company.

Grant Hardy, Ph.D.

Professor of History
and Religious Studies
University of North Carolina at Asheville

Professor Grant Hardy is Professor of History and Religious Studies at the University of North Carolina at Asheville. After serving two terms as the chair of the History Department, he is currently the director of the Humanities Program. He has a B.A. in Ancient Greek from Brigham Young University and a Ph.D. in Chinese Language and Literature from Yale University.

Dr. Hardy is the author or editor of six books, including *Worlds of Bronze and Bamboo: Sima Qian's Conquest of History*; *The Establishment of the Han Empire and Imperial China*, coauthored with Anne Kinney of the University of Virginia; and *Understanding the Book of Mormon*. His most recent book is the first volume of the *Oxford History of Historical Writing*, coedited with Andrew Feldherr of Princeton University.

Professor Hardy won UNC Asheville's 2002 Distinguished Teacher Award for the Arts and Humanities Faculty and was named to a Ruth and Leon Feldman Professorship for 2009–2010. He has participated in scholarly symposia on Sima Qian and early Chinese historiography at the University of Wisconsin–Madison, Harvard University, and the University of Heidelberg. He also received a research grant from the National Endowment for the Humanities.

Professor Hardy was raised in Northern California and has taught at Brigham Young University, BYU-Hawaii, Elmira College, and UNC Asheville. He lived in Taiwan for two years in the 1980s. He and his wife, Heather, have two children. One of the things he is most proud of is that he has written or rewritten most of the articles on imperial China for the *World Book Encyclopedia*, so his name is in every elementary school library in the country. ∎

Table of Contents

INTRODUCTION

Professor Biography i
Course Scope 1

LECTURE GUIDES

LECTURE 1
Life's Great Questions—Asian Perspectives 3

LECTURE 2
The Vedas and Upanishads—The Beginning 17

LECTURE 3
Mahavira and Jainism—Extreme Nonviolence 31

LECTURE 4
The Buddha—The Middle Way 44

LECTURE 5
The Bhagavad Gita—The Way of Action 58

LECTURE 6
Confucius—In Praise of Sage-Kings 72

LECTURE 7
Laozi and Daoism—The Way of Nature 87

LECTURE 8
The Hundred Schools of Preimperial China 102

LECTURE 9
Mencius and Xunzi—Confucius's Successors 117

LECTURE 10
Sunzi and Han Feizi—Strategy and Legalism 132

Table of Contents

LECTURE 11
Zarathustra and Mani—Dualistic Religion 147

LECTURE 12
Kautilya and Ashoka—Buddhism and Empire 162

LECTURE 13
Ishvarakrishna and Patanjali—Yoga 176

LECTURE 14
Nagarjuna and Vasubandhu—Buddhist Theories 191

LECTURE 15
Sima Qian and Ban Zhao—History and Women 205

LECTURE 16
Dong Zhongshu and Ge Hong—Eclecticism 221

LECTURE 17
Xuanzang and Chinese Buddhism 237

LECTURE 18
Prince Shotoku, Lady Murasaki, Sei Shonagon 253

SUPPLEMENTAL MATERIAL

Timeline 269
Bibliography 301
Credits 313

Great Minds of the Eastern Intellectual Tradition

Scope:

The men and women whose ideas have shaped the traditional cultures of Asia still have an impact on most of the world's inhabitants to this day; therefore, a basic understanding of Asian thought is indispensable for anyone traveling to that part of the globe, trying to make sense of international politics, or interacting with people and products with roots in Asia, or even for those who simply want a fuller picture of the human condition. It is not possible anymore to study only Western thought and history and then claim one knows everything necessary. The world is a smaller place than it used to be, and the variety and richness of the Eastern intellectual tradition is breathtaking.

This course is therefore an introduction to the most significant thinkers in Asian history. It is eclectic, with attention given to influential figures in philosophy, religion, history, literature, political science, and technology, from ancient times until the coming of the West. I will be talking about people and ideas that are relatively familiar such as Sunzi and his *Art of War*, Daoism, Yoga, Zen, Gandhi, and Mao, but also some that are virtually unheard of in the West, though they are all celebrated in their own lands (and deserve to be better known elsewhere).

The lectures are arranged in roughly chronological order as they track the intellectual development of the three major Asian civilizations—India, China, and Japan—with side trips to Persia, Tibet, and Korea. They provide some basic historical background so these great thinkers can be understood within their political and social contexts. Although we will jump from country to country, there are enough cross-cultural connections, particularly those provided by Buddhism and Confucianism, that the course as a whole will tell a coherent story.

After meeting foundational figures such as Mahavira, Laozi, and Prince Shotoku, we will examine the ways their ideas were developed and contested in subsequent centuries. In later lectures, we meet some of the people who first tried to synthesize Western and Asian ideas, usually pairing prominent intellectuals who represent either a more open versus a more critical perspective toward foreign values and the possibility of adapting them to Asian sensibilities. In the last few lectures, we will see some of the ways in which traditional Asian thinkers are still important in the modern world and why all this might matter to Westerners today.

Although the Eastern intellectual tradition is historically quite distinct from the West's, it is not entirely strange or exotic. The basic questions the great thinkers of Asia tried to answer are similar to those that have occupied philosophers and religious leaders in Europe and America: What is the nature of reality? How do we know what we know? How should society be organized? Why do people suffer? How can we find happiness? These questions will provide a constant theme throughout the course. In some instances, the search for answers came through practices such as meditation or yoga or aesthetic experience, but Asian thinkers also employed the sort of careful observation, vigorous debate, and logical analysis that we value in our own tradition. Whatever their sources, the insight and wisdom offered by the sharpest minds of the East often challenge our own assumptions and also provide opportunities for dialogue and deeper understanding. ■

Life's Great Questions—Asian Perspectives
Lecture 1

Is there an Eastern intellectual tradition and, if so, does it matter to people in the West today? In the West, nearly all thinkers and writers knew about their contemporaries and their predecessors; not so in the East, where two major but relatively distinct traditions developed—one in India, the other in China. Both addressed the same major questions that occupied Western thinkers. A person must understand the approach and the answers offered by Eastern thought to be a truly educated citizen of the world.

Asia has a 2,000-year written record of intellectual speculation and analysis in philosophy, religion, politics, literature, history, psychology, and science, from the anonymous Indian Vedas to the 20th-century texts of Mao Zedong and Mohandas Gandhi. Over the course of these lectures, you will meet these and several dozen more of the East's most important thinkers, spanning the entire continent.

The first eight lectures cover the origins of Eastern thought, including the Vedas and Buddhism in India and Confucianism in China. The next 10 lectures cover the major intellectual developments of the early empires of India, China, Persia, and Japan, followed by 10 on the great minds of the medieval era, where we will see how ideas moved from India to China and Tibet and from China to Japan and Korea. After one lecture on the science and technology of premodern Asia, we will conclude with seven lectures on the philosophy of the

Confucius was indisputably the founder of Chinese philosophy.

modern era, including those thinkers who sought to integrate Western ideas into Asian traditions.

So, the first major question we must ask is, is there an Eastern intellectual tradition? The official answer is "sort of." Most scholars agree on the core of the Western intellectual tradition, limited as it may be to the perspectives of the proverbial dead white males. These thinkers and their writings have been tremendously influential in shaping the world we live in, even if most people don't read them anymore. They are the origins of our "mental furniture."

The Eastern intellectual tradition, by comparison, is more diffuse; there is no equivalent to the West's "great conversation." Instead, we find two more-or-less parallel Asian traditions, independent in origins and outlook, although both were influenced by Buddhism: In India, we find a system of thought rooted in Hinduism and based on the idea of *darshana*—insight or understanding. In China, the tradition originated with Confucius and Laozi and focused on the idea of dao, a "way" or "path" to right living.

In many ways, Eastern thought is not particularly mysterious or exotic.

In many ways, Eastern thought is not particularly mysterious or exotic to Westerners. Asian thinkers are interested in the same sorts of questions that have engaged philosophers in the West: What is the nature of reality? How do we know what we know? How should society be organized? How should people treat each other? What is the cause of pain and sorrow? Can it be stopped? How can we find happiness? How can we give our lives meaning? Whether you are still seeking answers to such questions or just curious about others' conclusions, a study of Eastern thought will no doubt enrich your intellectual life. ∎

Suggested Reading

Carr and Mahalingam, eds., *Companion Encyclopedia of Asian Philosophy*.
Collinson, Plant, and Wilkinson, *Fifty Eastern Thinkers*.
Koller, *Asian Philosophies*.

McGreal, ed., *Great Thinkers of the Eastern World*.

Smart, *World Philosophies*.

Questions to Consider

1. How are the major intellectual traditions of Asia connected to each other?

2. What are the most important questions of existence?

3. What is the value of turning to the Eastern intellectual tradition for several independent perspectives on the nature of being human and the meaning of life?

Life's Great Questions—Asian Perspectives
Lecture 1—Transcript

Hello. I'm Professor Grant Hardy from The University of North Carolina at Asheville. It's a pleasure to be with you. And that's not just polite-talk; I'm thrilled to be here. Twenty years ago, I bought the first edition of the lecture series *Great Minds of the Western Intellectual Tradition*. Since I was teaching Chinese history at the time, I thought wouldn't it be wonderful if there was something like this for the Eastern intellectual tradition as well? And that's what we're here for. Our first task in this introduction is to set some basic parameters, so you know what to expect from this course. I'll make a few comments about the content and scope of what will happen—the where, the what, the who, and the when—along with some of the challenges that will arise. Then we'll look at two significant questions. Is there such a thing as the Eastern intellectual tradition? And second, why would this matter to people in the West today?

The where: We'll be doing 36 lectures about Asia: So that's India, China, and Japan, with a few side trips to Persia, Tibet, and Korea. There was certainly intelligent thought and rich cultural development in the Americas and in Africa, but Asia is the one place, aside from Europe and the Near East, that has a long written record of intellectual speculation and analysis—like a thousand years or more.

The what: We're not just doing Asian philosophy. In the West, and particularly within the last few centuries, the term philosophy has taken on a restricted meaning. It's a critical examination of fundamental questions of existence, values, knowledge, and language based on systematic, rational argument. In contemporary universities we sharply distinguish between the discipline of philosophy from religion, politics, literature, history, psychology, and science. Each of those have a different academic department. These distinctions though do not hold up in the pre-modern West, and they are certainly foreign to Asian thought. We'll be doing a little of all of those. Because this course will cover great minds from a number of disciplines, it might be useful to think of what we are doing in terms of the original definition of the Greek word *philosophia*—it's the love of wisdom.

Now the who: I will be introducing you to several dozen major figures in Asian intellectual history. I'll highlight those thinkers who have had the most influence within their own cultures. Over and over, "this is one of the most important thinkers in Asian history"—and that will always be true. Construct a little mental list of your own of famous thinkers from Western history: You might think of Moses, Aristotle, Jesus, Aquinas, Machiavelli, Shakespeare, Newton, Adam Smith, Marx, Freud, Einstein—and all of those are pretty familiar to you. We'll do something similar in this course, but we'll be talking about Asian figures that you would know pretty well had you grown up in those regions.

Now the when: We're going to cover a long time-span, beginning with the anonymous writers of the Indian Vedas beginning about 1200 B.C., and continuing with foundational figures such as the Buddha and Confucius around 500 B.C. We'll have about eight lectures on the origins of Asian intellectual history. Then we'll have 10 lectures on the development of major intellectual traditions in the age of early empires in India, China, also Persia and Japan. Then we'll have 10 lectures on great minds of the medieval era—that term is borrowed from Western history doesn't exactly work in Asia but it's convenient. In this medieval period we'll see how these cultural traditions mix as ideas move from India to China and up to Tibet, and from China to Korea and Japan. We'll end that section with a survey lecture on science and technology in pre-modern Asia.

We will finish with seven lectures on the modern era, where I will introduce thinkers who were instrumental in integrating Western ideas into Asian traditions, as well as Asian scholars who first introduced their own intellectual heritage to Western audiences. That will take us into the 20th century where we'll talk about people like Gandhi and Mao Zedong. We are going to bounce back and forth a little across timelines as we track developments in one region before we move to the next, so a little bit of India and the we'll come to China and we'll backtrack and go again, but I'll help you keep the times and places straight.

As we go through this you'll be aware of three challenges. The first is what to do about Islam, which begins in the Near East and then spreads throughout North Africa, but it also reaches into Asia as well. From the perspective of this course, Islam is a Western religion, with its emphasis on the one true God who created the world, it's monotheistic—actually it's the same god that's worshipped by Jews and Christians, and this god will someday judge the souls of men and women and then consign them either to paradise or hell for eternity. In fact, Islam is an important part of the Western intellectual tradition, with Muslim thinkers playing major roles in the preservation and the propagation of Greek ideas and philosophers like Plato and Aristotle. But it is worth remembering that there are three times as many Muslims living today in Asia as in the Middle East, I mean all put together. In particular, Bangladesh, Pakistan, India, and Indonesia have huge populations of Muslims, especially Indonesia. I will assume that you already know something about Muhammad and the religion he founded, and we will pick up the story of Islamic thought as it spreads eastward through Persia and into South Asia.

The second challenge that we have will be Asian names and terms—there's just no way to get around this. Sanskrit, Chinese, and Japanese are all difficult languages, and they don't sound much like English. I will try not to pile on too many of these foreign words, and I will sometimes spell them out as I speak, but the names are inescapable in a course about great thinkers. There are sometimes multiple English spellings for the same people in China and India. For example, Sima Qian, the great historian in Han dynasty China. His name is spelled S-i-m-a Q-i-a-n. So the *q* sounds something like an English "ch" sound. There are actually two Romanization for Chinese, which is why Daoism is sometimes spelled with a *t* and sometimes spelled with a *d*. It's always pronounced Daoism with a *d*, but there were some linguistic reasons why they used the *t* earlier. Don't worry, I'll help you through all that. Furthermore, in China and Japan, the family name comes before the given name. So Sima Qian's father is named Sima Tan; Sima is the family name. But this is part of what makes a course like this sort of interesting, different ways of thinking about how the world comes together.

Wherever I can, I will try to work in names and terms that may already be familiar to you. We'll talk about Confucius and Buddha, of course, but also yoga, karma, guru, mandala, nirvana, yin and yang, Gandhi, and the Dalai Lama. I will put each of these thinkers and ideas within their historical context and then at the end of the course you will have a good overview of how they all fit together.

The third challenge will be the sheer amount of material that we're covering. Prepare for meaning of life overload. We will be looking at several major religious and philosophical traditions, all of which have long, rich histories of debate, elaboration, commentary—commentaries on commentaries sometimes—as they're thinking about the nature of the universe, how we should live, and what life is for. It's important, though, that we talk about the leading figures all along the way, because intellectual history is cumulative rather than displacive. If you're taking a course in physics, you don't care that much about Galileo; we have new theories that work better than that. In the humanities in Asian intellectual history, Confucius and the Buddha still matter greatly all the way through. We'll go back to the well again and again just as people in these traditions do.

Many of these traditions organize their basic insights into lists and you are going to hear a lot of those, so there's the eight-this and there's the four-that. Don't just tune those out, they matter. Asian thinkers use lists partly because they are generally working within an oral tradition and they're easier to memorize. These are lists that were taught to students. Lists are also attempts, worked out over time, to be clear and comprehensive—so they provide sort of road markers for spiritual or intellectual progress. A lot of wisdom goes in those quick lists that I'll just tick off. I'll try to give them to you a couple of times so you can catch it as we're going.

We're just going to hit the highlights in this course, but you may still feel a bit overwhelmed by the time you get to Lecture 36. That's okay, it's a lot to digest, and you can listen to this course over again. This will give you a good overview, a comprehensive sweep through Eastern intellectual tradition. If you're interested in learning more, it will provide a solid foundation for further study. Which brings me to the first of my major questions: is there an Eastern intellectual tradition? An official answer is: sort of.

I'm going to take a quick detour here. Just a couple steps from my bed is a small bookshelf containing the 60 volumes of the *Great Books of the Western World*. I know the criticisms of this set—that it focuses nearly exclusively on dead white males, that many important works were left out, they could really use commentaries or introductions—but I still really like it. It's a handy collection of the kind of books that I enjoy reading, and I'm always in the middle of one or two, regardless of whatever else I'm working on. I don't know that I will ever make it through the whole set, but it seems like a privilege to listen in to what Robert Hutchins, one of the founders of the Great Books project, called the Great Conversation. These are books that have been tremendously influential in shaping the world that we live in, even if most people don't read them too much anymore. Our common ideas, our assumptions, our cultural conventions came from somewhere often from these thinkers, and I'm curious about those origins. If we can discover the origins of our mental furniture then we are free to argue with those thinkers; we can deliberately choose what we will or won't accept into our minds. Remember Socrates famously said, "The unexamined life is not worth living." I think of that every morning when I wake up and see those two shelves of cute matching volumes. It makes the history of the West look compact and handleable and inviting.

But because I teach Chinese history, I also wonder if there couldn't be a matching set called *Great Books of the Eastern World* that similarly offered a compact but relatively comprehensive window into the origins and development of Eastern thought. I'm not sure that this would be a best seller, but it would be fun for some of us. Nevertheless the results wouldn't be quite the same. A case can be made that there is a Western intellectual tradition, in the sense that nearly all the writers knew about both their contemporaries and then also about their predecessors. They read the earlier books in the set and many of them were responding to or criticizing what previous thinkers had said. As the philosopher Alfred North Whitehead had once remarked, which is a little bit of an exaggeration, European philosophy "consists of a series of footnotes to Plato." That's not the case with Asian thought. There is an intellectual tradition, but it is more diffuse and fragmented than a shelf of books or even a long-running conversation.

Let me give you an extended analogy. Imagine that you're in a big city with three major convention centers and there are three large conferences all going on at the same time. The first will represent India, and we'll put it at the Darshana Hotel. Darshana is a Sanskrit word that originally meant "to see" or "to view" but then eventually it came to mean "understanding" or "insight," particularly insight into the nature of reality. It's a common term to refer to Indian philosophies—they're darshanized—but those philosophies usually include some notion of salvation. They often have religious overtones. Remember that religion and philosophy are sort of bound together in Asian history, especially in India.

In this conference it begins with a plenary session on the Vedas, that is this collection of ancient hymns, and the Upanishads, which are some later texts that explore some of the ideas implicit in the Vedas—ideas about samsara, which is reincarnation; karma, which is justice; and moksha, or liberation. Eventually the audience breaks into smaller groups, and then the six orthodox darshanas, the philosophical schools in India, all argue with each other and they refine their ideas as they argue with each other on rational, logical grounds. There are also two groups who are at this conference that entirely reject the principles laid out in the first session—that is, they reject the authority of the Brahmin priests and the Vedas, the sacred texts, that they're associated with—so these two subgroups break out into their own sessions. These are the Jains and the Buddhists. Occasionally, Zoroastrian and Muslim visitors will wander in and join in the conversation.

A little while after things get started at the Darshana Hotel, another convention center begins hosting a second meeting. We'll call this the Dao Hotel since this is going to be in China. *Dao*, as you may know, is a Chinese word that means "a path" or "a road." It is usually translated in philosophical contexts as "the Way" with a capital *W*—the *dao*. We often associate this term *dao* with Daoists, that makes sense right? But all the Chinese schools of thought, beginning with Confucius, claimed to teach about the Way. In fact, there is a great book on Chinese philosophy entitled *Disputers of the Dao*. Everybody wanted to tell you about the Way. Now in this conference, we're in China now, there are some differences from what we saw in India. There isn't a caste system, Chinese thinkers tend to be aspiring government officials, and the discussions are more focused on the problems of this world rather than on metaphysics or concerns about the next life, or lives as the case may be. But the debates are just as vocal and lively. There are Confucians, Daoists, Legalists, Mohists, Naturalists, and Logicians—we're going to talk about all these people—and they're all arguing about the *dao*.

Some people say that the true Way is the path trod by ancient sage-kings, while others argue that the real Way is the way of nature, and so forth. There is a practical dimension to a *dao*. Chinese philosophers are not just interested in describing the world accurately; making they're definitions very keen and concrete, they are engaged in providing guidelines on how we should live. The word *dao*, which means path, is meant to be followed; it's like you would walk along the path.

And this brings us to the third convention, which will stand in for Japan. This is a more recent organization that is just getting started, so they send some people over to the Dao Hotel to see how they have arranged things there. Participants at this third conference, we're in Japan, have their own set of political and cultural concerns, but they begin as an affiliate of the second group, so we will put them in the Do Hotel—*do* is the Japanese pronunciation of the Chinese word *dao*. It's actually the same written character, same meaning. In Japanese they often borrow Chinese characters; they call them kanji there, and use them as part of their written language. We'll see that a lot of Japanese thought starts in China, not all of it but a great deal of it does.

In this Do Hotel in Japan, it's a smaller gathering, and the attendees end up arguing about issues of particular interest to themselves on their own terms. But there are always a few people going from the Do Hotel back to the Dao Hotel see what's going on there and bringing back ideas and training manuals, even though most of the participants in the Dao Hotel are not paying much attention to what is happening at convention center number three.

One more set of connections. There is a particularly active subgroup at the Darshana Hotel—these are the Buddhists—some of them make their way to the Dao Hotel and strike up conversations with the folks there, starting with the Daoists naturally enough. They manage to attract enough people to their side of the auditorium that eventually the other speakers who are speaking in the Dao Hotel start to adapt their pitches to respond to Buddhist concerns— we see that with Neo-Confucianism. Over time the Buddhists make their way to the Do Hotel as well in Japan, where they become very popular. In the meantime, there are almost no Buddhists left back in the Darshana Hotel, this is a fascinating turn of events having to do with the development of

Hinduism and with the arrival of Islam in India. Buddhism basic[ally died] in the land of its birth, in India.

Now we can return to the question, Is there an Asian intellectual trad[ition?] Not if we are thinking about a single conversation. Indian scholars d[on't] know much about Chinese thought, and vice versa, although Chinese idea[s] are very well known in Japan, Japanese thinkers are not discussed very much in China. But everyone argues with the Buddhists, so indirectly, Chinese and Japanese intellectuals do receive some influence from Indian thought. One way to think about this is to imagine two relatively distinct great conversations. They're is one focused in India and the other in China, and then considerable overlap into Japan and Korea, with Buddhist ideas moving all the way through Asia and even up into Tibet, where Buddhism will be central to Tibetan thought. In the lectures that follow, we will be jumping from one civilization to another civilization, but there are some connecting threads and as we move through the course you'll see more and more interaction between these different regions in Asia.

Which leads us to the next question, Why might all this matter to Westerners today? I've got several answers. The first one is that it's interesting. I'm always intrigued by how different life has been at other times and in other places. It's fascinating to study intelligent, thoughtful people who have conceptualized their lives in ways that are quite foreign to our own cultural assumptions. We'll see several examples of significant ancient texts that were re-discovered in the 20th century, so the conversation keeps going.

The second reason to study the Eastern intellectual tradition is that it's useful. That may be a bit of a surprise, but let me explain. It's a bit of a cliché to say that the world is getting smaller, but it's one of the true clichés. Today, the West is deeply connected to Asia through politics and the economy. You have probably encountered Asian companies, Asian products, and people at your work. You may have friends from Asia, you may have neighbors or family members, you yourself may have an Asian origin at some point in your genealogy. Or you may have traveled to China or to Japan. In any of those situations, you probably noticed some cultural differences. A course like this can help people better understand each other. The ancient Stoic philosophers used to speak of being cosmopolitan, which literally means

1. If you don't know something about Asian history, nd literature, you are missing a great deal of our leal of what defines the human condition. You won't the planet as a whole, the one that you live in. It's r own Western intellectual tradition, but that's not

 a third answer as to why you should care about this. That has with the meaning of life. I know that it's unfashionable these days to care about the big issues of meaning and existence, but they are as important as ever. All of us have choices to make as to how to spend our time, what our priorities should be, what matters most in life. You can just sort of fall into conventional ways of living—you know, you can do what other people are doing, you can do what you see on TV, you can just continue what you grew up with, or you can investigate things deliberately.

What we will find in the next 35 lectures is that, in many ways, Eastern thought is different, but it's not particularly mysterious or exotic. In fact, Asian thinkers are interested in the same sorts of questions that have engaged philosophers in the West. Again and again in this course we'll come back to five basic questions: you ready? First, what is the nature of reality? Does it include a god? What happens after we die? Second basic question: How do we know what we know? It's kind of an odd question—how do we know what we know? What counts as evidence? What is the nature of language and how does that help or hinder communication? The third question, how should society be organized? What is the proper role for government? How should people treat each other? What makes for a successful family? The fourth big question, Why do people suffer? We see so much pain and sorrow around us where does that come from? Can it be stopped? Fifth and last, how can we find happiness? It's a question worth thinking a lot about. How can we find happiness? How should we live our lives? What's worth spending our time on?

Some of you may be seekers—you may still be looking for answers to life's great questions, and if you're interested, you can actually become a Buddhist; you can convert. Or you can take up yoga, or you can adopt Confucian values, or you can devote your life to Japanese art. These are living traditions. Probably more of you, however, have already decided basically what you believe in politically or religiously and how you will spend your life. I'm actually in that category. I'm pretty secure in my own religious beliefs and my social values. In fact, I'm an outsider to all the traditions that I will be talking about—I'm not Buddhist, I'm not Hindu, I'm not Confucian, yet my life has been immeasurably enriched by engaging with Eastern thought. Sometimes my ideas have been challenged and I've been forced to refine what I believe or to think about things from another perspective. On other occasions I have adopted some aspects of Asian thought into my own worldview. Let me give you a quick example.

One day, as I was translating Chinese, I came across the phrase *wàng nián jiāo*, which was defined in the dictionary as "a friendship in which the difference in age between the friends is forgotten." Literally, the phrase means "a forget-the-years friendship." That was a new concept, I'd never heard of it before but once I thought of it in that way I started to categorize all the friendships that I knew, and the term fit some of them. I'd even been in some relationships like that myself. Where there was a difference in age and it didn't really matter so much. Once I learned that phrase, *wàng nián jiāo* this forget-the-age-friendships, once I had a word for it then I started to notice those particular friendships more and I realized what a wonderful gift they can be.

Let me give you just one more example. I learned Chinese when I was living for a couple of years in Taiwan. You learn Chinese, as with any language, by speaking it as much as possible. You make lots of mistakes, and gradually you get better but you need to talk with people. I discovered that as I was out and about if I saw a Chinese mother and some children, I learned how to say in Chinese, "You're children are really cute," which is just a really great sort of conversation starter. To my surprise, when I would say "You're child is very cute," Chinese mothers would invariably say, "Who? This child? This child is ugly, and ignorant, and naughty. Never does what I say." At first I was pretty shocked by this when it seemed to be a pattern. I thought we're going to have a whole nation of children who grow up with poor self-esteem. But that isn't really how it works because all Chinese mothers talk about their children in the same way so any individual child doesn't feel picked on or set apart from his friends. So it doesn't have that same edge to it. But also it comes from Confucian notions of politeness, that what you need to do is to disparage what's your own and then praise what's someone else's. I wouldn't recommend that you try this at home, in America if you tell other people that your children are ignorant and ugly, people are not going to understand, you're children are going to feel terrible about this. But in a Chinese Confucian culture it works.

There is certain wisdom, a graciousness, about being modest about one's own abilities, one's own accomplishments, and family, and then being generous with regard to what is someone else's. I know it sort of goes against American cultural values. When I came back to American from Taiwan, after two years there, I had reverse cultural shock. It was sort of amazing how rude and arrogant Americans were about everything that was great that they did. I had sort of adapted to this more Chinese mode of politeness. In a similar fashion when I would practice my Chinese and try to work on it, Chinese people would always say, "Your Chinese is great!" even though I knew that it was terrible, and I knew that they knew that it was terrible. But it kept us talking.

So in this course, we're going to keep talking about the Eastern intellectual tradition. Because we're outsiders for the most part, we're going to be generous and appreciate of how things are there. I'm going to try present these ideas in the best light possible. There may be some room later on for some critical approaches but to begin with I want you to be able to see these traditions as people from the inside who grew up with them, for whom they seem natural and regular would see them, who love these traditions. I want you to learn to love these traditions, at least to some extant to know what they are like. Then we can see from there what parts might be useful for you, what might feel comfortable, what you may want to incorporate in to your own life and into your own thought patterns. It will all begin with the Indian Vedas. So that's where we will start in the next lecture; I'll see you then.

The Vedas and Upanishads—The Beginning
Lecture 2

Nothing is known about the authors of the Vedas and the Upanishads, the oldest surviving texts of Indian thought. The Vedas are a collection of hymns to an ancient pantheon; the Upanishads contain the collected wisdom of the Aryan sages. Together, they describe the core metaphysical and ethical beliefs that would become Hinduism, as well as many aspects of the Indo-Aryan civilization that produced them.

The Indo-Aryans (commonly called Aryans) were the second great civilization of the Indus River Valley. These nomadic cattle herders entered the area sometime after 1500 B.C., mingling with the descendents of the previous Harappan civilization and eventually taking up agriculture there. Most of what we know about their culture comes from the Vedas and the Upanishads.

The Vedas are collections of hymns and ritual texts that were preserved orally for centuries before being written down between the 4th and 6th centuries A.D. (Hindus today refer to their most sacred texts as *shruti*, "that which is heard.") The most important Veda is the Rigveda, containing 1,028 hymns to a multitude of gods. Most were gods of natural phenomena, with human-like personalities and foibles, like the gods of Olympus or other European pantheons. In fact, the Aryans were originally from a region in the modern Ukraine, and their language, Sanskrit, is related to modern European languages.

The Vedic religion is often called Brahmanism, to distinguish it from its descendant, Hinduism.

Most Vedic hymns were written to accompany rituals, but some address creation, the order of the universe, and the origins of social conventions, including the caste system, with its four major divisions, or varnas: the priestly Brahmins, the warrior Kshatriyas, the common Vaishas, and the laboring Shudras. The Vedic religion is often called Brahmanism, to distinguish it from its descendant, Hinduism.

The Brahmins developed a set of texts called the Brahmanas that specified how rituals were to be performed in excruciating detail; ritual kept the universe running smoothly and ensured human prosperity. Some Indians began to wonder if this focus on ritual and material concerns wasn't missing the point. A few began to live as ascetic hermits, devoting their lives to understanding the nature of ultimate reality through rituals of the mind. These sages' teachings became the Upanishads. The word *upanishad* means "to sit close to," connoting leaning in close to a guru to hear some secret teaching.

There are 13 major Upanishads and about 108 total, dating from about 900 to 500 B.C. Most take the form of debates about principles like samsara (reincarnation), karma (cosmic justice), dharma (right behavior), moksha (liberation from the cycle of samsara), Atman (the unchanging, eternal self), and Brahman (the ultimate external reality that creates and sustains the universe).

The sages' great breakthrough is the equation Atman = Brahman—the essence of you is identical to the essence of everything else. In the West, this idea is called monism. Our experience of being separate from everyone and everything is an illusion. Moksha comes when we realize this and can be reabsorbed into Brahman, the great world-soul. ∎

Suggested Reading

Embree, ed., *Sources of Indian Tradition*.

Kupperman, *Classic Asian Philosophy*.

Puligandla, *Fundamentals of Indian Philosophy*.

Radhakrishnan and Moore, eds., *A Source Book in Indian Philosophy*.

Questions to Consider

1. How can religion give rise to philosophy?

2. Why might reincarnation be an attractive concept?

3. Is there anything permanent in the changing, multi-faceted world we see around us?

The Vedas and Upanishads—The Beginning
Lecture 2—Transcript

Hello, welcome back. We're going to start our survey of the Eastern intellectual tradition in India with two anonymous collections of writings—the Vedas and the Upanishads—and our first great thinker, Uddalaka, who may have been one of the first philosophers in the history of the world. He lived about 800 B.C. and is one of the many sages who appear in the Upanishads. Unfortunately, we don't know much at all about the authors of these texts. Sometimes for our earliest great minds, we know more about their thoughts than about their lives. But I can tell you something about the historical background of these writers, whoever they were.

You probably remember that many of the oldest civilizations started on river valleys. Around 3500 B.C. or so, in Sumerian civilization started in the Mesopotamia, the area between the Euphrates and the Tigris rivers. Then a few centuries later, the Egyptian civilization began on the Nile River. About a thousand years after Mesopotamia, so we're talking say 2500 B.C., another civilization began on the Indus River in what is today Pakistan. For this course, for most of it, I'm just going to talk about India but India at the time is going to be the whole subcontinent. It will include what's today Pakistan, India, and Bangladesh. The oldest civilization in this part of the world, in India, is called the Indus valley civilization, is sometimes called Harappan, after one of its major cities that archaeologists have discovered. The people of Harappa, or the Indus valley, flourished for about a thousand years, from 2500–1500 B.C. and, as far as we can tell from the archaeological remains, they were a rather impressive people. They controlled a vast area larger than Western Europe with hundreds of cities, with extensive trade, and with indoor plumbing—that's always a kind of impressive thing to us today. We don't know as much about them as we would like, because their writing system has never been deciphered. There isn't very much of it so it's hard to work with, it may never be deciphered. It is clear though, that about the time the Harappans began to decline, another people came into India from the West through Afghanistan. These are called the Aryans, or as scholars prefer to call them, the Indo-Aryans.

A quick note of caution before we move on, these Aryans had nothing to do with Hitler. As with so much else, the Nazis took a traditional term and then twisted its meaning so that it's something different than what it traditionally meant. The same thing happens with the swastika, which is an old traditional, actually ancient, symbol in Hinduism that represents the god Vishnu, or Brahma, or sometimes it's the symbol for good luck. So if you go to India today, you may see swastikas there but they have nothing to do with anti-Semitism.

The ancient Indian Aryans, the name means the noble people, were nomadic, cattle-herders who over the course of several centuries migrated from the Northwest into the Indus River valley, down the river. They gradually settled down, took up agriculture, and intermingled with the descendents of the Harappans. We know a lot more about the Aryans because of their literature, which somewhat remarkably, remained unwritten for almost a millennium. It was just passed down orally from Brahma priests who specialized in memorizing and were very good at precisely memorizing.

We're going to start by talking about the Vedas. These are collections of hymns and other ritual texts that began as oral literature—the kind that I told you about, carefully memorized and preserved by the Brahmins, the priests. The oldest, largest, and most important of the four Vedas is called the Rigveda. It includes about 1,028 hymns to various gods. Through them we can learn something of the Aryans' lifestyle, their clothing, their food, their social structure, and, of course, their religion because all of those things are mentioned in the Vedas. The Aryans worshiped a multitude of gods, mostly associated with natural phenomena such as the sun, the wind, air, and storms. One god, Indra, gets a lot of attention because he's the sky god who wields the thunderbolt and defeated the dragon-like Vritra who had been holding back the waters, that is, the rain. So that sort of makes sense that the lightening comes and then the rains come. Let me just read you a little bit from this:

> [He] who slew the dragon, freed the seven rivers, ... cave of Vala ... he, O men, is Indra. ... Even the heaven and earth bow down before him, before his very breath the mountains tremble. Known

as the soma-drinker [and soma is an ancient hallucinogenic of some sort], armed with thunder, who wields the bolt, he, O ye men, is Indra.

There is much that is strange here but there's also some familiar elements. The Vedic gods seem to be organized into a large family, they have human-like characteristics—they get angry, they get jealous, they have favorites, they scrap among themselves, and they can be influenced by ritual and by sacrifice. That sounds a little like the gods of Mesopotamia but even more like those of ancient Greece and Rome or even Scandinavia. Indra seems a bit like Zeus or Thor. There is a good reason for this. The Aryans were an Indo-European people, and their language and religion were related to those of other Indo-Europeans. Indo-European is a language family, the earliest speakers lived around the Ukraine or Southern Russia, and then they spread into Europe and then down into India as well. Just as Romance languages such as French, Italian, and Spanish are all descended from Latin, from Roman ways of speaking, most of the modern European languages, along with those of Persia and North India, are derived from Indo-European. So Sanskrit, the sacred language of the Vedas, is distantly related to Greek, Russian, and even English. As an example, the Aryans worshipped the god Agni, the god of fire. His name is cognate, it's a linguistically similar name, with our name igneous—if you remember your geology or "ignite." Even the word *veda* is related to our word *video*; it's something that is seen, which then came to denote knowledge or wisdom, as in "Oh, I see." In the same way Vedas mean wisdom.

It appears that most of the Vedic hymns were written to accompany rituals and sacrifices, and much of their content is just what you would expect in a hymn book. There's extravagant praise for the various gods and goddesses, along with pleadings for future blessings. But because religion often deals with the great questions of life, there were also hymns that addressed creation, or the order of the universe, or the origins of social conventions. For instance, the god Varuna was thought to know everything, to enforce justice, and to preserve the world's smooth functioning. He sees everything so he can reward or punish it. There was also a hymn to Purusha, a primordial deity who was sacrificed by the gods. Purusha's mind became the moon, his eye the sun, the sky came from his head, and the earth from his feet.

Perhaps most intriguingly, in the same hymn that we see the first indications of the caste system that was introduced by the Indo-Aryans, with its four major divisions. Up at the top are Brahmins, or priests, they come from Purusha's mouth. Then the Kshatriyas were the warrior-rulers come from his arms, because it wields weapons. And then the Vaishya, or the commoners. Those are going to be landowners and merchants from his thighs. Then the Shudras, those are the laborers, the servants, from his feet. This last, lowest caste was descended from people who had inhabited the land before the Aryans arrived and were excluded from the Vedic religion. Outcastes, who you may have heard of, are people who don't even fit into there. Like what do you do with a child who is born from a Brahmin mother and a Shudra father, what caste does he go into? Actually no caste. He's just out of it, the whole system; their lives were truly miserable.

It is not a coincidence that in this hymn, the Brahmins are mentioned first, and they are associated with Purusha's mouth. The priests memorized the Vedas and then they performed the sacrifices that accompanied them had an interest in upholding their social status. In fact, the Vedic religion is often called Brahmanism, to distinguish it from the later related, but distinct set of religious beliefs and practices that we call Hinduism. And remember as I said, even though the Vedas were first composed sometime between 1500 and 1000 B.C., they weren't written down until the 4th–6th centuries A.D. For a thousand years, they're preserved orally.

Hindus today refer to the most sacred revelations, which include the Vedas, as *Shruti*, that which is heard. As opposed to *Smriti*, that which is remembered—that's a secondary class of scriptures that includes the epics that we will be talking about in Lecture 5, the *Mahabharata* and the Bhagavad Gita. There is something magical about the revealed words themselves, as they were recited and spoken aloud. But even hymns thought to embody eternal truths could still be perplexing in many ways.

There's a multiplicity of gods and creation stories in the Vedas. Often times when you're talking about a god, he's the greatest god of them all. And then as I said there's a number of creation stories, they don't exactly match up; they're not consistent. From this comes perhaps a degree of skepticism. There's a famous quote from "Song of Creation":

> Who verily knows and who can here declare it, whence it was born and whence comes this creation? The Gods are later than this world's production. Who knows then whence it first came into being? [Then the answer's going to be:] He, the first origin of this creation, whether he formed it all or did not form it, Whose eye controls this world in highest heaven, he verily knows it, or perhaps he knows not.

How extraordinary that is. That even the god who oversees creation maybe he doesn't even really know how it all works.

Ritual maintains the order of the cosmos; there are sacred ceremonies that keep things working smoothly. That leads to religion as an idea of deal-making; you perform sacrifices and rituals in return for protection and prosperity from the gods. But they didn't always work and when things went poorly, kings tended to blame the Brahmins, the priests, who in turn argued that not every officiator was properly trained. Of course the gods would ignore sloppy offerings. Note that their solution required still more expertise and more royal support; they were not about to undercut their privileged position in society.

The Brahmins developed a set of ritual texts called the Brahmanas, which specified sometimes in excruciating detail exactly how rituals were to be performed. They said the precise amount and quality of the materials used; they gave the precise pronunciation of sacred words. These texts were added to the Vedas with the idea that if the sacrifices were performed exactly, then the gods would be compelled to respond. But these perfected rituals didn't always work either. And there were still others who thought that the whole business of ritual had gone too far. Was religion really a matter of ever-more specialized and detailed rule books? What was the real meaning of the rituals and sacrifices? Some Indians began to devote their lives to religious questions, living as ascetic hermits, rejecting ordinary, material concerns, giving up family life, and shifting their attention from prosperity in this life to the nature of ultimate reality. They compiled their speculations into texts called the Upanishads.

There's external fire that's part of all of these Vedic rituals and sacrifices now that's getting shifted to internal fire; there's a power that comes from asceticism. Self-denial for religious reasons as in fasting, or celibacy, or meditation, which is in some ways a fasting of the mind. This might be a familiar process for you. Catholics have Lent, where they give up something to help focus their attention on spiritual matters. Muslims don't eat during daylight hours during the whole month of Ramadan. So we see these sorts of practices elsewhere. Other people argued, this is still in India now, that the most important thing was not the ritual itself, but it was the spiritual reality behind the ritual. So, to go through a ritual step-by-step in one's mind might be as efficacious as actually performing the actions and words out loud. These teachings eventually became attached to the Vedas as part of the vast oral literature of India. It is in the last stages of this tradition, the Upanishads that we start to see serious philosophizing, as thinkers struggled with the basic questions of death, existence, and knowledge, and that element of skepticism starts to come in.

The word *upanishad* means "to sit close to," and the idea is that you're sitting close to a teacher, a guru, leaning in to hear some secret teaching. The Upanishads, like the Vedas are considered *Shruti*—remember that's revealed oral texts—in this case, they're revealed by sages who have gained insight into the nature of the self and the cosmos and are willing to share that. There are 13 major Upanishads, and some 108 total, dating from about 900–500 B.C. Most of them take the form of a dialogues or debates; they are frequently long, complex, and rather opaque. Because they were composed over a period of centuries, by numerous anonymous thinkers, they do not offer a comprehensive, consistent system of thought, but they do develop some basic principles. Among the most important are samsara, karma, dharma, and moksha. We'll talk about each of those.

Samsara is reincarnation. The idea is that after we die, we will be born again in another body, perhaps a human perhaps an animal, but in a regular cycle of birth and death, rebirth and re-death. This concept is foreign to many in the West, but imagine what might be attractive about reincarnation, or what it might explain. First thing that might come to mind is that you get lots of chances. In this life if you don't get things quite right you get another chance later on. Perhaps this is one reason while in India, often times religious controversy seems less intense sometimes elsewhere in Europe and the Middle East. If you're wrong you'll have a chance to fix it sometime. Think about déjà vu; I know that psychologists give scientific explanations of how this happens, where you feel like you've been someplace where you know you've never been before, or done something that you've never done. I assume though that people have been feeling this as long as people have been having modern human brains. Reincarnation gives you an explanation. Or think about people who have some sort of precocious genius, maybe Mozart, who seems to almost be born with gifts beyond other people. Reincarnation says it's because he developed them earlier on. Or there might be different experiences between rich and poor and you wonder why that might be like, and in reincarnation you get a chance to try them all—even gender is not eternal. Have you ever wondered what it is like to be on the other side of the gender divide? Every male in this life will someday be female, and vice versa.

Another example, or another possibility of something, is immediate friendships. Have you ever hit it off just right away, or maybe disliked someone right away, reincarnation says perhaps you had some connection earlier on or then perhaps some romantic possibilities. I once published a book and in the dedication that I made to my wife, I used the Chinese phrase that means "in all of the worlds and lives to come may we always be reborn as husband and wife." I don't believe in reincarnation myself, but I still think that's about the sweetest thing you could ever say to somebody. If I had to do it over again I would still choose you, again and again.

But perhaps the most important thing that reincarnation gives is some sense of justice. There are disparities people are richer, or are healthier, or are smarter and why is that? Reincarnation says it has to do with what happened in the past the world is a just sort of place.

Next term is karma, which means action. The idea is that all actions have consequences, good or bad. The law of karma says that is that's what will determine your next life. It's sort of a cosmic justice. There's no judge there's no forgiveness there's only this natural eternal law. Reincarnation doesn't happen randomly. If you're good you will be reborn in a better situation. If you're bad you may be reborn in a worse situation as a person, or if you're really bad you may not even be a human you may be reborn as a dog, or as a rat, or as a cockroach even. Animals are in this process even the gods are in this process of being reborn. You may have played the game *Chutes and Ladders* growing up. That's a game that Americans get from England where it's called *Snakes and Ladders*. The British got it from India when India was a colony then. It had to do with reincarnation that you could go up in your next life or you could slide down on the back of a snake if you deserved something lower.

The third term is dharma, which means right behavior, a duty, or morality, in particular caste duty. I guess it could also be justice, truth, or reality. This is the ordinary norm for whatever situation in life you're in. Some people who criticize this say dharma sounds like a tool to keep lower classes in their place. Perhaps, if you're born a servant your job is to be the best servant and just see how it goes until the next life. But also there's an element of compassion that comes because when you see someone that is unfortunate you think that could have been me once, or that might be someone I once loved in a past life. So I'm not sure that religions are good or bad in themselves, they all have potential for kindness and compassion, as well as judgment and less pleasant sort of interactions.

The fourth term is moksha; this is the extraordinary goal. Rather than just trying to get a good next life you want to get out of this cycle of existence entirely. This is release or liberation. The Indians realized that most people's lives are not good, most of them are miserable. Living life over and over gets sort of pointless. It's sort of like, you may recall the Bill Murray movie *Groundhog Day*. The same day lived over and over and over, after a while he just wants to escape. Even the same life, 50, 60, 70 years over and over—it doesn't mean much. If you're looking for permanence, for peace, for freedom from suffering you want to escape that cycle entirely through moksha. How do you do that? One of the key ideas is liberation through knowledge.

I'm going to give you three more important terms, two are Indian and one is Western. Brahman, this is the one underlying substance, the one unchanging absolute being, the ultimate external reality that creates and sustains everything that we see around us. It's beyond all description. The next term is Atman: the unchanging eternal self. It's ultimate introspective reality that can only be perceived by direct experience, maybe through meditation. It's the answer to the question, What am I at the deepest level of my existence? The great breakthrough in the Upanishads is the equation Atman = Brahman, which to the ancient Indians was every bit as exciting as $E = mc^2$, that is to say. Atman = Brahman, means the innermost essence of what makes up you is identical to what makes up everything else. Take for example this podium and myself, what's the difference between us? Sometimes my students would say, you're about as interesting as that, but I'm made up of molecules, those are made up of atoms, those are made of subatomic particles (protons and neutrons) and so is this podium. There is some way in which I'm connected to the outside world, but it's not like modern science in that it's like a machine sort of just materialism. In India this connection, Atman and Brahman, is a spiritual, great consciousness.

I told you three terms, one more: Monism. This is the term from Western philosophy. Monism is like mono, it's one thing. The world isn't two things or many things, it's just one thing. It is an illusion that everyone and everything are separate. With this realization, we can be freed from ego, from reincarnation, and from the suffering that we experience when we are reabsorbed into Brahman, into the great world-soul. Indians say it's like a drop of water returning to the ocean. You can realize that you're not separate, you're the same. Salvation comes from moral purity, introspection, meditation, mystic knowledge of the self, which gives us access to Brahman. That's Moksha, but you're not saved as an individual; you sort of lose your individuality as you come to realize that you're part of this whole.

Now we're to our first philosopher, Uddalaka. There are over a hundred sages that appear in the Upanishads, actually including some sagely women, but to give you a better sense of these texts, I will talk for a few minutes about one of the earliest and most famous of these seers, these people who have insight, Uddalaka. He lives about 800 B.C. In the Chandogya Upanishad, the story is told of Uddalaka and his son Svetaketu. Svetaketu went away to study the Vedas with a teacher when he was 12 years old. He studies for 12 years, and then he comes back to his family really proud of what he learned, a little bit arrogant. His father Uddalaka asked if he had gotten the wisdom that allowed him to hear the unheard, to perceive what is unperceivable, to know the unknown. It's sort of like, if you think you're so smart tell me about this. Svetaketu has no idea what his father is talking about, and at that point Uddalaka employs a series of metaphors and analogies to enlighten his son.

Uddalaka tells him that by knowing one lump of clay, he can know about all clay things, and one gold nugget can tell him about all objects that are made from gold. The idea is that single substance, like gold, can take many forms so you concentrate on that single substance. He talks about Brahman, this pure being, absolute being. Then he tells Svetaketu, "You are that." The boy doesn't quite understand, so Uddalaka compares it to honey, which is made by bees from many flowers, but in the end is simply one, indivisible substance—you can't tell exactly which flower produced that bit of honey that you're using. He continues:

> These rivers, my son, run, the eastern toward the east, the western toward the west. They go from sea to sea. They become indeed sea. And as those rivers, when they are in the sea, do not know, I am this or that river. In the same manner, my son, all these creatures, when they have come back from Being, know not that they have come back from Being. [This is the Brahman.] Whatever these creatures are here, whether a lion, or a wolf, or a boar, or a worm, or a midge, or a gnat, or a mosquito, that they become again and again. That which is that subtle essence, in it all that exits has its self. It is Being. It is the Self, and you, O Svetaketu, are that.

Then Uddalaka goes on to give perhaps the most famous demonstration of all. He asks his son to go get a Banyan fruit and then to cut it open. "What do you see," he asks. And his son replies, "I see some small seeds." "Break open a seed and tell me what is there." He cuts it open and says, "Nothing, really." Uddalaka explains that there actually is an infinitely small, invisible substance there that is the essence of the Banyan tree. And then he says again, "You, Svetaketu, are that." Of course, his point is that Brahman and Atman are one and the same, and after a few more examples, the Upanishad records that Svetaketu finally understood this teaching. I guess this is a great moment in father-son bonding, though from this lesson that he's trying to teach him aren't they really the same? And aren't they really the same with the rest of the cosmos?

Let me give you some comparisons to Western philosophy. Like the Greek pre-Socratic philosophers, the search for what is lasting and unchanging is what matters. You may remember Thales who said that everything is water underneath the surface. And Heraclitus said, no it's fire; everything is a form of fire. There are also differences with Greek philosophy. In Greek thought individualism and competition are unimportant, not so much in India. In India they give much more attention to suffering. There's not very much socialization with the caste system, and they concentrate on ritual instead of politic, which was a major concern in city-states in the ancient Greece.

How about some comparisons with the Hebrews. They're similar in that Hebrews cared about creation and relationship of human and divine. They do in India as well, but in India history is not as central, it's not that you can know god by seeing how he has acted in history. The Indian religion is a little more flexible. Obviously Indian religion, Brahmanism is polytheist, with lots of different gods and goddesses, but it might also be monotheistic from a certain perspective. There is just one Brahman, the gods are all one they just go be different names or they just have different forms. You may have heard of avatars, where a god may take another form and be a manifest on earth. So the Krishna is an avatar of Vishnu. Or India may also be atheist. It may be that it's all just an illusion in the end. There's also a different view of nature from India and the ancient Hebrews. No sharp divide between creator and created animals, and humans, and gods are all sort of on the same spectrum.

Just as the concept of a single creator God, who intervenes in history, and will judge all men and women underlies the religions of Judaism, Christianity, and Islam, so also the metaphysical package of samsara, reincarnation; karma, which is cosmic justice; dharma, duty; and moksha are at the heart of three great Asian religions: Hinduism, Jainism, and Buddhism. But there are some subtle differences in how these ideas are understood in those religions. We'll talk about that in the next two lectures on Jainism and Buddhism. See you then.

Mahavira and Jainism—Extreme Nonviolence
Lecture 3

India gave rise to faiths besides Hinduism, the most influential of which are Jainism and Buddhism. Jainism accepts the basic ideas of samsara, karma, and moksha but also teaches that all material objects have souls and that moksha comes from working off bad karma through self-sacrifice. Although Jainism has always been a minority faith, the Jain principle of ahimsa, or nonviolence, would affect people the world over through the life and work of Mohandas Gandhi.

The founder of Jainism, Vardhamana, was born into the Kshatriya caste in northeastern India in the mid-6th century B.C. It is believed he was raised in luxury and wealth but gave up his possessions at the age of 30 to live as a wandering ascetic. After 12 years of fasting and meditation, he attained enlightenment, became a jina ("conqueror"), and was thereafter known as Mahavira ("the great hero"). Jains revere him as the 24th and last tirthankara—"ford finder"—the founders of their faith. For the remaining 30 or so years of his life, he was a spiritual teacher.

Mahavira's teachings made several significant departures from mainstream Brahmanism. He taught that nearly everything—animate and inanimate—has a soul; these souls are not part of Brahman but are distinct entities caught in the agonizing cycle of samsara. Karma was almost a material quality; cruel acts attracted heavy karma that dragged the soul down to the lower levels of existence. Through an arduous process of self-purification, one could permanently break free of samsara to achieve nirvana, a state of infinite knowledge, perception, energy, and bliss.

According to Mahivira, one could only rid oneself of bad karma through self-sacrifice and refusing to harm other entities. He took this principle of ahimsa (nonviolence) to its logical extreme; by refusing to harm even plants, he eventually starved himself to death at 72.

All Jains take five great vows: no violence, no stealing, no sexual immorality, no falsehood, and no grasping. Those on the ordinary spiritual path practice vegetarianism, monogamy, meditation, occasional fasting, and generally lead lives of material simplicity. The extraordinary path is a solitary, monastic lifestyle, including celibacy, wandering, traveling only by foot (and barefoot), nudity, and begging for food or self-starvation, which is seen as the highest good.

Although Jainism is very strict, there is much to admire in the faith; for one thing, its extremism is voluntary and directed against the self, not against others. The emphasis on ahimsa gives Jains a keen awareness of suffering and the obligation to alleviate it. Interestingly, there is no creator god in Jainism; its ethics are derived not from divine decree but rational argument.

Although Jainism is very strict, there is much to admire in the faith.

The familiar tale of the blind men and the elephant is used in Jainism to critique ordinary epistemology—how we know what we know. Their concept of many-sidedness acknowledges that the world is complex and that there is no single perspective from which reality can be completely comprehended. Combined with ahimsa, this gives Jains little reason to argue heatedly over faith and motivation to agree to disagree.

In terms of our big questions, Jainism asks us to consider whether our happiness depends on the suffering of others and to make an effort to correct this problem. It is an impressive way of life, disciplined, rational, and even noble, but it was too much for many people, which is why Mahavira's followers were eventually outnumbered by those of his near contemporary, the Buddha. ■

Suggested Reading

Embree, ed., *Sources of Indian Tradition*.

Puligandla, *Fundamentals of Indian Philosophy*.

Radhakrishnan and Moore, eds., *A Source Book in Indian Philosophy*.

Questions to Consider

1. When is our happiness directly connected to the suffering of others?

2. What kind of life results when religious principles are taken to their logical conclusions?

3. What is the connection between metaphysics and ethics?

4. Given human limitations, is there ever such a thing as impartial, absolute knowledge?

Mahavira and Jainism—Extreme Nonviolence
Lecture 3—Transcript

Hello again. In the last lecture, I introduced the classical Indian Vedas and Upanishads with characteristic teaching of monism—remember that Atman and Brahman are the same thing, that you're inner most self and ultimate reality are the same thing—along with the terms samsara, reincarnation; karma, cosmic justice; dharma, duty or morality; and moksha, liberation. That package of ideas turned out to be a powerful combination of ideas, fueling Hinduism and the six orthodox philosophies associated with that religious tradition. But not everyone in India was convinced, remember the discussions in the Darshana Hotel. For the next two lectures, we're going to talk about the two most significant heresies. Those are Buddhism and Jainism, they're heresies in that they reject the authority of the Vedas as well as the speculations and sacrifices of the Brahmin priests.

But first, I want to talk about a third heresy, Carvaka. We sometimes think of India as a particularly spiritual place, and indeed most of the prominent thinkers and philosophies have been concerned with religious answers to life's questions. Not because no one ever thought to question these assumptions. The Carvaka school is one of the most irreligious, skeptical systems of thought ever devised, and it comes out of ancient India. It is true that the school did not exactly thrive. The earliest texts, dating back to about 600 B.C., have been lost, but it was influential for some time. From what we can piece together from scattered references and later works, these thinkers posited a type of materialism in which the only things that could be perceived directly, only those things were thought to exist. It had to come through the senses. If it can't be seen or heard or touched, it doesn't exist. According to Carvaka philosophers, there is no soul, no reincarnation, no gods. In fact they said that religion is a fraud devised by men to take advantage of others. Carvaka was also known by the term Lokayata, where *loka* means "this world." What we imagine as a soul or consciousness is simply a side-effect of a healthy body; when the body dies, consciousness disappears. There is no existence apart from a physical body. The parallels with materialistic philosophies in the West, such as Epicureanism, are rather striking. So if this life is all there is, with no purpose or meaning, and if ideas of right and wrong are simply human conventions, that make no difference whatsoever to the cosmos, how should we live? Carvaka philosophers said you just do the best you can. Enjoy pleasures where possible and avoid pain. There's really nothing else to worry about.

So as you can see, huge variety of speculation in ancient India, from profoundly religious ideas of the Upanishads to the uncompromising materialism of Carvaka. Into this world of debate, and discussion, and intellectual turmoil came Mahavira, the founder of Jainism. He wasn't known as Mahavira when he was born. Mahavira is a title that means "great hero." His name was Vardhamana; he was born into the Kshatriya caste, the warrior-ruler caste, in northeastern India in about the 6th century B.C. The traditional dates are 599–527 B.C., though recent scholarship moves this forward by half a century, to 540–468 B.C. This was a time of political and social change—ancient clan ties gave way to regional kingdoms, trade and wealth was increasing, cities were getting larger, and there was a greater disparity between rich and poor that was being noticed by a lot of people. It started to bother a lot of people.

Documented information about Mahavira's life is hard to come by but traditions are that he was raised as a prince. He was in fact the second son of a king and raised in luxury and in wealth. From an early age he was deeply interested in spiritual matters. He was dissatisfied with the life that he saw around him—the increasing inequities, the turmoil, and the warfare that he saw. At about the age of 30, after his parents died, he gave up his kingdom—he has an older brother who's going to be the heir, but he gives up any claim to royal privileges—he gives up his possessions, and his family. For the next 12 years he wandered as an ascetic, someone who denies himself physical pleasures in a quest for spiritual progress. He fasts he meditates until finally at the age of 42, he gained full enlightenment. At that point, he became a Jina, that means a conqueror, and he was known as Mahavira. Jains see him, Mahavira, as the 24 and last Tirthankara that means a Ford-finder. The world is imagined as a terrible river of suffering and misery and he finds a way across it. He doesn't build a bridge. He gets across it and then you have to follow his path. The world Jain means follower of the Jinas, you're going to follow his example.

For the rest of his days, some 30 more years, he taught others what he had learned about the great questions of life. He accepted doctrine of samsara, reincarnation, but with a slight twist, one that makes a tremendous difference in everything else. Rather than believing that only humans, animals, and gods have souls, Mahavira taught that nearly everything is alive. Everything is made up of jiva, living intelligences, trapped in matter. He divided the world of living beings, which is almost everything, into five categories. There are beings with five senses, the regular five senses we talk about. That includes humans and larger animals. Then there are creatures with four senses, they can't hear. That includes flies, wasps, and butterflies. Then you're down to three sense animals, they're deaf and blind. That includes ants, fleas, and moths—I guess moths flying into candle flames made it seem like they couldn't see very well. And then two-sense animals, with only taste and touch. Those include worms, leeches, and shellfish. Then finally, creatures with just one sense: touch. These are plants microscopic organism, earth like dirt, wind, water, drops, and fires. This is by far the largest category. The one thing they all have in common is that they can all feel pain. They're whole existence is to be able to feel pain.

A modern scholar has described it in this way:

> Thus the whole world is alive. In every stone on the highway a soul is locked, so tightly enchained by matter that it cannot escape the careless foot that kicks it or cry out in pain, but capable of suffering nevertheless. When a match is struck a fire-being, with a soul which may one day be reborn in a human body, is born, only to die a few moments afterwards. In every drop of rain, in every breath of wind, in every lump of clay, is a living soul.

Sometimes when I teach my classes about this, I ask if there's anybody who's a smoker and might have a lighter with them. I ask them to produce a little flame and then it goes out, I then point out that that was a soul that was born as a flame and died as a flame. It may be reborn someday as a student of mine. There's another ancient Jain scripture that asks you to imagine the infinite number of times you have been hunted and torn apart when you were a deer; or caught with hooks and nets, scaled and gutted when you were living as a fish; or when you were a tree, you were chopped down, stripped of bark, and cut into planks; or when you were a piece of iron, you were pounded and beaten every day, it says "always in fear and pain and suffering, without a moment's reprieve, life after life."

There is no all-encompassing Brahman; instead there are an infinite number of souls that are eternally distinct that are caught in an endless cycle of agony. But it's not exactly endless, because Mahavira also taught a version of karma and moksha. In his conception, karma, which is cosmic justice, was almost a material quality. Cruel and thoughtless acts attracted a heavy karma, almost like clouds of sticky, dark but still invisible particles that weigh down a soul at the time of death and send it toward the lower realms of existence. Whereas acts of kindness and generosity resulted in a lighter soul, which then can move up this ladder of existence. By acts of self sacrifice you can work off this bad heavy karma so that the goal is to accept suffering for yourself, but not to cause other people to suffer. If you can do that you can eventually be freed all together form matter and from samsara.

So rather than killing mosquitoes that landed on him, Mahavira would willingly share his blood with them and let them fly off. Or while he was wandering around, other ascetics would carry sticks or staffs with them to keep off dogs, but Mahavira according to tradition would let dogs bite him rather than inflict harm or pain on them. Mahavira took this principle of ahimsa, which means non-violence, or, doing no harm. Ahimsa is a key term in Jainism. He takes that principle to logical extreme, eventually he doesn't wear any clothes because even the clothes that we wear come from the cotton or flax or some living creature that has to suffer so that we could manufacture it into clothes that we can wear. He just goes naked he also in the end starves himself to death at the age of 72. You get more bad karma from eating larger animals, less for eating smaller, and even less from eating vegetables but you still get some bad karma so he just eats nothing at all—then goes into nirvana.

Through an arduous process of purification through self-denial and self-mortification, all karma from past actions is exhausted and when a person dies, he or she enters into the state of nirvana, never to be reborn again. Nirvana is not quite like the Christian notion of heaven. It has no material attributes whatsoever, you can't talk about streets paved with gold, but nirvana is described as a state in which a soul has four things according to Mahavira: infinite knowledge, infinite perception, infinite energy, and infinite bliss.

So if everything is alive, and you want to avoid the bad karma that comes from causing suffering to other living creatures, how do you act? Or perhaps more importantly, what do you not do? You don't want to cause suffering. All Jains take the five great vows: no violence, that's ahimsa; no stealing; no sexual immorality; no falsehood; and no grasping, this is nonattachment. In addition, there are two broad spiritual paths available. There's the ordinary path and the extraordinary path. Regular Jains practice vegetarianism, remember you want to eat as low in the food chain as possible. They're monogamous. They limit acquisitions and wealth by charity by giving away extra possessions that they have. They limit their travel. They observe special periods of fasting, of meditation. Sometimes they sweep the ground in front of them so they don't accidently step on little creatures. At times they might wear face masks so they don't accidently breathe in little creatures and thus kill them. They strain their water. And they also don't eat at night, I guess you don't eat at night because if it's dark you may accidently bite something and swallow something living. They don't eat root vegetables, no potatoes, garlic, onions, carrots. That may seem a little strange but the idea there is that root vegetables have very complex souls that have lots of souls within them. You also have to kill them to harvest them, so stay away from those.

By tradition, Jains avoided farming, instead becoming merchants or bankers. They live these very strict lifestyle but the religion survived. They found that as merchants sometimes they did a little better, had a little more prosperity than their Hindu farming neighbors. There still Jains around today, maybe 4–5 million in the world today. They're a little bit hard to count because sometimes they are counted among Hindus. But the honesty of Jains businessmen is proverbial.

I said there were two paths. The ordinary path where you just try to live the best you can get a good afterlife and move up gradually. Then there's the extraordinary path where you want to end this existence now in this life. That's where you would take as a monk or as a nun. No family; no sexual immorality means strict celibacy; they wander about from place to place, they don't get attached to a place, don't own a home; they walk wherever they go; they are barefoot; beg for food and just accept whatever people are willing to give them; they suffer all insults without response; and then occasionally they may choose to follow Mahavira and choose to starve themselves to death and that's the highest good.

Eventually, there were arguments about some of these practices and consequently two divisions of Jains, each with their own version of the Jain scriptures. The Digambaras, the sky-clad monks, the only clothes they wear are air, they wear absolutely nothing. It's only men who do this. They also eat with their hands, they don't use utensils at all. They also say there is no enlightenment for women. A woman will do the best she can but she's not going to be a sky-clad monk. Maybe in the next life she'll be reborn as a man then go into nirvana from there, a moksha. There are also the Svetambaras. Like the monks, they wear white, light clothing, and women can achieve moksha.

Moksha, or liberation, comes at the end of a fourteen stage process. I won't go through all 14 stages, but basically these are steps towards enlightenment. These lists of places you should be make it seem more rational or scientific. It's sort of like physics where you start with a certain types of math and understand them you move in a regular progression. Faith comes in stage four from a flash of insight. You don't adopt this difficult lifestyle out of blind faith but your motivation increasing as you gain a little more insight from progressing along this path of enlightenment.

Jainism might seem extreme, but there is a lot to admire in this. It is a sort of religious extremism but it's directed against one's self rather than against other people. Sometimes in some Western traditions, you show how devoted you are by going out and killing heretics or persecuting others. In this one you your devotion is all directed towards yourself. There is also a tradition that Mahavira ties into, remember he's from the priestly caste—once you become a Jain caste doesn't matter, but he comes from that tradition of conquest. Rather than military or political conquest, which was his class tradition he instead moves toward spiritual conquest—ahimsa (nonviolence), renunciation, and asceticism. It's difficult, you have to be disciplined. Those are all warrior caste virtues. Except for Mahavira this path is open to everyone.

I like the way that it's rational and consistent. The metaphysics leads to ethics. If you believe that the whole world is alive and capable of feeling pain, then the way that Mahavira asks you to live makes perfect sense. The emphasis on ahimsa, on non-violence, is attractive. It influenced Mahatma Gandhi, he grew up in an area where he knew Jains and admired their moral principles. There's a keen awareness of suffering that comes in this religion; Christianity also has a concern for the poor and afflicted, but not to the same extent. Jainism is going to avoid a big problem in many monotheistic religions, a problem of theodicy. How can a god be all powerful and all loving, and still produce a world in which there's so much suffering. In Jainism that's not a problem because the world wasn't created by a god. These little alive beings have always existed. That's just the way it is and he's showing a way to end that.

There's a tradition of literature and scholarship in the followers of Mahavira. The first one is going to illustrate the pervasiveness of suffering and the power of desire to keep souls in karmic bondage. The story is there was a poor man leaves home to find a better life. He got lost in a thick forest; he's hungry; he's thirsty; he's afraid. Then he suddenly sees an elephant, a rather large elephant, this is a deranged elephant that's charging him with an upraised trunk. He turns and at the same time he sees an un sees an ugly, evil demoness who's laughing loudly and holding a sword. So he's caught between the two. Terrified, he runs for a Banyan tree. He tries to climb it but finds he can't climb it because the lower limbs are too far off the ground, so he jumps down into a well that happened to be nearby and hanging on the side of the well to a clump of reeds growing out of its wall. He's hoping to prolong his life even if only for a few minutes.

He looks down below and there are horrible snakes at the bottom of this well, it's an old dried up well, and a giant python that hisses and opens its mouth. The man thinks, "I'm only going to live as long as these reeds hold out," but when he raises his eyes up to the reeds he sees two mice that are gnawing at the roots of the clump of reeds. The wild elephant, enraged, butts the Banyan tree again and again until a beehive that was hung over the well was dislodged. It falls down, hits the man on the head. He is stung by a swarm of angry bees, but then, by chance, a drop of honey from the honeycomb in the hive falls on his head, rolls down his face and into his mouth. He tastes that momentary sweetness and he forgets everything—he forgets the elephant, the demon, the pit, the snakes, and the bees—and he thinks, "this is kind of tasty. Can I get some more of this?"

Commentators explain that the elephant is death, the demoness is old age—this is an allegory—the tree is salvation, which is unobtainable for ordinary men, the well is life and the snakes are passions down at the bottom. The mice are the weeks that eat away at life and the stinging bees are diseases. The honey, of course, represents trivial pleasures, which should be inconsequential to those who understand the whole situation, like how perilous and how tormenting this all is. But those trivial pleasures sometimes seem so irresistible. The point of the story is to give up those minor pleasures, look around and see what's actually happening. You need to escape from the terrors and the terrible situation of this life. Don't be suckered by the little joys and pleasures that may come your way occasionally.

I promised you two stories. The second story is the familiar tale of the blind men and the elephant. It's a story that gets told in some other Indian traditions but it's prominent in Jainism. Once there was a king, he was perhaps as a practical joke, brought together five blind men and asked each of them to touch an elephant and then describe the beast based on his experience. The first man who touched the elephant's trunk, said that it was like snakes. The second one, who grabbed the tail, said no it's more like a rope to me. Then there was one who felt the side of the elephant and said it feels like a wall. The one who put his arms around the leg said elephants are more like pillars. Then the fifth, feeling the ear of the elephant said, elephants are like winnowing fans. The men soon fell to arguing heatedly, since each was sure from his own direct experience that what he said was right. Of course all of them were right, but only in a partial way, from their own limited perspective.

That's a simple enough story, and one that has been retold many times in several traditions, but for Jains it illustrates a sophisticated philosophical critique of ordinary epistemology. Epistemology is science of how we know what we know, the study of how we know what we know. There are a number of Jain philosophers that do a lot of analysis along these lines. They developed the theory of many-sidedness, which acknowledges that the world is complex, that there are multiple viewpoints, each of which may be partially true. Therefore, rather than confidently pronouncing that "X is Y," a thoughtful observers should restrict their assertions to "X may be Y, at least that's the way it seems to me." Or more precisely, "relative to a certain standpoint and to a certain aspect, this object appears blue." They don't say, "This is blue." All judgments are limited and tentative; there is no single perspective from which reality can be completely comprehended.

When a disciple asked Mahavira if the world is finite or infinite, he explained that from the perspective of substance, it is one. Because of that it can be counted so it's finite. There's just one world. It is also finite in terms of its area, which has to do with Jain cosmology and how they thought about the cosmos. At the same time it is infinite in with regard to time and it is infinite as well from the standpoint of modification—given the countless modifications of color, taste, smell, shape, weight, and so on that the world encompasses. So it's both finite and infinite at the same time, it depends on the perspective that you view it from. Mahavira's ideas on the doctrine of viewpoints and the doctrine of maybe are developed much further by his disciples over the centuries, but if you think about it; does it really make sense for Jains to argue heatedly about anything? The principle of ahimsa, or non-violence, is much better served by agreeing to disagree. Truth is relative to a certain perspective. Surely there is some sense in which everyone is right, at least partially, just as there are ways in which everyone is wrong. Why fight over it? It just wouldn't be the Jain way.

Now we come to the big questions. I talked about these in the first lecture: What is the nature of reality? How do we know what we know? How should we live? Why do people suffer? How can we find happiness? And Mahavira gave answers to each of those questions. You might think about how the answers he gave could be applicable in our lives. It's a thought question. Does our happiness ever depend on the suffering of others? I have two children and both of them are adopted. I have gained a great deal of delight in being a father, watching my children grow, develop, and mature but when I watch that and enjoy that I'm always aware that somewhere in the world are two mothers who at the same time are missing children that they gave up for adoption. Now it was a freely chosen sort of thing, I think it probably works out in the best interest for everyone, but there's always that understanding that there's a different perspective there. Think about sporting events; to the exact degree that you are elated when you're team wins someone else is disappointed that their team loses. That's true in all competition. Think of how much competition there is in life—in jobs, in partners, for grades. Think about where the goods that you enjoy come from your clothes, your food, toys that you give to your children—often times they come at the end point of a long production process that sometimes involves a fair amount of suffering for people from a Jain perspective, even for things.

As I said, Mahavira offers a keen awareness of the pervasiveness of suffering and an example of how to escape being complicit in it. Remember that he's a Ford-finder, he shows you the way out of this comprehensive world of suffering and sorrow. You have to follow his example, and his example is based on ahimsa. Mahavira taught a rather impressive way of life: It's disciplined; it's rational, it may even be noble but it was too much for many people. It was just too difficult to actually practice, even the ordinary norm as opposed to those who wanted to become Jain monks and nuns. That's why Mahavira's followers were eventually outnumbered by those of his near contemporary, the Buddha, who taught the middle way, between regular life and what he saw as extreme asceticism. We're going to talk about that in the next lecture when we pick up Buddha and the doctrines that he taught. See you then.

The Buddha—The Middle Way
Lecture 4

> The second major heterodox school in India is Buddhism, which bills itself as "the middle way" between extreme asceticism and ordinary life. Buddhists practice mindfulness—intentional, rather than accidental, karma. The Four Noble Truths of Buddhism lay out both a diagnosis of the ills of the world and a prescription for their cure, known as the Eightfold Path. The aim of Buddhist practice is not to live with suffering but to learn to eliminate it.

Siddhartha Gautama was born in what is now Nepal around the year 563 B.C. Like Mahavira, he was a prince, born to luxury in a time of political and social turmoil. Miraculous legends surround his conception and birth; what is more certain is that, at about 29 years of age, he abandoned his life of privilege for that of a wandering ascetic.

The Buddha (Siddhartha Gautama) experienced the extremes of wealth and poverty, power and humility, and settled on a "middle way" as an ideal.

After six years, Siddhartha found the extremes of the ascetic life were hampering his spiritual progress. He resumed washing and eating but spent the bulk of his time in deeper and deeper states of meditation. At last, he achieved enlightenment, coming to a full understanding of the human condition and how to eliminate suffering. Adopting the title of Buddha (meaning "the awakened one"), he began to teach. After 45 years as a wandering teacher, he fell ill from eating offered food and died, escaping the cycle of samsara and passing into nirvana.

The Four Noble Truths

- Suffering is universal.

- Desire is the cause of suffering.

- Letting go of desire—including the desire for nirvana—can minimize or eliminate suffering.

- The Eightfold Path is the way to eliminate desire: right views and right intention (achieving wisdom); right speech, right action, and right livelihood (ethical conduct); and right effort, right mindfulness, and right concentration (mental development).

Buddhist practice focuses on the process, not the goal. It retains ideas of samsara, karma, dharma, and moksha, but unlike Brahmanism and Hinduism, which teach that people and animals have souls, and Jainism, which teaches that everything has a soul, the Buddha taught that nothing has a soul. All sentient beings are transient; any grasping at permanence ends in failure and suffering. Nirvana is achieved by overcoming the illusion that there is a self.

> **Nirvana is achieved by overcoming the illusion that there is a self.**

A lay Buddhist is expected to avoid greed, hatred, and delusion; to try to practice vegetarianism and avoid intoxicants; and to avoid doing harm through violence, theft, and sexual immorality. Buddhist monks and nuns—known collectively as the sangha—follow a much stricter lifestyle, including celibacy and mendicancy.

The Buddha didn't claim to have any special status or divine authority; his path to salvation was empirical, practical, and available to anyone. It was demanding but not extreme and therefore held a lot of appeal for both his contemporaries and for many people today. ■

Suggested Reading

Embree, ed., *Sources of Indian Tradition*.

Kupperman, *Classic Asian Philosophy*.

Puligandla, *Fundamentals of Indian Philosophy*.

Radhakrishnan and Moore, eds., *A Source Book in Indian Philosophy*.

Questions to Consider

1. Why is there so much suffering in the world? Is there any reliable way to escape it?

2. Are there more aspects to human beings than the familiar duality of mind and body?

3. How stable is our sense of self? Why do we cling to it?

The Buddha—The Middle Way
Lecture 4—Transcript

Hello; it's good to be back with you again. In the previous lecture we talked about Mahavira and Jainism. We are going to today talk about the second major heterodox school in India, which is Buddhism. It bills itself as the Middle Way between extreme asceticism, this was their critic of Mahavira, and ordinary life on the other side. When I teach a course on Buddhism, I usually invite students to try a class assignment in the beginning of the semester. I ask them to try to live like a Buddhist for three consecutive days, which means no injuring creatures, eat vegetarian; no stealing; no sexual activity, including no thoughts about sex even; no false speech; and no intoxicants. For those who say that's the way I pretty much live now you can also go further with three more extra credit assignments: no eating after noon, so 12 noon then you don't eat anymore—have a big breakfast; no entertainments, no music, dancing, performances, perfumes, or cosmetics; and no oversleeping. Those are for monks. Then I say, I don't care whether you find this pleasant or terribly difficult and unpleasant, I mostly just want you to try it out. The point is mindfulness; to try to live your life very mindful of everything that you do. Often times students will try and then they'll mess up and then they'll try again until they get three consecutive days.

I once had a student who pointed out in the original assignment, I had said no accidental killing of insects or creatures and they said that's more like Jainism where you get bad karma for non-intentional actions. Buddhism is very much attuned towards psychology and to the mind; intention matters greatly. According to the Buddha, if you want to kill a fly, say you swat at it and miss you still get the bad karma for killing it, whereas if you accidently kill an insect it doesn't matter so much.

I'm going to talk about the basic principles of Buddhism and its appeal, but first we have to start with a review of the Buddha's life story. He was born in modern Nepal, just north of the border with India, lived about 563–483 B.C. Scholars have sometimes said maybe it was a century later than that. But either way, this was a time of social and intellectual turmoil. He was a contemporary of Mahavira just about and he was also a prince. This is the time as I said in the earlier lecture of kingdoms start getting larger, warfare, there are inequities in society, the caste system is there, and the Vedic religion—Brahmanism, which is based on the Vedas—started to be seen as ritual, it didn't have deep spiritual answers.

The first extended biography of the Buddha is written by a man, Ashvaghosa, in Sanskrit. It's late; it's late 2nd century A.D., maybe 700 years after the Buddha life. The story is that there was a miraculous birth, not a virgin birth. His mother was married at the time but apparently had a hard time getting pregnant and once dreamed of a white elephant that came and entered into her side and she found herself pregnant. The real miracle comes later when he's born, because he's born without any pain or discomfort to his mother what so ever. What a lovely miracle. As soon as he was born he took seven steps, that would have been unusual, and then he spoke. He said: "I am born for enlightenment, for the good of the world. This is my last birth." I'm sure it would have been surprising to his mother to have this young infant start speaking right away.

These miracles weren't added later to the story. In the earliest Buddhist texts that we have the Buddha is sort of more than human it seems. His biography begins before he was born. There are a lot of stories called *Jataka* stories, about previous lives where he did all sorts of miracles. Then he was finally born as Siddhartha Gautama in his last incarnation. Shortly after his birth, his mother died and he was raised by his stepmother who was also his maternal aunt—so his father married his mother's sister after she died. He had a rather unusual upbringing. There was a prophecy that he would grow up to be a chakravartin, which is a great king, or he would grow up to become a holy man.

His father, who was the king, wanted to influence events because he wanted his son to inherit his kingdom and make it more powerful and larger, so he kept him at the palace and never let him out and surrounded him with all sorts of luxuries, music good food and there were women around, and he got married and it was just lovely. But he was very curious what life was like outside of the palace. So he asked to go on a fieldtrip. His father arranged things so that when he went out he wouldn't see any unpleasant things. But the gods sort of interfered and when he went out he saw someone who was old. He said to his chariot driver, "what's wrong with that guy?" The chariot driver said, "That's what happens to everyone if you're lucky enough to live long enough." He went out again and saw someone who was sick and decrepit. Then he went out again and he saw a corpse, the first that he'd ever heard of death. He realized that the life that he was living was pretty artificial. He went out one more time and saw a man wandering, an ascetic, a holy man. He realized it was possible to achieve peace and contentment even if you're living in a world that's full of suffering. He made up his mind that that was the path he was going to take.

At the age of 29 when everyone was asleep one night, he left the palace; left his family as well. It's unpleasant to think of the Buddha as a deadbeat dad, he did have a wife and a son, but from an Indian perspective this is actually a good thing because he's produced an heir for his father. He's done his duty, his family obligation, his dharma and now can move on. For six years he wandered around with other ascetics, other holy men. He practiced meditation, and fasting he was very disciplined—he got down to where he was eating just one grain of rice a day the legend says. But then he came to his limit of his progress and said, "I'm not getting any wiser. I'm just hungry." So he started eating again and washing, and his fasting companion said, "We knew he didn't have the disciple, he couldn't hack it." But the Buddha doesn't care; he vows that he's going to sit under a bodhi tree until he has achieved enlightenment, until he has answers.

He sits down and then he goes into a series of deeper and deeper meditative states, where he sees his own previous lives, past incarnations; he sees the past lives of others and then he becomes enlightened. The word *buddha* means "the enlightened one" or "the awakened one." He didn't want to learn just how to live with suffering, or block it out, he wanted to eliminate it entirely. Once he became enlightened, his first inclination was to just go into nirvana, and then some of the gods induced him to stick around and teach others. His first sermon was taught to his five former companions at a place called Sarnath, in India. You can still go there and see a stupa there that commemorates this great occasion when the Buddha set in motion the wheel of the law; he starts everything going. He spends the next 45 years wandering about teaching, organizing followers. At the age of 80, became sick after eating some food that had been offered to him and he died. He passed into nirvana.

What he taught his disciples, well they weren't his disciples yet but his old friends, were the Four Noble Truths. The Four Noble Truths are: All life is suffering. Suffering is caused by desire; if you stop desire you can stop suffering. You can stop desire by following the eightfold path. Let me give you an explanation for each of those. Life is suffering; that may be the obvious for people who face grinding poverty, malnutrition, disease, abuse, warfare, political oppression, but also for those of us whose suffering comes primarily from interpersonal relationships and health issues—think about where the suffering in your life would come from, hopefully interpersonal relationships and health issues, but life is suffering for those people as well. Partly it's because nothing lasts forever, is one of his insights. So if you say my life isn't all suffering, I would challenge you and say name something that's not suffering. You might say ice cream or spending time with friends and family, or as some of my clever students say, listening to you lecture Professor Hardy is not suffering. Ok, I'll grant you that perhaps. But wherever there are pleasures they're temporary. The more that you enjoy them, the more you will miss them when it ends. Everything comes to an end sooner or later. The Buddha described it in this way: "Birth is suffering; decay is suffering; illness is suffering; death is suffering." That all seems reasonable. "The presence of objects we hate is suffering; Separation from objects we love, is suffering; not to obtain what we desire, is suffering."

Suffering comes from desire. That seems maybe a little strange for us because in our modern economy, there's advertising. The whole point of advertising is to encourage desire in people who didn't have them before and that fuels our economy. In the end, our desires always exceed our resources and leave us unhappy, unsatisfied. One translation of this first Noble Truth, is not that all life is suffering but that all life is unsatisfactory. In some ways you're not going to always get everything that you want.

The third Noble Truth is: You can stop suffering by stopping desire. Don't get attached to material goods or even to people. Even the desire for nirvana, the desire for escaping desire can be the kind of desire that might keep you in this cycle of existence. It's a little tricky.

So (1) Life is suffering; (2) suffering is caused by desire; (3) if you stop desire you can stop suffering, we're to the fourth Noble Truth which is the eightfold path. It says right views, right intention, right speech, right action, right livelihood, right effort, right mindfulness, and right concentration. I know that's a lot to keep in mind, lots of commentaries on how exactly to do all of those, but basically that list of eight can be divided into three parts. The parts are wisdom, right views and right intentions the first two things; the next three have to do with conduct, right speech, right action, and right livelihood—so you can't be an arms manufacturer; the next three are mental development, right effort, right mindfulness, and right concentration. These are not sequential; you can work on all of these things at the same time.

The Buddha has given a diagnosis—the problem is that all life is unsatisfactory, he's told you the cause for this disease, and the cure for it, and a prescription, something you ought to do. He's described it as being like medicine, you have to actually put this into practice. Buddha didn't talk much about nirvana. The word literally means a snuffing-out, or extinguishing, but he focuses on the process rather than the goal. Nirvana is some indescribable state. He asks the question, Where does a flame go when it goes out? And that's what nirvana is like, who knows. But the one thing is focusing on what we can do at this time.

Suffering is caused by selfishness, that is, the desire for our own pleasure, well-being, for our own continuance. The Buddha undercuts this with a twist on the metaphysics of the Upanishads. He retains the ideas of samsara, karma, dharma, and moksha, but unlike Hinduism, where people and animals have souls, and Jainism, where everything has a soul, the Buddha taught that nothing has a soul. All sentient beings, all creatures that can perceive and feel, including animals, spirits, gods, and humans are composite, transient, and soulless. Any grasping at permanence will end in failure and suffering. Enlightenment is simply the realization that there is no part of you that is eternal and lasting. Instead you are a combination of the Five Aggregates: a body, feelings, perceptions, disposition, and consciousness. We'll talk about those in more detail later. All these are changing all the time. Some may outlast your body and be reincarnated in another collection of matter, but if I could overcome the illusion that there is an entity named Grant Hardy, who has needs that must be met and ambitions and desires, then my aggregates would simply dissipate at my death, and I could find—right there's not "I" at the point but something related to me—could find peace and permanence in nirvana. So birth and death and rebirth, and all the suffering that goes with them, in the end comes from ignorance: It's the illusion of self and has needs and can try to find happiness. The solution to selfish desire is the realization that there is no self there.

Some refinements, a bunch of lists here, remember the oral origins of Buddhist teachings. They were passed on by word of mouth for centuries. The three characteristics are: All things are impermanent, unsatisfactory, and not-self. There's no self in there.

The Five Aggregates, or sometimes called the skandas: You are made up of a body, that includes six senses—the five regular senses plus the mind according to the Buddha is a sense organ. It can sense dreams, imagination, and mental states. Then you have sensations that come in that are pleasant, unpleasant, or neutral. To use a slightly more modern way to think about it, you can think about your sensations that are coming in your nerves. The next are perceptions; this is the way you process sense objects and mental objects. You categorize or label them; you say, that's a dog or a house, or I'm feeling rather uneasy now or nervous. Your sensations are coming in and you can only pay attention to one at a time, this is the perceptions. If I mention it now you might realizes that in addition to hearing my voice you can also see whether the temperature is warm or cool, or whether you're hungry or not, or you can feel the pressure of your seat or chair on your rear end, and you only pay attention to some of those. What you choose to pay attention to, that has to do with the fourth of these aggregates, is your psychic dispositions. That includes instincts, habits, impulses, emotions, and personality—have you noticed that some people are happier than others? Or some appear to be angry all the time? I'm not sure that their lives are exactly different but some people just choose to focus on those events that are frustrating or irritating, and it's a habit of mind and it colors their personality. The fifth aggregate is conscious thoughts where you try to plan out and try to grab on to things that are unpleasant and try to escape those that are unpleasant.

All of those five things are changing all the time. There is a Buddhist scripture where a monk goes and talks to the king. The king asks the monk, how did you get here? And the monk replies, in a chariot. Then the question comes up, what's a chariot? Is it the poles, wheels, axle, chariot body? It's not any one of those. So the king said, so is it all of those together? No, you can imagine all of those things laid out on the ground. It's all of those things together at a particular time in a particular orientation to each other. That's what you are like. There's no soul, but there's still reincarnation. There's something that passes. Buddhists say it's like a candle lighting another candle—there's no lasting entity that is transferred. Or it's like a rope, there's no single strand that goes all the way, things are wound up together they end, they continue, but they're joined up together from into something that has some relationship between the beginning and the end of the rope. Or a more modern example, there's an old joke about George Washington's axe that he supposedly cut down the cherry tree with. Someone says, we've got that in our family. It's been there since George Washington's time, we still use it. We've had to change the handle four or five times and we've had to change the axe head twice, but it's still the axe. Is it the axe or not? That' sort of what this is like. Buddhism provides a sophisticated critique of the mind/body dualism; it's just more complicated than that.

There are the Four Immeasurables: The Buddhist worldview has been characterized as pessimistic, but he would have called it realistic. We are able to enjoy luxuries we do because we are unaware of the costs and the future. How much entertainment is escapism? You're trying to forget someday you and everyone you love will die and things will come to an end. But his ideas can also be thought of as optimistic—if we strip away our illusions and ignorance, we can attain the Four Immeasurables, which are friendliness, compassion, sympathetic joy, and equanimity. Imagine beyond all of that illusion itself and that drive to do everything, somewhere there is unadulterated friendliness, compassion, sympathetic joy, and equanimity. Doing good to others weakens the hold of egoism and selfish desire. The religion has kindness as it's sort of center.

Now that you can recite the Four Noble Truths, are you enlightened? No, it's like medicine you have to put it into practice. Buddhism is the middle way between the extremes of asceticism and materialism. It's challenging, but not impossible.

How to become a Buddhist? First are the three refuges, told you lots of lists, you acknowledge the Buddha; the Dharma—remember that meant duty, particularly caste duty in Hinduism. In Buddhism that means teaching of the Buddha; and the Sangha, which is the community of monks and nuns. Then you avoid greed, hate, and delusion, which are the three poisons, or the three fires. What a great list! What are the sources of evil in the world, is there anything not included in greed, hate, and delusion? Then you lead a life, as much as you can, of kindness and compassion. No animal sacrifices that's going to be criticism of Vedic religion, they encourage vegetarianism. And all Buddhists take the five precepts—we're back to the exercise I gave my class: no harming or killing, no stealing, no sexual immorality, no lying, and no intoxicants—which sounds like some of the 10 commandments, with the exception of the no intoxicants, but you don't want to drink alcohol to forget your troubles in life you want to focus on those so that you can escape them.

As in Jainism there's an ordinary path and an extraordinary path. You might live the best that you can and then hope for a better life the next time around you. If you want to be a monk or a nun and move into nirvana directly from this life there are more rules: strict celibacy; no possessions of any kind except for a set of clothes and a change of clothes, two robes, sandals, a begging bowl, razor, glasses; you don't eat after 12 o'clock; no entertainment stuff, no music, dancing, or entertainments; no ornamentation, some monks and nuns shave their heads; and no use of money. They beg for food, it's not like asking strangers for things rather they go around and people recognize who they are because of their robes and they're shaved heads, and they give them things. They actually don't ask, they just accept what's given. They spend their time in scripture study and in meditation. They are about 250 rules for monks, nearly 350 for nuns—it's a little more difficult. The Buddha himself was hesitant to allow nuns into his religion that he was starting. He was perhaps concerned about the vulnerability of single women, or he was concerned with the respectability of this movement that he started and people wouldn't support the Sangha if there were rumors about things going on, but for whatever reason he eventually accepted nuns and of course monks as well. The Sangha, the community of nuns and monks, is the longest continuously existing social organization in the world. Jainism might also be a competitor for that claim, but that's an astonishing thing. Monks ordain other monks, who ordain other monks and that goes back to the Buddha himself. There's a close connection between the monks and the Buddhist laypeople because beg for their food and they give people opportunities to gain merit by giving gifts and then they teach the people in return. It's a little bit like professional athletes. A village might have a monk that lives there. That monk is capable of doing spiritual achievements that are beyond anything you can do. You're cheering him on and trying to help him as much as you can and hoping for the best that he will conquer and go into nirvana. Just like perhaps you cheer on your favorite athletes that are doing things down on the basketball court or football field, who are doing things that you could never do in a million years—okay well maybe in a million years, but not in this lifetime. You're happy to cheer them on and to help them as you can by being a fan, buying tickets and watching what goes on. Think of monks as spiritual athletes.

Why is Buddhism then so attractive to people? Partly because it's not brand new, it still draws on these ideas of samsara, karma, and dharma though there are some redefinitions for how those go. Then this idea of moksha or nirvana, which again is not a place it's hard to even talk about it as a state of being. You can't really say much about it all and the Buddha didn't say much about it. There's also a certain urgency that comes. There's a sermon that the Buddha teaches called the fire sermon, where he says you're on fire. Your senses are burning with passion, desire, hatred, delusion, so you need to do something about that. Notice that he's tying into Vedic imagery, the fires that accompany sacrifice. He says no your whole life is on fire. Buddha was agnostic on many issues. He acknowledged that there were gods but they themselves are in a cycle of birth, rebirth, and death, and they're not all that important for liberation. They can't be enlightened for you, you have to follow the example of the Buddha yourself. There are also multiple heavens and multiple hells, but they're not permanent. You may be a terrible person and die and be reborn into a Buddhist hell, then you'll be there for a while suffering terrible doing all those hellish things sort of like in Dante, but that's not forever. You'll eventually die in the hell and then be reborn perhaps this world as a human being, maybe an animal, whatever your karma gives you.

Another reason that the Buddha was successful in teaching was that he taught in local languages rather than Sanskrit, which was the classical ancient language that the Vedas were written in that the Brahmans used. He taught people in languages that they could understand. Later on those are going to become written down in a language called Pali, which is a literary language that is related to those vernacular languages. The scriptures are sometimes wonderful in Buddhism. Let me give you an example from the Dhammapada:

> The thirst of a thoughtless man grows like a creeper; he runs from life to life, like a monkey seeking fruit in the forest.
>
> Whomsoever this fierce thirst overcomes, full of poison, in this world, his sufferings increase like the abounding Birana grass.
>
> He who overcomes this fierce thirst, difficult to be conquered in this world, sufferings fall off from him, like water-drops from a lotus leaf.

What a lovely image, like water drops from a lotus leaf your suffering will come off. Or describing people like a monkey, running here and there trying to get what they want and it will never work out for them.

Most people are interested in suffering issues and how to get out of that, how to escape that. That's attractive to people. The Buddhist has this idea that the main problem is main problem is ignorance, it's not as in some Western religions where the basic human problem is sin or pride, you just don't know what is really happening. There's a story about Kisa Gotami, who was a young mother who had a son who died. She was of course devastated by this and she went around to people saying, "Can you please heal my son?" People would look at her and say, "Your son is already dead there's nothing we can do." But she was beside herself, so they said, "Why don't you go talk to the Buddha, he knows about this sort of stuff." So she went to the Buddha and asked him to help her. He said, "First I need you to go find some mustard seeds, but I want you to find mustard seeds from homes in where no one has died and I want you to bring those back to me." So she went house to house and said, "I need to do something for my son, would you please give me some mustard seeds?" They would say sure we can help. But she would say, "I need it to be from a home where no one has encountered death." And people would say, "That wouldn't be here maybe try somewhere else." After she goes all over she realizes that there are no homes that are entirely free from death and from sorrow. She realizes that it's not just you, this problem isn't special to just you. She then buried her son and returned to the Buddha and eventually became enlightened.

The solution is knowledge, it's understanding how the world works. There's an understanding of the causes of suffering and there's an understanding for how suffering can be stopped as well. It's a very logical, systematic analysis. It also is consistent enough that the Buddha says Buddhism itself will come to an end someday. He didn't claim special revelation or divine authority, he just figured out how the world was.

One more thing that people like about Buddhism is that it's empirical and practical. In the Kalama Sutra the Buddha said to the people, don't believe just because you hear something, or because it's tradition, or it sounds reasonable, or it's in the scriptures, or because your teacher said it. You need to try it out yourself. So Buddhists follow the example of Buddha like him they have to awake to this dilemma of the world that they are on fire, they become aware of the falseness of ordinary life, and then they have to give it up. It's not exactly like wearing a WWJD bracelet (what would Jesus do?) Christians want to follow the example of Jesus in some way but they don't want to follow the example and suffering for the sins of the world. No one can do that, just Jesus where as with Buddhism you actually follow the Buddha through every step that he took. You become enlightened in the same way that he became enlightened.

His last words as he died and went on to nirvana were, "And now, O monks, I take my leave of you. All the constituents of being are transitory work out your salvation with diligence." All things, whether good or bad, eventually come to an end, including this lecture. But we're not done with the course yet. Next time, well talk about the Bhagavad Gita, a book that that was, at least in part, a response to the challenges posed by Buddhism. See you then.

The Bhagavad Gita—The Way of Action
Lecture 5

> The Bhagavad Gita is a section of the Hindu epic Mahabharata that recounts a conversation between a prince and a god on the necessity of duty. It puts forth the idea of karma yoga: that one should focus on action, not on the fruits of the action. Karma yoga combines the religious sensibilities of the Upanishads with concerns of ordinary life, including obligations to one's family and community. It argues that moral action is only possible if there is no concern for reward or punishment.

The authorship of the Bhagavad Gita and the Mahabharata is uncertain, but it was composed sometime between 400 B.C. and A.D. 200 and influenced nearly all subsequent Indian literature and philosophy, including the work of Gandhi, as well as Western thinkers such as Ralph Waldo Emerson and Henry David Thoreau. It argues that a person can live a spiritually meaningful life without becoming an ascetic and champions a life of action.

Set against the background of an Indian war of succession, the Bhagavad Gita is a didactic dialogue between Prince Arjuna, who is concerned about causing suffering, accumulating bad karma, and destroying his family, and the god Krishna, an avatar of Vishnu, who responds with five reasons to fight:

The god Vishnu appears as the charioteer Krishna in the Gita.

- Atman, the self, is eternal, so no one is ever really killed.

- It is sinful to reject one's caste duty; in Arjuna's case, the duty of a warrior is war.

- Withdrawing from action is still an act, with karmic consequences.

- The source of evil, and thus bad karma, is desire, not action in itself.

- There are several ways one can act without attracting bad karma: jnana yoga, the recognition of the eternal nature of the soul; bhakti yoga, dedication of one's actions to Krishna, who will absorb the karmic consequences; and karma yoga, acting without attachment.

Karma yoga requires a person to focus on their actions without regard for the results of the action. In situations of anxiety or high emotion—such as public speaking, test taking, and so forth—emotions such as fear, desire, and embarrassment can interfere with our performance. Practicing karma yoga allows us to be "in the moment," acting without concern for the outcome. This can improve both our performance and ease our minds; in Hindu theological terms, it also frees us from the karmic consequences of the action.

Karma yoga requires a person to focus on their actions without regard for the results of the action.

When divorced from desire for the consequences, a person's sole motivation for action is duty; thus karma yoga emphasizes social responsibility. It also emphasizes the actor's state of mind, as the same actions can have very different karmic consequences depending on attitude.

Given recent Western history, not to mention much of its philosophy and religion, the idea of ignoring the consequences of one's actions might seem dangerous, if not horrifying. But there is also value in decisive, emotionless action: Think of the duties of a fire fighter or emergency room doctor. Even parents, for example, can be more effective in correcting their children when they can act calmly, without feeling anger, disappointment, or guilt.

Karma yoga is not entirely foreign to Western thought. Jesus, in the Sermon on the Mount, derided hypocrites who prayed or gave alms only to ensure

God's blessings or glorify themselves. Some have even argued that the only truly moral actions are desireless, selfless actions. ■

Suggested Reading

Embree, ed., *Sources of Indian Tradition*.

Kupperman, *Classic Asian Philosophy*.

Puligandla, *Fundamentals of Indian Philosophy*.

Radhakrishnan and Moore, eds., *A Source Book in Indian Philosophy*.

Questions to Consider

1. Is it possible to make ordinary life sacred?

2. In what circumstances can emotion interfere with effective action or with doing one's duty?

3. What are the differences between the way of knowledge, the way of devotion, and the way of works? Do other religions offer a similar variety of paths to enlightenment?

The Bhagavad Gita—The Way of Action
Lecture 5—Transcript

Hello, welcome back. In this lecture we're going to talk about the Bhagavad Gita. Like the Vedas and the Upanishads the authorship is uncertain but there's a great mind behind this book. And certainly the Bhagavad Gita is a landmark in Asian intellectual history. The Bhagavad Gita is a brief section from the *Mahabharata*, which is probably the longest poem in the world. It's about eight times the length of the *Iliad* and the *Odyssey* put together. It was written sometime between 400 B.C. and 200 A.D. It's traditionally ascribed to Vyasa, there's a name attached to it but he's more of a legend than an actual person. He's an important figure early on in the epic, in fact he's the grandfather of the main characters but he's certainly more mythical than Homer. *Mahabharata* is a massive epic; the Indian say that "what is not here is not found anywhere else." In other words all the stories in the world are contained within the *Mahabharata*. The names may be a little bit different some of the details may be changed but it's all pretty much there. In the middle of this huge work a section of 18 short chapters, maybe 700 verses out of 90,000, that's the part known as the Bhagavad Gita—sometimes we'll refer to it as the Gita for short.

This text became an independent text; it was circulated separately from the vast *Mahabharata*. It became one of the most important and beloved works of Hindu scripture, with great deal of significance for Indian literature and also philosophy. We'll see later in this course a number of important figures write significant commentaries on the Bhagavad Gita, people like even Mahatma Gandhi, who for many years read the Gita every day and referred to it as his spiritual dictionary. Certainly the Bhagavad Gita is the Hindu text that has attracted the most attention from foreigners.

Here's the question that the text is trying to get at: Can someone live a life that is spiritually meaningful, in a serious way, without withdrawing from family and society? So you might hear a little bit of criticism of Jains and Buddhists, for whom the ideal life is to become a monk, or that's even true of Hindu ascetics, some of the people from the Upanishads. Leaving family and possessions, wandering about, spending your time meditation, it's not really a viable option for most people, and what if everyone did it? Society would come to an end, families would come to an end very quickly. So the Bhagavad Gita is about the value of an active spiritual life as opposed to a life that's withdrawn from society in renunciation.

Let me talk about two background stories here in this long epic the *Mahabharata*. There are two sets of cousins that are competing for the throne. Our heroes are the five Pandava brothers, the eldest of whom, Yudhisthira, loses his claim to the kingdom in a dice game. His evil cousins challenge him to a match, so they're going to play this game and the winner will get the kingdom eventually. The evil cousins have confidence to do this because there's a bad uncle, he's kind of a cardsharp but with dice who's going to help him out so they challenge Yudhisthira to this game. Because he comes from the Shudra class, that's the warrior class, it's against his dharma to withdraw when someone challenges him directly, so he accepts this challenge. Then he gets so caught up in the passion of the game that he loses everything. It starts with a few small things that are wagered then its double or nothing and then more. He loses not only his possessions but also his kingdom, then he even sacrifices the freedom of his brothers, he wagers his brothers and he loses they become slaves. He wagers himself and then at the very end he wagers Draupadi, who is his wife. Oddly enough she's actually the wife of all five brothers, it's sort of a unusual family situation that's not replicated anywhere else in Indian history, just this one particular family. At the terrible climax after he's lost everything, a jackal cries and everyone in the court recognizes this as a bad omen.

The blind king who's overseeing this decides to grant Draupadi three wishes. Her first wish is I would like freedom for Yudhisthira, the oldest brother who has done all this gambling. The king says, "Alright. What's your second wish?" She says, "I would like for my husbands, for his brothers, to be free as well." And that's granted. Then the king turns to her and says, "What's your third wish, you get three?" And she says, "Nothing. I don't actually want anything more." The idea here is that if you push things too far, there will be consequences. Be wary of desire. Draupadi says, "Greed destroys dharma." You've probably heard stories of three wishes before, have you ever heard a story like this where the third wish is no thanks, I don't need any more wishes?

The two sides work out a deal whereby the Pandavas will go into exile for 13 years, after that time they can come back and reclaim their kingdom. As you might guess, when the time is up, they come back to the kingdom and the cousins won't budge. War is then inevitable. The two groups of cousins, along with all their allies and armies, are set to fight each other in a climactic battle. One of the Pandava brothers, Arjuna he's the great archer, looks over toward the opposing forces and he recognizes their friends and loved ones, his teachers are there and he decides that the kingdom is not worth the cost. He doesn't want to kill those people, he doesn't even want to fight. Overwhelmed with sorrow and anguish, he slumps down in his chariot and casts aside his bow and arrows and says, that's it. He has a chariot driver, who's the god Krishna—actually this is Vishnu who's taken a human form of Krishna, that's accompanying him. Krishna tries to persuade Arjuna to do his duty. The conversation between the two, a man and a god, is what makes up the Bhagavad Gita. As I said, Krishna is an incarnation of the god Vishnu, he's the supreme god who is beyond desire, yet interferes when necessary when necessary in human affairs in human-like form.

Let me just say a couple of words about avatars, not so much to explain the mind of the author of the Gita but to set up some connections for later lectures. Avatars are incarnations of a god or manifestations. There are several lists of avatars of Vishnu, the most famous has 10 incarnations in it. It includes Rāma, number seven. He's the hero of the epic the *Rāmāyan*, which is the second epic in addition to the *Mahabharata* in Indian history. The story of this is that his wife, Sitā, is kidnapped by the demon Rāvana and Rāma is able to rescue her with the help of the monkey king, Hanuman. We will see Hanuman, or something very much like Hanuman again, when we talk about Xuanzang—he is the famous Buddhist pilgrim; a translator who goes from China into India and then brings back scriptures. There are stories told about him where he's accompanied by the monkey king, the monkey god. Incarnation number seven is Rāma.

Number eight is Krishna, the one we're talking about today. Number nine is the Buddha; this is sort of interesting because when Buddhists in India start to have conflict with Hindus, Hindus are able to say, "When you worship the Buddha, you're actually just worshipping Vishnu in another form so it's okay, you can still be Hindus." This is part of the reason that Buddhism is eventually going to die out in India; it gets sort of reabsorbed into Hinduism.

Back to *Mahabharata* and the Bhagavad Gita. I've given you the literary context, but there is a larger historical context to this work. It was a time of increasing warfare and social conflict associated with growing kingdoms, urbanization, more trade, more awareness of the larger world and suffering. It's the same situation that called forth Jainism and Buddhism. The key concepts of the Upanishads—atman, Brahman, samsara, moksha—are merged with Vedic duties and ceremonies. Krishna is an incarnation of Vishnu, but ultimately he represents Brahman—remember that's the absolute ultimate, external reality. He's both finite and infinite, god and ultimate being. There's a dialogue in the Bhagavad Gita between a knower and a seeker, Krishna is the one that knows and Arjuna is the one that tries to find answers. The title Bhagavad Gita means "Song of the Lord." It's a poem, it's in verses. It's about the search for permanence, calmness, and serenity in a world of change.

In the middle of the story is where you're going to start this; there's a lot of names. Arjuna is concerned about causing suffering, about bad karma, and about destroying family. Krishna gives him five reasons why he should fight—though the Bhagavad Gita is not this systematic, it's more literary; but I'll pull out the main ideas. The first reason: Because the atman, the self, is eternal, no one is ever actually killed; they are simply sent into the next phase of reincarnation. "He who takes the Self to be the slayer, he who takes it to be the slain, neither of these knows. It does not slay, nor is it slain."

The second reason that he should fight is because of duty and honor, this is caste duty. Remember dharma, caste duty, this is what Arjuna was born to do, he's a warrior. It is not sinful to fulfill your station in life; in fact it's better to do your own duty poorly than someone else's done well. For example if you're from the warrior caste and not much of a fighter but you're a great potter. It's still better to fight poorly rather than to do someone else's caste duty.

The third reason that Krishna gives Arjuna why he should fight is inaction is impossible. Withdrawing from action itself is a deliberate act. AS he throws off his bow, that's still something. Not making a choice is still a choice. In some ways this is a jab at Buddhists, who say withdraw from society entirely. Krishna is going to say you can't not choose, you can't not act.

The fourth reason is the source of evil, of bad karma, is passion and desire. It doesn't necessarily come from the actions themselves.

The fifth reason he's going to explain that there are ways to act where you can do what you need to do but not get bad karma. There are three ways that are noted in the Bhagavad Gita. The first is Jnana Yoga, the way of knowledge; this is based on the Upanishads. It's the idea that life and death are not real, selfhood is an illusion; monism—remember that atman equals Brahman; what's deepest inside you is the same as the same as what's outside in the world, and in particular Krishna is everything, he's the incarnation of Brahman. Here's another quotation: "He who sees Me in all things, and sees all things in Me, he never becomes separated from Me, nor do I become separated from him." If you're able to realize that oneness of all things you can escape the bad karma that comes from acting in this way.

The second way is the act of devotion. This is going to be developed more fully later in Hinduism, but it's still there in the Gita. The idea is that you can dedicate your actions to Krishna and he in return will take upon himself any karmic consequences. You sort of sacrifice of self, surrender your own will. Rather than spending it in expensive ceremonies and sacrifices, you make everything you do a loving sacrifice to God and everything that you do.

The third way to escape bad karma is karma yoga, the way of works. This is the big idea in the Gita and we'll talk about it later, but the way it works is by acting without attachment. You do something but you're not too concerned about the consequences of your action. It's a form of partial renunciation, you still do what you need to do but you're not entirely invested in it.

Each of these three paths is appropriate for different sorts of people. For Brahmins it would be the way of knowledge. For commoners and women, perhaps the way of devotion is more appropriate. For the Kshatriya, the warriors, it's the way of works, sort of more active. There's a theory behind this. According to the Gita, everything is made of some combination of three qualities, they're called the three *gunas*. These are *sattva*, which is bright and intelligent; *raja*, active and passionate; and *tamas*, heavy and lethargic. In Brahmans *sattva* is dominant, or that intelligent brightness. In Kshatriyas it *raja*, it's more active and passionate. For Vaishyas, these are merchants, commoners, land holders, it's a mixture of *raja* and *tamas*, which is sort of a dark lethargic. And for Shudra, the lowest caste, they're just mostly *tamas*. We'll see this theory of *gunas* again when we talk about yoga in Lecture 13.

The climax of the Gita comes when Arjuna asks to see Krishna in his true form, and the god obliges by producing a terrifying manifestation of his full glory and power, which encompassed the whole universe. Arjuna is humbled, awestruck, and obeys the god's command and accompanies him into battle. With karma yoga the focus is on action, not on the fruits of the action. There's no concern as to success or failure, costs or rewards. One is able to concentrate completely on the task at hand, without over-analysis, distractions, or emotion. When might this be useful? Perhaps for athletes, perhaps you've heard about being psyched out, where you get on the field and you get distracted by thoughts of your parents in the stands or a recruiter, and you can't perform to the best of your ability. Or you may have experienced yourself, stage fright at a piano recitals; or if you've had the opportunity to be in drama perhaps you've forgotten some of your lines, or public speaking, or test anxiety—it sort of breaks my heart sometimes when I look at tests and there will be a multiple choice section in there and a student will have the right answer, then they'll cross that out and put the wrong answer. Sometimes they even cross that out, put the right answer, cross that out and put the wrong answer. I say you're thinking about it too hard, it wasn't a trick question. It might be useful in applying for jobs, a time when you're so caught up in desire that you can't really say the right things, you don't come off as well as you could. There are many situations in which emotions such as fear, desire, anger, embarrassment, or excitement can interfere with one's performance, or where thinking too much can get in the way of acting.

If you act with karma yoga, not attached to the fruits, according to the Bhagavad Gita you'll be more effective. Krishna says, "Thinking of objects, attachment to them is formed in a man. From attachment longing, and from longing anger grows. From anger comes delusion, and from delusion loss of memory. From loss of memory comes the ruin of [understanding], and from the ruin of [understanding] he perishes." That actually sounds a little bit like some of my high school wrestling matches, where I got caught up in desire, then frustrated, then angry when I didn't do well, then I forgot everything, and it was a complete disaster. If you can act in accordance with karma yoga you'll be at peace.

Here's another quotation: "But the self-controlled man, moving among objects with senses under restraint, and free from attraction and aversion, attains to tranquility" Or as it says elsewhere, Krishna says, "He whose mind is not shaken by adversity, who does not hanker after happiness, who has become free from affection, fear, and wrath, is indeed the [sage] of steady wisdom." What a lovely image. To be the sage of steady wisdom, calm, steady, unperturbed, regardless of what might come. Sometimes I feel like it might be a failure on my part that I'm so affected by the weather. When the sun is shining, when it's a lovely day, I feel great. When it's overcast and drizzling, I'm sort of a little bit down but then I think isn't it time to take control of your own life? Why are you so affected by something so external?

If you live according to karma yoga, you can be free from karma, bad karma in particular. A quotation, again: "Forsaking the clinging to fruits of action, ever satisfied, depending on nothing, though engaged in action, he does not do anything." It's sort of a non-karmic action, which may sound a little bit like the non-action from the *Daodejing*, which we'll be talking about in the future.

Karma yoga offers a way to combine the religious sensibilities of the Upanishads with ordinary life that will include obligations to one's family, profession, social status, and nation. Unlike the solitary asceticism practiced by Hindu holy men, Jains, or Buddhists, karma yoga emphasizes social responsibilities and community. Note also the emphasis on mind that might be a response to Buddhism, which also cares a lot about mental processes. The same actions can have very different consequences in terms of karma, depending simply on one's attitude.

Karma yoga offers a resolution of military conquest versus spiritual conquest, remember that was Siddhartha Gautama's dilemma that there was a prophesy that he was either going to be a great ruler or a great spiritual leader, he couldn't be both. But in the Gita, Arjuna is offered both of those. It's an eloquent rebuttal to those preaching the doctrines of renunciation. Ultimately, karma yoga, along with the paths of knowledge and devotion, offer liberation, moksha; union with the god Krishna; and union with the universe, Brahman.

Some implications: What might these ideas mean in our culture? I confess that when I first heard of karma yoga, I was a little bit horrified. Isn't it morally hazardous to ignore the consequence of one's actions? The ideas in the Gita seem a little dangerous. They minimizes the reality of suffering and evil—you're not really killing people, don't worry about that. There's no critique of society, about how the caste system may be unfair. It disconnects actions from their results, and it potentially absolves evil by means of devotion or duty, which sounds a little bit like what Nazis said in World War II, in the Holocaust. We were just doing our duty, they said. But at the same time, if the goals are admirable, there is something to be said for calm, decisive, emotionless action. Imagine a corporation that is struggling financially. Perhaps for the very survival of the company, some workers have to be let go. An effective CEO can't worry unduly about each person. Imagine you're the stockholders, you hired him/her to make tough decisions and if he/she can't, then he's/she's not a real CEO. You need to get someone else who will fulfill his/her role; it's just his/her duty.

Obviously karma yoga is going to be applicable to soldiers, it was the original context, but think also of government officials who must trim costs, or doctors who have to inflict some pain in order to cure, or professors who, in all fairness, sometimes have the difficult job of handing out Fs, or parents who must discipline their children if they are not to turn into monsters. Those people all might benefit from karma yoga, which highlights the dangers of acting with emotion.

Let me take the last example, the one about parents. Sometimes my children need correction. I find this very unpleasant—remember the line "this will hurt me a lot more than it will hurt you?" But it is something that my duty as a father requires. Yet I believe that it is important to never discipline a child in anger, in the heat of the moment. You might have seen this in a public place, like a restaurant for example. Where a couple will bring their children and the children start acting up. After a while they start getting bad parent looks from other people, like why did you bring them here? Why can't you control them? The parents get more and more frustrated and embarrassed and they lash out at the children sometimes in ways that might make you uncomfortable. As dispassionately as possible, as a parent, it's important to enforce the rules. I've tried to do this, I've tried not to let my own embarrassment or ego or frustration interfere in doing what I think is right and fair.

Let me give you another example. This example I'll call Karma-yoga driving. I'm taping this in Washington DC, I live in North Carolina. I actually have friend here, we come up at least once a year sometimes more. When I get ready to drive up, particularly I-95, I give myself a little pep talk. I say to myself, "When you get out on the freeway there are going to be bad drivers there. There are going to be people who cut you off. They're going tailgate. They're not going to signal. And there's nothing you can do that's going to change that situation. But you're not going to let it bother you. You're just going drive as calmly as you can, you're going to focus on your goal. You're not going to worry about being late or all of that. You're just going to get there as effectively as possible." Road rage is never a good idea. Sometimes getting too emotionally involved can be counterproductive.

So when you read the Bhagavad Gita, you will need to make up your own mind. It is valuable or is it in some ways reprehensible? In which circumstances would karma yoga be appropriate or perhaps not so? The ideas of Bhakti Yoga, the way of devotion, and dharma yoga, the way of action, are not entirely foreign to Western thought. There are some parallels. You may remember some of the sayings of Jesus in the New Testament. He once said, "Whosoever will save his life shall lose it, but whosoever will lose his life for my sake shall save it." It's the notion of surrendering one's will to Jesus. Also a notion of disinterested action: On the Sermon on the Mount, he said, don't be like the hypocrites who give alms or fast or pray to be seen of others, "they have their reward." Is what Jesus says. They're just doing it for the rewards, to be seen of others. You should do it for God, without concerns for others.

Some people, some philosophers, have even argued that truly moral action is only possible if there is no concern for reputation, payback, or even for heaven or hell. Desireless, selfless action is the only action that truly counts as moral. If you're less religiously inclined, being totally absorbed in a task is another way to lose one's self. Think about in your life, what kinds of things might be like that? Something where you're engaged in doing something then the next time you look up at the clock the whole afternoon has gone by, you hardly noticed it. It might be reading, writing, figuring out a puzzle, fishing, making music, or maybe constructing something in your garage—whatever it is, it would be some activity that you find so engaging that you can give it your single-minded attention. You don't have to work to really be part of this, the time just seems to zip by. You might even forget to eat. That's a really satisfying mode of action and it can be incredibly productive as well. There's something about karma yoga there too. It might be a problem with multi-tasking or the internet. There are so many distractions, it makes for fewer opportunities for that single-minded, very effective, satisfying action that's quite close to what I think the ideal of karma yoga is.

I like the idea of happiness from internal rather than external causes. The Bhagavad Gita shows a method of self-control that leads to peace in an uncertain world, regardless of success or failure. For these, and for other reasons, partly because it's very short, the Bhagavad Gita has had an great influence outside of India. The earliest translation from Sanskrit to English was made in 1785, just after the American Revolution, by a merchant with the British East India Company. His name was Charles Wilkins. People were very excited about this at the time. In 1809, William Blake, the great English poet and artist, exhibited a drawing that he entitled *The Brahmans*, that showed Wilkins working with his Brahman collaborators translating the Gita. In 1845, Ralph Waldo Emerson wrote this in his journal. He said,

> I owed—my friend and I owed—a magnificent day to the Bhagavat Geeta. It was the first of books; it was as if an empire spoke to us, nothing small or unworthy, but large, serene, consistent, the voice of an old intelligence which in another age and climate had pondered and thus disposed of the same questions which exercise us.

It's interesting he notices that the Bhagavad Gita even though it's so old and ancient and old and comes from such a foreign culture is still relevant. It addresses the same sort of questions that occupy us. In that same year, Henry David Thoreau took a copy of the Bhagavad Gita with him to Walden pond and read it avidly. A hundred years later, in the desert of New Mexico, the physicist Robert Oppenheimer watched the blinding flash and mushroom cloud of the first atomic bomb test. Saw this explosion and remembered two verses from the Bhagavad Gita, which has had studied in Sanskrit, he had an unusual education for a physicist. He remembered the lines, "If in the heavens, the [light] of a thousand suns burst forth all at once, that would be like the [light] of that mighty one …I am death, the destroyer of the worlds." Somehow fits this atomic explosion.

Whoever wrote the Bhagavad Gita was certainly one of the great minds of the Eastern intellectual tradition, and his influence has now spread out of Asia and across the globe. It's amazing that this ancient text, which can be both distressing and inspiring, has the potential to still speak to pressing concerns in the world today about effective action, the integration of spiritual values with ordinary life, balancing personal fulfillment with obligations to family, profession, to society. In my own case, I'm still working on the details of karma-yoga lecturing. We'll see how it goes next time, when we talk about Confucius.

Confucius—In Praise of Sage-Kings
Lecture 6

> Confucius was the first Chinese philosopher and one of the most influential thinkers in world history. His central idea was to address contemporary lawlessness and social disintegration by looking to the sages of the past. He was a strong advocate of education, ritual, and social hierarchies, as well as government that leads by moral example, not the threat of punishment. More than simply a master of aphorisms, Confucius offered the world a comprehensive program for personal ethical development.

Confucius (in Chinese, Kongfuzi: "Revered Master Kong") is probably the most significant thinker in Chinese history, yet he considered himself a failure, having never occupied a significant political post where he could implement his ideas—although several of his students did, and within a few centuries of his death, most Chinese people had accepted his analysis of what was wrong with the world and how to remedy it.

Confucius, like the Buddha and Mahavira, lived in a time of political turmoil, social breakdown, and tremendous suffering. Born around 551 B.C. to a minor, impoverished aristocratic family, he received a good education. He spent most of his life as a teacher of culture, ritual, ethics, and statecraft, with only a brief, unsuccessful tenure as a government magistrate.

Confucius's answer to his world's problems was a return to the morals of the past.

Confucius did not write down his own ideas, but his followers collected them after his death in a volume called the *Analects* (Chinese *lunyu*, "conversations"), a jumbled collection of stories, sayings, and answers (sometimes without questions). The advice is practical and concrete but not systematic. A common theme is to practice *lin*, or reciprocity—as a certain Western thinker would later say, to treat others as we wish to be treated.

Confucius's answer to his world's problems was a return to the morals of the past; ethics come from sages, not revelation or innovation.

Values of the *Analects*

- Education, especially in the classic texts.
- Moral behavior of those in government.
- Proper performance of ritual, including basic etiquette.
- Individual effort at morality, including the practice of *ren* (kindness or benevolence).
- Awareness of one's place in the social hierarchy.

To Confucius, all relationships were unequal—ruler/subject, parent/child, husband/wife—and obedience to authority was absolutely crucial. To those in the modern West, this focus on hierarchy might smack of oppression, but Confucius's point was that there are no autonomous individuals; each of us exists within a web of relationships that defines our identities. As in the Bhagavad Gita, duty to one's station and community is a prime moral virtue.

The Confucian model for government, unsurprisingly, is the family, the relationships where we first learn the ethics and traditions we carry into the wider world; even in modern China, *guanxi* (relationships) are central to the function of business and bureaucracy. Confucian rulers lead by example and enforce the law not through the threat of punishment but by instilling proper attitudes in its citizens. Similarly, Confucian ethics are not based on the promise of individual reward—earthly or heavenly—but on a desire to benefit humankind in general.

Any system that emphasizes knowing one's place can be turned to oppressive ends, but this is a gross distortion of Confucianism. In the web of relationships, respect and *ren* move in both directions. Confucius didn't advocate rules for rules' sake but to better society and ensure individual happiness through mutual respect, personal responsibility, and striving for wisdom and justice. ∎

Suggested Reading

Chan, *A Source Book in Chinese Philosophy*.

Chin, *The Authentic Confucius*.

Confucius, *The Analects of Confucius*.

De Bary and Bloom, eds., *Sources of Chinese Tradition*.

Ivanhoe and Van Norden, eds., *Readings in Classical Chinese Philosophy*.

Kupperman, *Classic Asian Philosophy*.

Lieberthal, *Governing China*.

Reid, *Confucius Lives Next Door*.

Questions to Consider

1. What are the keys to social harmony? How can morality best be taught?

2. To what extent is a person's life defined by his or her relationships? When might hierarchical distinctions have value?

3. What role do music and ritual play in a full life?

Confucius—In Praise of Sage-Kings
Lecture 6—Transcript

Hello again. Are you ready for a little change of pace? We've been following events at the Darshana Hotel for some time, up into the 1st century A.D. We're now going shift our focus to China, the Dao Hotel, and then jump back in time to the beginning of the conference going on there. The first Chinese philosopher was Confucius, who like the Bhagavad Gita was concerned with community and social obligations, but he comes at these issues from a very different historical background. Confucius may be some body that you've heard of, but perhaps do not know a lot about. He lived about 500 B.C.; contemporary of Buddha, about 100 years before Plato in ancient Greece. Confucius was probably the most significant thinker in Chinese history, which would have come as a surprise to Confucius himself. When he died at the age of 73, he thought about himself as a failure. His main ambition in life was to serve in government, to put his ideas into action. He never really held a significant position, and as a fall back he became a teacher. It's sort of sad that he's a failure in life and then he becomes a teacher. But apparently he was a pretty good teacher because some of his students got jobs, which may have been a little bittersweet for him. He was happy for his students but at the same time reminded of his own failures at what he really wanted to do.

Confucius, like Socrates or Jesus, never wrote anything himself. But after his death his disciples put together a collection of his teachings called the *Analects*, which became the most influential book ever written in the Chinese language. It was studied, memorized, and analyzed for 2,500 years by students in China, Japan, and Korea. It's undoubtedly one of the most influential books, not just in China's history, but in world history. It's very quotable; in this lecture you'll be hearing me give a lot of quotes from the Confucius *Analects*.

Within a few centuries of his death most Chinese people had adopted his analysis of what was wrong with the world and how best to remedy it. Confucianism is not just a philosophy it's more like a religion in that it provides a comprehensive world view. It provides meaning in life, specific guidelines for living. Today in East Asia people live by Confucian principles even if they're not exactly sure where they come from.

Chinese history divided into dynasties. Confucius lived toward the end of one of the longest of those. It's called the Zhou dynasty. It was founded some 500 years before he was born, about 1045 B.C. It had followed the Shang dynasty. It became older and corrupt, lost the mandate of heaven. There were some kings, kings Wen and Wu, who took over and started the Zhou dynasty. These are sage-kings.

The kingdom of China was much too large for any single person to rule over. So they ended up with a system sort of like feudalism in the medieval West. They divided the territory up into lots of units and put some rulers in each local area, like junior kings. They have lots of relatives, those are the people you can trust to make your junior rulers. And those relatives had lots of sons, each of whom deserved some part of the kingdom. Eventually some 200 kingdoms or little states all over china, semi-autonomous but related by blood, sometimes distantly, to the Zhou kings.

Over time those ties of kinship started to weaken. And these states started to compete with each other for resources and territory. By competition I mean warfare. They're starting to fight with each other and take each other over, to annex each other. There is a period called the Spring and Autumn Era from about 722–479 B.C. Confucius lives at the very end of this period. In that 240 years the number of states goes from about 100, already been reduced from their height, to 40. You can see how this process is going. In the same 240 years, there were maybe 500 battles between states, 100 civil wars. It is a time of violence and increasing civil disorder; there are assassinations, murders, ministerial who stage coups and take over, and a lot of deadly intrigues among aristocratic families. Battle was no longer elegant competition among aristocrats fighting in chariots, sort of like in the Iliad or the *Mahabharata* in the Gita, but large-scale slaughter that came as huge infantries of commoners were put in the field to fight with each other.

The old ceremonies were treaties that were sealed by killing a sacrificial animal, then smearing its blood on ones lips while swearing an oath to the gods to uphold the provisions of that treaty. But the gods were the ancestors of the weakened house of Zhou, remember that ancestor worship is the fundamental religion in China, people began to speak of *kóu xĭe wèi gān*, which means to "break an oath while blood is still wet on one's lips." You just couldn't trust anyone; things are falling apart moral confusion, universal distrust, warfare, and of course tremendous suffering. This is the world that Confucius is born into.

We don't know a lot about his life, the first biography was written 400 years after his death but from the *Analects* we can piece together some information. He was born in 551 B.C., to the lowest level of aristocracy, in state of Lu. It's a small state but it has a cultural heritage that goes back to the earlier Shang dynasty. It's now in Shandong peninsula in China in the northeast of china. His name was Kong Qiu. The Jesuits, missionaries coming in in the 16th century coined the term Confucius, which is a Latinized form of Kong Fuzi, which means Revered Master Kong, which is a name they picked up somewhere. Chinese don't actually use that term very much, they just call him Kongzi, Master Kong. We'll call him Confucius. His father died when he was three, he was raised by his mother. They were a poor family but he did manage to received an education but not a job. He once said, "If there were any of the princes who would employ me, in the course of twelve months, I should have done something considerable. In three years, the government would be perfected." But that's wishful thinking, because he didn't really get a job. That's the kind of thing you might say at an interview.

At about 30, he became a teacher of traditional culture, ritual, ethics, and statecraft. At the age of 51, he was employed as magistrate, for at first a minister of public works then a minister of justice. It looked like a career was starting but then he had a falling out with the ruler. He left his native state Lu at age 55, wandered around from state to state with his students looking for jobs, looking for someone to employ him. He was turned down by everyone, dozens of rulers in multiple states. He finally returned back home at the age of 68 and then he died a few years later in 479 B.C. Lived into early 70s, but by that time his adult son had died, as had his favorite disciple—on that occasion he said, "Alas, Heaven has destroyed me." Confucius probably thought that was the end of it.

But we have a book. A book called the *Analects*. That's the Greek word for selections; the Chinese term *lunyu* is more like conversations. You can imagine after his death, his students sitting around saying, do you remember when Confucius said this or he said that. Then they said, we're getting older we should write that down before it's all lost with us. So they put together this book. It consists of 500 brief quotations or anecdotes that are arranged into 20 books. They call them books but they're chapter length books. The whole thing isn't that long. Scholars today still argue about how this book *Analects* came together. It was probably put together over several centuries, there were additions and revisions but for our purposes, take the collection as a whole, as it was known in imperial China. You can read it in an afternoon, it's not that long. When you open it up you'll find this odd, fortune-cookie kind of format. Let me give you some examples.

The very famous first lines of it say, "The Master said," (when they're talking about the Master it's always Confucius—"The Master said, Is it not a pleasure, having learned something, to try it out at due intervals? Is it not a joy to have friends come from afar? Is it not gentlemanly not to take offence when other to fail to appreciate your abilities?" He had some personal experience with the last, he felt unappreciated. These are rhetorical questions, the answers going to be yes to these. But they do focus one's attention. Even now when I have friends that show up at my house they pull up into the driveway after a long trip, I think is it not a joy to have friends come from afar? Of course it is.

Another quotation, these are almost at random: "The Master said, 'Learning without thought is pointless. Thought without learning is dangerous.' " Let's do another one, "The Master said, 'Zilu, shall I teach you what knowledge is? When you know a thing, to hold that you know it; and when you do not know a thing, to allow that you do not know it;—this is knowledge.' " He Plato said something sort of like that, to know what you don't know is the beginning of the knowledge. These are very practical and concrete sorts of suggestions rather than a theoretical, systematic philosophy. Basically Confucius is answering questions. Sometimes in the *Analects* we get the questions, sometimes we just get the answer without the question. They're also some stories about Confucius, that are thrown in there, some sayings of disciples, and the topics are all mixed up; they're not thematic at all. Confucius was a teacher, so sometimes the same question is asked by different students and he'll give different answers. I'm not sure that this is because Confucius is being inconsistent or forgot what he said before; I think he's addressing the particular needs of particular students. Some of them he urges forward and others he tries to hold back a little bit. You can imagine how frustrating this might have been for students to hear all of these different answers to these questions. One of his students, Zigong, once asked "Is there one single word that can serve as a principle of conduct for life?" Just give me one thing that I can focus on. Confucius replied, "Perhaps the word 'reciprocity' will do it. Do not do unto others what you do not want others to do unto you." I'm not saying that Jesus stole that, but Confucius was there first by about 500 years.

So you have all these nice sayings, slogans, aphorisms but do they add up to a coherent social vision? I believe they do. The problem Confucius was facing was the breakup of society—violence and lawlessness, his answer was to return to the morality of the past, that of the sage-kings of the early Zhou dynasty. Social standards come from sages, wise men, rather than revelations or from innovative thinking. Confucius himself said I'm a transmitter I'm not a innovator.

Confucius didn't exactly found a school of philosophy. Even though we call it Confucianism that's not what they call it in China. He belonged to a scholarly movement that's called Ru, we might call it Ruism, which preserved ancient texts and ceremonies. Even today, the Chinese term for Confucianism is *rujia*, or the school of the Ru. Ru means something like ritual classicists or specialists. But Confucius was the most prominent figure within that tradition. This matters, because they were masters of traditional music and dance. Confucius taught us about harmony, learning by doing, by example. Those examples he's going to find in family and in the government.

I'm going to be more systematizing than Confucius is in the *Analects*. I will give you five major themes that can be found there. The first one is education. If you want to return to the morality of the past you need to know about the past. You need to know something of history. You need to know something of literature traditional works that have been passed on especially the five Confucian classics. The Ru school sort of adopted these ancient Chinese text and made them they're own. They include the *Venerated Documents*, *Classic of Poetry*, *Spring and Autumn Annals*, *Record of Ritual*, and *Classic of Change*, which some of you may know as the Yijing, a divination manual. Confucius is doing a little like the way the Upanishads did developed ideas from the Vedas. He's taking these traditional texts and developing ideas within them.

Education was the first, the second is moral government. Here's a quote, Ji Kang, a ruler, was distressed about the number of thieves in his state, and inquired of Confucius how to do away with them. Confucius said, "If you, sir, were not covetous, although you should reward them to do it, they would not steal." He basically says if you want your people to stop stealing from each other you should quit stealing from them. You can imagine the response was next, show me some other candidate for this job. Confucius once compared the rulers to the wind and the people to the grass. Whichever way the wind blows the grass will bend, people will follow the example of their rulers.

The third principle is ritual and music. The Chinese term is *li*, which means ceremony, manners, etiquette, and customs. The idea here is that there are certain specified behaviors that will help you become a better person, that will channel emotions. For example think about the death of a parent, which can be a very traumatic, heart-wrenching experience; people hardly know what to do with themselves but we have a series of rituals. There's a viewing, a funeral, you put the casket into the hearse, everybody drives to the cemetery with your lights on, when you're doing those things it gives you a way to channel and focus those otherwise chaotic and overwhelming feelings. On the other hand if when you're parents die, your first response is "Yes, now I get the house," which is completely inappropriate. Going through those rituals might help you develop the right sense of attitudes. It's not just rule books it's an adaptation the scholar, the gentleman will know how to harmonize these requirements. Lin fang, one of his students asked, What is the root of ritual? The Master said, Big question! In ceremonies, prefer simplicity to lavishness; in funerals, prefer grief to formality. The Confucian school is going to have some flexibility.

The fourth theme is individual effort. He talks about *ren*, which means benevolence, humaneness, goodness, it's sort of the culminating virtue. The Chinese character is the number 2, or the character for 2, alongside a piece that means people. It has to do with how people interact with each other. He talks about a gentleman versus an inferior man. Here are some quotes,

"What the [gentleman] seeks is in himself. What the [inferior man] seeks is in others." "The gentleman agrees with others without being an echo; the small man echoes without being in agreement." Is Confucius conservative, he's looking back to the old ways of doing things? There's an element of that but there's also something new here. He's saying that a gentleman is not just someone born into a noble family, that is the traditional definition, but he says anyone can act according to these principles. It's merit not birth that matters. That's a radical idea in early China.

His fifth and last theme is hierarchy. A quotation, Duke Jing asked a question about government "Confucius replied, 'There is government when the prince is a prince, and the minister is minister; when the father is father, and the son is son.'" What? What he has in mind is that if every father acted as a father should, was concerns with the welfare of his children, made sure they were educated, protected them, took care of them, and if every son acted as a son should showing respect for his father and obedience then every family would run much more smoothly. So also for those other relationships. Confucians talk about five relationships: ruler/subject, parent/child, husband/wife, older brother/younger brother, and friend/friend. Each of those relationships are unequal with the possible exception of the last. There is a superior and a subordinate. I myself am the oldest of six children, of five brothers it seems like a great idea to have my brothers be obedient to me but I'm not sure they'd see it the same way.

Would the divorce rate be lower if all wives were obedient to the husbands? At this point this sounds controversial, but stay with me here. I think the answer is yes, but certainly at a cost. There would be a number of women who are trapped in unhappy relationships, but they would be staying together for their families, which would remain intact. Now sometimes I have students who hear this and say, Professor Hardy, if you're just looking for hierarchy couldn't you get the same result if all husbands were obedient to their wives? Sure, but Confucius would never have thought that way. He does belong to ancient China. He actually doesn't say very much about women. That's a lack that's going to be remedied by a woman scholar, named Ban Zhao, and we'll hear more about her in Lecture 15. In some ways my example is a fair comparison because Confucianism does stress the importance of sacrificing oneself for the good of the group, the family. In other ways it's unfair because Confucius would put a lot of emphasis on the duties that husbands had to their wives. Woman as mothers have a tremendous amount of authority over their children, even their adult sons. In the end age is a more important differential than gender.

One of the most important moral obligations is filial piety. This is respect for parents. It's an awkward term because we don't have anything in English that captures the full extent of this Chinese virtue this isn't just little children obeying their parents, this is an adult virtue. You're not just respect, obedience, taking care of them in their old age. Truly filial children, we're talking about adults, will do anything to make their parents happy and will continue to follow the ways of their parents for at least three years after their parents have died. They should be in mourning throughout those three years. Confucius of course is going to give you very practical advice about how this should happen. "When his parents are alive, a son should not go far abroad; or if he does, he should let them know where he goes." Another piece of advice, "Behave in such a way that your father and mother have no anxiety about you, except concerning your health." He also says, children should know how old their parents are at any time. Just for the record as of today my father is 73, my mother is 71.

In Confucianism, hierarchy does not equal oppression. That's how we sort of think of it there's always a natural clash between those above and those below. Instead there are these hierarchal but non confrontational relationships think about mentoring, well clearly there's a superior and subordinate but that relationship works harmoniously for the good of both parties. When I think about my parents' marriage, they have a more traditional marriage than I have. When I was growing up, my father was the head of the household, what he said is what happened. When I got a little older and started to look at how my parents actually interacted I realized that my father never really said this is what we're going to do until he knew what my mother wanted to happen. So who's in control of this relationship is hard to say but it's not really about being in control.

According to Confucius we're not autonomous individuals; our identities are defined by the web of relationships in which we live. We're parents, we're children, we have siblings, we have a boss, perhaps you are a boss. The result of all these five things, education, moral government, ritual, individual effort, hierarchy, is a society that is spontaneously cooperative, rather than competitive or antagonistic.

The model for government is the family, rather than a legal contract with rights and responsibilities. The family is where we learn morality, which then can carry over in to wider world. Today in China, in my opinion, there hasn't been a strong tradition of rule of law; things get done through relationships—a thing called *guanxi*. There's also not a lot of room for rights or privacy, think about the one child policy. Even the most intimidate decisions that a couple makes the government is there. It's a very paternalistic government. Remember that in the Confucian ideal paternalism is not necessarily bad. There's such a thing as a good father who cares about his children. It depends on the morality of the rulers whether this system works or not.

Let me offer some general observations. Confucius doesn't put so much focus on rules and punishments, as much as on instilling proper attitudes and habits. A very famous quotes says,

> The Master said, "If you try to guide the common people with coercive regulations and keep them in line with punishments, the common people will become evasive and will have no sense of shame. If, however, you guide them with Virtue, and keep them in line by means of ritual, the people will have a sense of shame and will rectify themselves."

To apply that to filial piety, if you want your people to show respect to their payments say after your parents turn 65 you pay them this much every month. But then people will start to hedge on that. They'll say yeah but I gave my dad a gift and it was worth this much, or I took my mother to the grocery store three times… If you give very specific rules people will start to argue with the rules. Confucius says it's much better to give rules to the attitude. I live in the South now, and Confucius would love the custom of teaching your children to say "yes, sir; no, ma'am"; that respect is for not just parents, but older people in general as well. Confucius wasn't entirely opposed to law and punishments; he was after all involved with government.

Good rulers will not have to employ them very often; they will guide their people through example.

When someone tells you that you should be moral in this way or that way it's fair to ask why. Why should I do that? It's interesting what Confucius does not say. Confucius doesn't say that you should live like this because if you don't god will punish you, or you'll go to hell. In fact here's another quotation, Jilu one of his disciples asked about worship of gods and spirits. Confucius said, "We don't know yet how to serve men, how can we know about serving the spirits?" "What about death?" was the next question, and Confucius said, "We don't know yet about life, how can we know about death?"

Confucius is not irreligious; ancestor worship is there it's the basic religion of China. Ancestor worship rituals are part of *li*, of ceremony. Confucius talks about the mandate of heaven, which isn't a personal god it's more of an impersonal moral force in the sky that watches over. It does not reward or punish immediately, so it's not exactly religion that's going to keep you in doing these ritual things. It's not prosperity either. Confucius says that sometimes choosing the right can leave you poor and unemployed but that's still what you should do, that was his experience. He says you should live in this way because it's the right thing to do. It's good for humankind generally, because it worked in the past in the ancient ways of the sage-kings, because it fits human nature.

Some later history for Confucianism: It was eventually adopted as the official ideology in the Han Dynasty, 200 B.C.–A.D. 200. It was associated with imperial China through the civil service exams that lasted until 1905. They were tested on their classical Confucian knowledge. For a couple thousand years boys learned to read by memorizing the *Analects*. They didn't have any idea about what the principles were but the words were in their heads. There's a certain flexibility that comes with Confucianism. These fragmented quotes are open to new interpretations. The most important of which was Neo-Confucianism in 12th century.

We need to address two more questions before we quit. The first one is, Is Confucianism even practical? Would it work for a society, for a family, for an individual? A philosophy that emphasizes deference to those in authority and knowing one's place can be turned to oppressive ends. In late imperial China, Confucianism was associated with foot-binding, concubinage, inability of widows to remarry. Many people in the 19th century blamed Confucius for China's poverty and backwardness. This I think is a distortion, originally Confucianism was intended to allow all members of society to flourish, reach their potential, remember that status not fixed at birth. Indeed, sometimes, Confucius said, being filial meant speaking up, respectfully of course, but telling your parents when you thought they were making a mistake. Now if they didn't listen to you, you just had to go along with it, but sometimes there's that.

Would it work for a nation? Confucius wanted to make a difference, as did his followers, to change things for the better, to be progressive while still holding on to what is most valuable from the past. But in some times and places that may be impossible, especially when the government is corrupt or tyrannical. In those cases, good Confucians don't seek office, but they retire from public life and focus on immediate surroundings, like family.

Can Confucianism work for a family? For some years we had some discussions about putting a poster for teenage daughter's room with a quotation from the *Analects* that would have reminded her of several of the ideals of the Confucian gentleman, who as it says takes care "when observing, to see clearly; … when listening, to hear distinctly … when in doubt, to ask questions; when angry, to ponder the consequences; … when gaining an advantage, to consider whether it is fair." I'll leave it to your imagination as to what kinds of problems made it seem like a good idea. In one's personal life, there's an openness to learning in all situations, from both the good and bad. Confucius said "When I walk along with two others, they may serve me as my teachers. I will select their good qualities and follow them, their bad qualities and avoid them."

I want to leave you with more than a sense of Confucianism is sayings. Confucius was a truly inspiring person. Not just random pieces of advice, but a program for lifelong moral development. You might think about where you are in this. The Master said, "At fifteen I had my mind [set] on learning; at thirty I stood firm; at forty I had no doubts; at fifty I knew the decrees of

Heaven; at sixty my ear was [attuned]; at seventy I could follow what my heart's desired without transgressing what was right" What a lovely idea, I can follow my heart's desire without transgressing what was right. Imagine that you're facing a difficult decision, a moral dilemma, and if you're like me you might be tempted to take the easy way out. You might be tempted to choose the path that would benefit you personally, but because of your moral upbringing, your integrity, thanks to your parents, because you're basically a decent person you make yourself do what you know you should. What would it be like if your first natural impulse was to do the right thing.

Another quotation, the Duke of She asked Zilu about Confucius, and Zilu didn't have an answer he went back and said what should I have said? Confucius said: "Why didn't you tell him that I am a person who forgets to eat when he is enthusiastic about something, forgets all his worries in his enjoyment of it, and is not aware that old age is coming on." Again a lovely ideal! To be so engaged in what you love that your worries disappear, hardly notice that you're getting older.

Confucius was not a dour moralist. He loved goodness, enjoyed life, and exhibited an infectious enthusiasm for learning and teaching. His is a practical philosophy that can only be truly understood by putting at least some of his principles into action. Remember that famous opening lines of the *Analects*, "Is it not a pleasure, having learned something, to try it out at due intervals?" And now is your chance. Thanks.

Laozi and Daoism—The Way of Nature
Lecture 7

Daoism is the second of the three major philosophies of China. Laozi's Daodejing ("the way and its power") responds to the political, family-centered morality of Confucius with a poetic, cryptic treatise rejecting man-made hierarchies and arguing the value of simplicity and humility over power and ambition. The dao (way) is the way of nature in a universe that consists of opposites in harmony, and de (virtue, integrity) is an innate human strength. Following the dao brings humans freedom, serenity, and longevity.

In many ways, Confucius established the baseline for all later Chinese philosophical debates. Among the first to dispute Confucius's system was a person or persons known as Laozi—a name that means "old master"—whose philosophy is collected in the late 4th-century B.C. book of poetic proverbs called the Daodejing. Much of its advice is cryptic, even paradoxical; its enigmatic nature has inspired more than 350 commentaries in Chinese over the past two and a half millennia. Composed during China's Warring States period, it offers a solution to the current turmoil not in the wisdom of the past but in a return to the way of nature.

The Daodejing consists of two parts. Chapters 1–37 focus on the dao, or "way," while chapters 38–81 discuss de, an innate human strength, often translated as integrity or virtue. The dao is hard to define; it is sometimes described as "the mother of the world," not unlike the Upanishads' Brahman. The universe itself is described in terms of binary distinctions: "When everyone knows goodness, this accounts for badness. / Being and nonbeing give birth to each other / Difficult and easy complete each other." This is related to the notion of yin and yang, but it is a mistake to reduce the idea of white and black to good and evil; both elements are necessary, and everything in creation has its share of both.

Following the dao means rejecting man-made distinctions, including Confucius's esteemed hierarchies. Politically, Laozi recommends nonintervention and effortless action—avoiding whatever doesn't come naturally. The universe enforces a law of unintended consequences: Every action brings its opposite; emphasizing any virtue highlights a corresponding vice: "When knowledge and wisdom appeared, / There emerged great hypocrisy. ... When a country is in disorder, / There will be praise of loyal ministers." Rather than great, wealthy empires, the dao leads to small countries and simple lifestyles.

> **Every action brings its opposite; emphasizing any virtue highlights a corresponding vice.**

Laozi offers several pieces of practical advice to both rulers and individuals. Individuals should live in unity with nature, be humble and shun ambition, embrace material simplicity, and generally go with the flow. Governments should be as minimal and unobtrusive as possible. One might ask, if each quality inherently brings its opposite, wouldn't humility bring power, and so forth? Yes, but that's the point: We should embrace what comes to us and not struggle against the universe. Forceful action always brings a backlash; better to practice nonaction.

In summary, Confucianism is associated with hierarchy, order, social responsibility, conformity, moralism, activism, service, and seriousness. Daoism prefers individualism, freedom, nonconformity, nature, retirement, tranquility, mysticism, and wit. Both are wary of competition, confrontation, and coercion; both are attractive and have much to teach us about how to live the best life. ∎

Suggested Reading

More than any other text mentioned in this course, students will benefit from reading multiple versions of the Daodejing. Fortunately it is quite short, and there are a few dozen reputable translations. I recommend the following:

Hendricks, *Lao-Tzu: Te-Tao Ching*.

Ivanhoe, *The Daodejing of Laozi*.

Lau, *Lao Tzu: Tao Te Ching*.

Mair, *Tao Te Ching: The Classic Book of Integrity and the Way.*

Chan, *A Source Book in Chinese Philosophy.*

De Barry and Bloom, eds., *Sources of Chinese Tradition.*

Graham, *Disputers of the Dao.*

Ivanhoe and Van Norden, *Readings in Classical Chinese Philosophy.*

Kirkland, *Taoism.*

Kohn, *Daoism and Chinese Culture.*

Kupperman, *Classic Asian Philosophy.*

Moeller, *The Philosophy of the Daodejing.*

Questions to Consider

1. Is nature an appropriate model for human behavior?

2. Are making distinctions and judgments necessary for progress? For happiness?

3. Why would it be useful to base a philosophy or even a religion on a text that is open to multiple interpretations?

Laozi and Daoism—The Way of Nature
Lecture 7—Transcript

Hello, I'm glad you can join me again. In this lecture we're going to be talking about Laozi and Daoism. But first, a word about spelling: There are two Romanization systems for Chinese. In older books you'll see Daoism with a *t* in newer books you'll see it with a *d*. Similarly Laozi used to be spelled with a *-tzu* at the end and now it's a *-zi*. In both cases the Chinese character hasn't changed, the pronunciation hasn't changed, it's just a different way of rendering that sound into English letters into the alphabet. So it's Daoism and Laozi.

Daoism is the second of the three major philosophies of China, Confucianism and Legalism are the other two; we'll be talking about Legalism in the next lecture. Like so many other early Chinese thinkers, Laozi offers a response to the idealistic, political, family-centered morality of Confucius. In many ways, Confucius established the baseline for later Chinese philosophical debates. Things are sometimes a little bit more complicated than they seem. Laozi was not exactly a founder of a movement, and Daoism is not exactly a philosophical school. The label was given retrospectively to a number of writers who thought about similar lines. I'm not sure they all would have considered themselves Daoists.

Laozi himself, there's a question as to whether he's an actual person. We have a book that was written by somebody, called the *Laozi*. Early Chinese books were often named after their authors, but the name literally means the "Old Master," and in fact Chinese doesn't distinguish between singular and plural so it may mean the old wise ones, the old masters. It was probably not written by a singular individual. It's more like Vyasa, remember the author supposedly of the *Mahabharata* in the Bhagavad Gita but unlike in India, the Chinese love history. They have always felt the need to historicize legendary figures by giving them birthdates and genealogies.

Here's the story about Laozi, this legendary figure. He supposedly lived about 500 B.C., so about the time of Confucius. In fact according to one story Confucius came to him for some advice about ritual, learned from him, and then of course was actually criticized by him as well. Laozi was the curator of Zhou archives, after a whole he got tired of a life in China and so he decided he was going to leave China and go to the West. As he was leaving there was a guardian of the frontier pass who said, Laozi don't just leave us with nothing. He quickly wrote down this book, the *Laozi*, gave it to the border guard and went out of China riding on the back of a water buffalo. I don't know about this story but we have a book.

It's called the *Laozi*, sometimes it's called the *Daodejing*, the *Classic of the Way and Its Power*. This book is very short. It has about 5,000 characters; it's divided up into 81 chapters and these chapters are only about a page or so. It comes out of 4th-century B.C. China from someone one, some way. I'll follow convention when referring to the author of this book, he or she or they whoever, we'll just call them Laozi. A modern scholar, Wing-tsit Chan, has said that "No one can hope to understand Chinese philosophy, religion, government, art, medicine—or even cooking—without a real appreciation of the profound philosophy taught in this little book," the *Daodejing*.

I'll try to give you a feel for it today with a number of quotations, but you really ought to read it yourself sometime. It's not that long. When you open the book, it's obviously in a very different tradition from that of Confucius; instead of practical, concrete sayings and advice, you find a cryptic, poetic style, with proverbs, paradoxes, wordplay, and rhymed passages. The very first lines are "The way that can be spoken of / Is not the constant way; The name that can be named / Is not the constant name." In Chinese it's, *dao ke dao / fei chang dao*; *ming ke ming / fei chang ming*. You can hear it has sort of a lilt to it and it's easy to memorize. Deeper into the book you'll find striking imagery, there are lots of contradictions, which may be part of its development as a book of aphorisms. Even we have our own sayings maybe "look before you leap," or "he who hesitates is lost." You notice that those have opposite meanings, though you might find them in the same book of proverbs. When you read the *Daodejing*, it seems like it means something, even if it's not exactly clear what that is. In Chinese there are over 350 commentaries on it, and almost that many translations into Western languages. When I encourage you to read the *Daodejing*, do so but you should really read two or three different translations to get a flavor for how things might be interpreted differently. The translations are quite different.

The book is divided into two parts: Chapters 1–37 focus on the Dao, or the Way; while chapters 38–81 give particular attention to De, an inner strength that is often translated as virtue, power, or integrity. *Daodejing*, the classic of the way and the power. In 1973, there were two versions written on silk were discovered in a tomb dated to 168 B.C. In 1993, a even older version, written on bamboo slips and dating to before 300 B.C. was found. There are some minor differences among these version but the most immediately evident is that the order of the two major sections is reversed, that is, the 2nd-century B.C. manuscripts, they have the power part first and the Way part second. We'll just use the standard version.

The *Daodejing* was composed during the Warring States Era in China, about 475–221 B.C., it's after Confucius's death. Like the Confucian *Analects*, it also offers a solution to the problems of social disorder and violence. But Laozi's advice is not to return to the morality of the past to those old sage-kings; instead he argues for a return to the Dao, that is, the Way.

What exactly is the Dao? Which is kind of a tough question. In chapter 56 there's a warning: Those who know, do not speak. And those who speak do not know. I'm going to be talking for the next 20–25 minutes, be forewarned what I'm saying really isn't the real Dao. The Dao that can be spoken of is not the real Dao but it seems to have something to do with nature. Let's begin again, and we'll take the quote a little further:

> The way that can be spoken of / Is not the constant way;
> The name that can be named / Is not the constant name.
> The nameless was the beginning of heaven and earth;
> The named was the mother of the myriad creatures.
> Hence always rid yourself of desires in order to observe its secrets;
> But always allow yourself to have desires in order to observe
> its manifestations.

It's somehow beyond words, it's ineffable. There's something about mysticism here; you notice something about femaleness, the mother of all things; something about desire. There's seem to be two themes that come out of the first chapters of the *Daodejing*. The first one is the unity of multiplicity: Sometimes the Dao is described as "the mother of the world"; the Dao gave birth to the one, which gave birth to two, from which came three, and then the ten thousand things. The origin of all things, It may be something like the concept of Brahman in the Upanishads.

There's also a theme of the resolution of opposition. Once again, we will go back to the text:

> When all under heaven know beauty as beauty, already there is ugliness;
> When everyone knows goodness, this accounts for badness.
> Being and nonbeing give birth to each other,
> Difficult and easy complete each other;
> Long and short form each other;
> High and the low fulfill each other;
> Tone and voice harmonize with each other;
> Front and back follow each other—it is ever thus.
> For these reasons, the sage dwells in affairs of nonaction,
> carries out a doctrine without words.

What does that mean? That sounds so different than what we saw in the Confucius *Analects*. One way to try to get at that is to ask the question, do you think I am short? I am 5'7". The answer may be it depends. Compared to the average American male, I'm on the short side. Compared to the average Chinese male I'm probably more closer to the average. How many things are like that? Where the answer is it depends. The Dao transcends common, binary distinctions that we make all the time. There's a difference between weak and strong, hard and soft, light and darkness, useful and useless, right and wrong—all of those are human distinctions according to Laozi. The Dao doesn't make those distinctions it accepts everything as natural. Even the difference between male and female. You might say, wait a minute that's a natural distinction? But gender is more than anatomy, perhaps some of you men out there have a feminine side or vice versa. I'm reminded of a cartoon from *The New Yorker*, that plays with the idea of up and down in a power sense. In this cartoon there's an elevator operator standing in front of an elevator. Up above the elevator there's a circle with an S in the middle, this symbol of yin and yang. The caption says, "Actually I'm going up and I'm going down." I know that elevators go up and down all the time, but can an elevator go up and down at the same time? I think the answer is yes. If you were in space, say on the moon, looking down through a telescope and there was an elevator right at the South Pole. When that elevator went up, in respect to the earth, it would actually be going down with respect to the moon.

Laozi would love those kinds of contradictions and puzzles. The idea that the universe consists of opposites in harmony can be seen in the related notion of yin and yang. There are these two elements, yin is dark, passive, female, persevering and yang is light, active, male, initiating. But they can't be reduced to good and bad; it's not like yang is good and yin is bad or vice versa It's more like the opposition between Heaven and Earth. Both elements are necessary and everything has its share of both of them. Yin and yang, ebb and flow over time, like a pendulum like in the summer it'll get hot, too much yang and then it will swing back the other way of yin to winter, then it will swing back the other way. The movement of the Dao, according to the *Daodejing*, is reversal. Think about all of the artificial, human distinctions that we make, like what gold is valuable and dirt is worthless. From the perspective of the Dao, those are both naturally occurring substances. Even though from the perspective of people, people kill each over the former, gold, but they don't really care about the other. But once again if you're trying to grow crops, dirt is going to be much more valuable than gold, which is hard to plant seeds in.

There's something of a contradiction here with Laozi. He says that these distinctions don't matter, like weak and strong, but he actually likes the weak. Laozi's going to lean toward the unlikely term. In the distinction between solid and empty, he likes the empty. It's the doors and windows that make a room useful, or it's the space between spokes that make a wheel, or it's the space within a jug that give it its utility. With the distinction between weak and strong, most people are going to say I like strong, but Laozi's going to say maybe you should give weak a second look. He says "when alive human beings are supple and weak; when dead they are stiff and strong."

Then he uses lots of images. He talks about the uncarved block, what shape is that? It's hard to know before it's cut up. He likes water, which is takes the low position, it's submissive. But he says, "Nothing under heaven is softer or more yielding than water, but when it attacks things hard and resistant there is not one of them that can prevail." So he says water is very soft, it takes the shape of whatever container you put it in, you can put your hand right through it, but for wearing down mountains over time, or carving valleys there's nothing like water.

Laozi gives particular attention to women, but does not advocate for the equality between the sexes. Rather, the *Daodejing* celebrates stereotypical female virtues such as yielding, softness, and humility, and it suggests that men would be more better off if they adopted these attitudes. Laozi says, "Know the masculine but keep to the feminine."

Harmony comes from following the Dao, rejecting man-made distinctions and hierarchy. So in this case it's the opposite of Confucianism, which says if everybody knew their place in society and acted in accordance with it, things would run smoothly. Laozi said just forget all of those social distinctions, they don't matter. Another quote:

> In the pursuit of learning one knows more every day; in the pursuit of the way one does less every day. One does less and less until one does nothing at all, and when one does nothing at all there in nothing that is undone. It is always through not meddling that the empire is won. Should you meddle, then you are not equal to the task of winning the empire.

Notice that political application at the end. Remember early Chinese philosophy is often played out before rulers as people are trying to get jobs and give political advice. So in this quote there's an idea of *wu wei*, of non-action, non-intervention. It's translated as effortless action. It's not exactly doing nothing, but it's avoiding whatever doesn't come naturally. Don't do things that you have to work too hard at, do things that are effortless.

Laozi's going to give you two cautions here about ordinary ways of doing things. He says when you emphasize a virtue you highlighting a vice. Or the quotation is, "When all under heaven know beauty as beauty, already there is ugliness." What could that mean? I want you to think of someone who is beautiful. I'll just throw a name, how about Scarlett Johansson, and for those of you who are female let's say Denzel Washington. When I say that Scarlett Johansson is a beautiful woman, I am also secretly implying that women who don't look like Scarlett are not quite so beautiful. You can't define something without showing the other side of it. It's like two sides of a coin. Highlighting a virtue also emphasizes a vice, or deficient.

The second caution is the law of unintended consequences that assertive actions bring their opposites, sort of like a backlash. If you're pushing too hard at work for a pet project that can make your colleagues more resistant to it. Or politicians whose ads feature their families a little too prominently make people suspicious of infidelity—why does he have to go that far? It's almost like I think he protests a little bit too much.

Both of these ideas, this backlash and virtues and vices being inseparable undercut Confucian ideas of morality and government activism. Another quote from later on:

> When the great Dao declined,
> The doctrines of humanity and righteousness arose.
> When knowledge and wisdom appeared,
> There emerged great hypocrisy.
> When the six family relationships are not in harmony,
> There will be the advocacy of filial piety and deep love to children.
> When a country is in disorder,
> There will be praise of loyal ministers.

In other words, you wouldn't be talking about filial piety if people were already respecting they're parents The fact that you're talking about it means there's a problem. Loyal ministers are only praised when disloyalty is common. Laozi says if you get rid of sageliness and wisdom, benevolence and righteousness—all of those Confucius values—then people would be benefitted a hundredfold.

Laozi's going to look back to an era before the Zhou dynasty, to the legendary Yellow Emperor. He thought of that as a time when there were small kingdoms and people are content with simple things and few possessions. Toward the end of the *Daodejing* he gives his vision of what an ideal society would be like. He says, "Even though neighboring states are within sight of each other, even though they can hear the sounds of each other's dogs and chickens, their people will grow old and die without ever having visited one another." They're just perfectly content with what they have.

Let's try some applications here. Based on his understanding of a unified, harmonious cosmos where opposites work together, like yin and yang, Laozi offers several pieces of practical advice to both rulers and individuals. He says union with nature, if you take the perspective of Dao, that will bring freedom, serenity, and longevity. Simplicity and humility are preferable to power and ambition. You should cut down on wants, don't try to be number 1. If you try to be number 1, number 2 and number 3 will all try to gang up and bring you down. He says—he doesn't say, but my paraphrasing does—how about you try to be number 9? Nobody will really care about you then. Let the big guys fight it out, remember this is a time of a lot of warfare, and you will sit on the sidelines and last longer. Don't work too hard, quit while you're ahead, take it easy, go with the flow. I grew up in California this all sounds very familiar to me.

You may ask, Doesn't talking of simplicity and tranquility, doesn't that bring its opposite? Remember this backlash sort of thing, if you push too hard the opposite will come? The answer is yes, but that's part of his point. The Dao is silent, there aren't any arguments, there's no confrontation. The way that can be spoken of is not the real way. The best teaching uses no words, because language is one of the main ways that humans divide nature into this and that, make distinctions, and assign values; the Dao just encompasses everything non judgmentally.

Since forceful action brings a backlash, it's best to practice non-action. Because civilization is the source of many problems, government should be as minimal and unobtrusive as possible. Laozi says the worst rulers are despised by their people; somewhat better are those that are feared by their people; better yet are rulers who are loved, in the West we might stop there, but Laozi goes further; the best of all are those rulers who are hardly even noticed by their people.

Could this really work? It certainly could work for individuals. When I was living in Taiwan the first quotation from the *Daodejing* that I heard, people said to me, "Great wisdom looks like stupidity." Should I be flattered by that? There's the great wisdom but there's the looking stupid part as well. For individuals you might be able to adopt some of these principles.

How about in a larger social setting? I sometimes ask my class, if we were a Daoist class how would we do things different? They come up with some ideas. We can sit in a circle so there isn't one person in charge, preferably we go outside. No attendance policy. Not on a strict schedule, we wouldn't have to get through a syllabus, we could spend time on what we were interested in. There certainly wouldn't be any tests, and no grades since grades are after all an artificial distinctions, they're not arbitrary I try to be very fair. But when I think about what my ideal student is, it would be someone that comes to me years later and says, Professor Hardy you're class changed my life. How do I know at the end of a semester who's going to fall into that category? I certainly don't. So no grades, no tests, not a strict schedule—would you study in a class like that? Maybe not, but maybe yes as well. Daoism isn't necessarily a philosophy for lazy people. Daoists can work very hard, but at things that come naturally to them. I really like my job; I enjoy reading and preparing lectures, and teaching it's actually not work. It just comes naturally even though I put a lot of time into it. Actually think about this Teaching Company course—no grades, no tests, will you keep listening? Sure, if it catches your attention. You might find yourself deeply engaged in this.

What about for nations? Could there be a Daoist country? President Ronald Reagan actually quoted from the *Daodejing* in his 1988 State of the Union Address. He said, "And as an ancient Chinese philosopher, Lao-tzu, said: 'Govern a great nation as you would cook a small fish; do not overdo it.'" Perhaps that works, the not meddling part, but that may be easier said than done, especially in country the size of ours. I'm not sure that Laozi would have been thrilled with the lifestyles or the governments of our modern world.

Many Chinese have been Daoist in some aspects of their life and Confucian in others. This isn't exactly like regular distinctions in Western religions. It's hard to be Catholic and Protestant at the same time, or Jewish and Muslim at the same time, but you can certainly be Daoist and Confucian at the same time. The two philosophies, despite their differences, have worked together like yin and yang to enrich Chinese culture. The differences between the two can be summarized as follows. Confucianism is associated with hierarchy, order, social responsibility, conformity, moralism, activism, service, and seriousness. Daoism on the other hand prefers the ideals of individualism, freedom, nonconformity, nature, retirement, tranquility, mysticism, and wit. Daoist philosophers are funny in a way that Confucians hardly ever are. I tried to make those lists kind of balanced because both of those are attractive, and both of those philosophies have their place in life.

There are commonalities as well as differences. Daoism and Confucianism are both wary of competition; they're hesitant about direct confrontation, they want to avoid that; they're suspicious of words being used other than their regular meanings; and they dislike coercion. They come out of the same historical circumstances, warfare, uncertainty, and chaos, and they're looking for social harmony. They both claim that they've found the way.

Later on, when Buddhists arrive in China, they find that the can talk to Daoists. I mean not just ideas about being and nonbeing, the subtle nature of reality, and the dangers of desire, but also specific meditative practices. You can imagine Buddhists coming in and saying, we meditate like this. And the Daoists had been doing some meditating as well and said, well we tend to like this sort of practice of doing it. They have something to talk about, they have a fair amount in common. In fact enough was in common that in China some people said, "Do you remember when Laozi left China and headed out West?" He probably went to India where he became the Buddha. This is why these ideas are coming back to us in Buddhist form. That's not exactly what happened but there are these commonalities.

Eventually, Daoism became a religion, complete with priests, rituals, and scriptures. Laozi himself was worshipped as a god. One wonders what would he have thought about that. I'm sure he would have been amused. These Daoist ideas get deep in all sorts of things in Chinese culture. For example you have two souls: a *yang* soul (*hun*) and a *yin* soul (*po*), which matters in ancestor worship. Your yang soul, which is light, can sort of go up to the other world wherever that may be, while your yin soul stays around the grave and can appreciate the offerings that are made in ancestor worship.

I'll try to give you a balance on some of these. Daoism may not be universally appealing. For example, Laozi argues against education. He thinks many people would be happier without education, which gives you desires and makes you frustrated when you get a degree and then can't find a job. He appears to promote a dangerous sense of irresponsibility—go ahead and quit, don't work so hard, and there may be circumstances where that's not good advice. His advocacy of subtle political maneuvering can seem almost Machiavellian. He once said,

> If you wish to shrink it
> Be sure to stretch it.
> If you wish to weaken it
> Be sure to strengthen it.
> If you wish it cast aside
> Be sure to raise it up.
> If you wish to take from it
> Be sure to give to it.

These opposites, what do they mean? Here's an application perhaps, an illustration: Imagine that you have a particularly obnoxious co-worker and you might encourage that co-worker to apply for a promotion. You might even write a glowing letter hoping that that person would get promoted to that position that they're entirely incompetent at and then they'll get fired. Remember if you want to weaken something, first strength in it. Or if you want to break it, you stretch it first.

In spite of all of that, Daoism has inspired centuries of magnificent Chinese art, architecture, literature, and poetry, not to mention medicine and cooking, which sometimes mixes things in yin yang kind of terms. You might have seen these wonderful Chinese landscape paintings. They have these magnificent mountains that just tower way above, and then very small at the bottom are some people. It's a nice contrast with Western art that tends to put portraiture like people, front and center everywhere. But if you think about it how important in the big scheme of things are human beings, really? From the perspective of the Dao, are human beings all that much more important than say microbes, or bacteria? Actually bacteria will probably be around much longer than human being will be.

One final quotation to end up, "When the Way is expressed verbally, We say such things as 'How bland and tasteless it is! We look for it, but there is not enough to be seen. We listen for it, but there is not enough to be heard. Yet, when put to use, it is inexhaustible!' " Laozi's *Daodejing* is like that; the book is inexhaustible. It's so clever, so mind-bending, so profound, so confusing. You can read it over and over, and always learn something new, which is what makes the *Daodejing* a classic and is what makes Laozi one of the great minds of the Eastern intellectual tradition. Thanks.

The Hundred Schools of Preimperial China
Lecture 8

The Warring States era (475–221 B.C.) brought a great deal of chaos and suffering to China, which, paradoxically, also allowed for a remarkable degree of social mobility. Talented, ambitious men vied for political appointments and often wrote about their ideas. Collectively called the Hundred Schools, these philosophies represent a golden age of thought and intellectual freedom in China. Here we will discuss the founders of three of them from the 4th century B.C.: Mozi, Huizi, and Zhuangzi.

Although Confucius and Laozi were by far the most influential thinkers in China's premodern history, they were by no means the only great philosophers of ancient China. About 100 years after the end of the Warring States period, a historian named Sima Tan divided the Hundred Schools of Chinese philosophy into six major schools: Naturalists, Confucians, Mohists, Terminologists, Legalists, and Daoists. Only two of these (the Confucians and Mohists) were self-identified schools; the rest are amalgams of schools with similar teachings.

The Mohists followed Mozi, the first great rival of Confucius. He wrote formal, extended arguments, rather than Confucian-style insights. His main idea was impartial caring, sometimes translated as universal love. He argued that large states attack small ones, great families overthrow the lesser, and the strong oppress the weak because of partiality; peace can be brought about by striving to love everyone equally.

Mozi's primary criterion for moral judgment was utility, followed by precedent and veracity. Things that met people's material needs—food, clothing, and shelter—are good; everything else is wasteful, including the beloved Confucian rituals. He condemned war as the greatest waste of all. He felt that social standing should be based on merit and stressed *yi* (righteousness) over *ren*. Where Confucius refused to speculate on the afterlife, Mozi promoted a religious vision where fear of ghosts and punishment from heaven kept people in line.

Huizi is categorized as a Terminologist, or logician. He composed a series of paradoxes that point to the relativity of time and space; for example, he writes that the moment a being is born, it begins dying. His paradoxes are often compared to those of the Greek philosopher Zeno, who lived a century earlier, especially his observation that if you take a foot-long stick and cut it in half every day, you won't use it up in ten thousand generations. Unfortunately, this list is all that remains of Huizi's work.

Zhuangzi was a great Daoist thinker, second only to Laozi, and unlike Laozi, we are confident that he was a single, real person. He was an elegant, witty writer whose ideas are similar to but more extreme than those found in the Daodejing. Laozi argued that ordinary distinctions were meaningless, but he generally had a preference for the less valued. Zhuangzi really has no preference, even between life and death or dreams and reality; he is famous in the West for being unsure whether he is a man dreaming he is a butterfly or a butterfly dreaming he is a man.

Zhuangzi ... is famous in the West for being unsure whether he is a man dreaming he is a butterfly or a butterfly dreaming he is a man.

Laozi argues for radical skepticism, saying all judgments are based on limited, incomplete perspectives. He is particularly wary of the limitations of language. He sees no point in fearing death nor in clinging to life; how can we be sure which is the better? Rather than present reasoned arguments, he prefers to illustrate his points with clever stories, some of which feature himself and his friend Huizi the logician as the main characters. ∎

Suggested Reading

Chan, *A Source Book in Chinese Philosophy*.

De Bary and Bloom, eds., *Sources of Chinese Tradition*.

Graham, *Disputers of the Tao*.

Ivanhoe and Van Norden, eds., *Readings in Classical Chinese Philosophy*.

Kohn, *Daoism and Chinese Culture*.

Kupperman, *Classic Asian Philosophy*.

Zhuangzi, *The Complete Works of Chuang Tzu*.

Questions to Consider

1. Why does social chaos sometimes lead to intellectual vitality?

2. Is a universal ethics possible? Can it be based on utilitarian principles? Religious principles? Or both at the same time?

3. How can philosophers use words to explore the limits of language?

The Hundred Schools of Preimperial China
Lecture 8—Transcript

Hi, welcome back. The Warring States Era in China goes from 475–221 B.C. The name sort of says it all, the Warring States Era. The interstate conflicts of that time brought a great deal of chaos and suffering to China, but the intense political competition also allowed for a remarkable degree of social mobility. There were talented, ambitious men who went from state to state looking for a ruler who would put their ideas into practice, we saw this earlier with Confucius. Many of the books they wrote have survived and their ideas promoted by these itinerant debaters has been collectively called "the hundred schools of philosophy."

There were Confucians and Daoists, of course, but also agriculturalists who claimed new techniques for increasing farm yields, which was important with all of this warfare when you put large armies into the field you need to supply them and to feed them so you need larger crop yields, there were also cosmologists who boasted of being able to harness the forces of nature. Some of these thinkers wanted to establish small, cooperative communes in which rulers worked alongside peasants in the fields rather than relying on taxes, sort of withdrawing from the larger competitive social situation, while other thinkers unashamedly recommended complete selfishness. There were military strategists like Sunzi who we'll be talking about in a later lecture, and there were some philosophers who argued that what the world really needed was just more love—they don't last a long time, the Mohists, we'll be talking about them before we're done today.

In the Han dynasty, about 100 B.C. after all of this is over, a historian named Sima Tan—he's the father of Sima Qian, who's going to get a whole lecture before long—wrote an essay in which he listed the six major schools of the Warring States Era: He's in a period of time when china is unified and he's looking back to this fragmented chaotic time, and he's trying to make sense of it. In his introduction to this list, he says:

> The Great Commentary to the Classic of Changes says, "All under Heaven share the same goal, yet there are a hundred ways of thinking about it; they return to the same home, yet follow

different pathways there." The Naturalists, Confucians, Mohists, Terminologists, Legalists, and Daoists all strive to create order in the world.

He says there are these different paths but they're all headed the same way. Then he's going to give you a quick list of how these thinkers differ from each other. He starts out by talking about the Naturalists. In Chinese this is the yin-yang school. They focus on omens, taboos, things that should and should not be done according to the seasons. You don't want to draft people in the military during the season of the harvest because you need people to tend to their lands, makes sense.

There are also the Mohists, that according to Sima Tan practiced frugality. They looked back to the simple lifestyles of the sage-kings Yao and Shun who were before even the founders of the Zhou dynasty that Confucius loved so much. The Mohists also encouraged agriculture.

There were the Confucians, who we've already head about. According to Sima Tan their areas of specialty were the classics and commentaries, rules of ritual, relationships between ruler and subject, father and son, husband and wife, elder and younger.

The next school that he talks about are the Terminologists, sometimes called the Logicians. They analyze argumentation and language itself.

Then there are the Legalists. Their area of focus is the strict application of law, regardless of social position. They said that rulers need to assign specific duties of officials and then hold them responsible for that. We'll have a lecture where we talk more about the Legalists.

And then finally the Daoists, who according to Sima Tan do nothing, but get everything done. They live in spiritual harmony with nature and adapt the good things from all the other schools. Sima Tan likes the flexibility of the Daoists, but he admits that sometimes it can be hard to understand what they're talking about. If you remember our readings last time from the *Daodejing*.

Only two of these schools were self-identified schools that's the Confucians and Mohists. The others were later labels that grouped together thinkers who had similar teachings. We'll talk about the Legalists in Lecture 10 and we'll talk about the Naturalists when we discuss Han dynasty Confucianism in Lecture 16. But here I want to introduce three more great minds of pre-imperial China: Mozi, Huizi, and Zhuangzi, all of whom lived during the 4th century B.C. in the Warring States Era. A word about the *-zi* that syllable at the end of a name means Master, so Master Mo, Master Hui, and Master Zhuang. That's why they all have that similar syllable.

Mozi is the first great thinker we'll talk about. He was the first great rival to the Ru school of Confucius, remember the Ru school is the school of classicists that's what the Chinese called what Confucius was a part of. Unlike many of the other intellectuals of the time, he founded an organized, distinct school of thought and actively recruited students. He lived in the generation after Confucius, probably from about 480–390 B.C. That makes Mozi a contemporary of Socrates. He is a man and a text, sort of like the Laozi. So his name is Mozi and we've got this book that's also called the *Mozi*.

His name is a little mysterious; it means tattoo. Some people have wondered if he was a convict because that was one of the legal penalties at the time, tattooing one's face. Or it also refers to an ink line and people have wondered if he was an artisan or craftsman because he put so many illustrations of people who work with their hands into his text. The *Mozi*, the book, presents formal, extended arguments. They're somewhat repetitious but it's obvious that persuasion has developed since the time of Confucius, who offered insights rather than arguments. *Mozi*'s main idea was "impartial caring," sometimes translated as "universal love." Rather than grounding his ethics on the idea of family, as Confucius did, Mozi argued that everyone should care for everyone else's parents just as much as their own. Here's how the argument goes. I'll just paraphrase it for you. Mozi says that the problem is that large states attack small ones, great families overthrow the lesser families, the strong oppress the weak, and all because of partiality, which means they're partial to themselves, their own interests. But he says it's not fair to criticize something without suggesting a better alternative. His alternative is impartial caring. You should love everyone equally. You might

107

say, that's stupid. How can you care for another person's father the way you care for your own dad? Or could you love other countries as much as you love your own country?

But imagine, and this is Mozi's own thought experiment, imagine that someone is about to travel abroad, or is about to go into battle. Would he entrust his parents, his wife and children that he's living behind to someone who cares for his own family first, or to someone how cares for everyone equally. "In such cases," he says, "there are no fools in the world." You may say that family-based morality is the best, but when it comes time to actually act on principles, you would side with someone who is committed to universal love.

A few more ideas form Mozi. His primary criteria of moral judgment was utility. If something helped to meet the people's material needs, we're talking about food, clothing, and shelter, basic needs, then it was good. Otherwise it was wasteful. He put the beloved Confucian traditions of music and rituals, including expensive funerals that show how much filial piety you have, into that latter category. Those are wasteful. And he condemned war as the greatest waste of all. What he recommended was frugality for individuals but also for governments.

Mozi taught that social standing should be based on merit. The Confucians talk about merit but they basically acceptance aristocracy and hereditary offices and they want to be advisors to those. Advisors are chosen by merit but the actual rulers are going to be born into those positions. Mozi rejects that he thinks that every position should be filled by merit. He also says that rulers should set the standards for their people just as Heaven set the standards for rulers. How are these standards determined? Mozi says there are three objective, universal criteria: precedent, what's worked in the past; veracity, like let's listen to the common people and learn from their experience; and utility, is it practical, does it add to people's material well-being, does it provide food, clothing, or shelter. Those are the principles, precedent, veracity, and utility, that we can use to figure out right and wrong.

Rather than *ren*, remember that's the Confucian principle of human-heartedness or benevolence, Mozi is going to stress *yi*, a righteousness.

He believed that righteousness was connected with the will of Heaven. For Confucius Heaven is kind of an impersonal, moral force that oversees the world but for Mozi, Heaven is more like a personal god. In fact, Mozi promoted a religious vision of society in which the fear of ghosts, spirits, and punishment from Heaven would keep the people in line. He's a much more religious thinker than Confucius.

Mozi's followers seem to have been artisans merchants, maybe small property holders, rather than not aristocrats. They were a disciplined cadre of activists, who shared his message with missionary zeal. They're always eager to debate people from other persuasions. They often rushed to the aid of small states that were under attack, which will be a problem because they are often on the losing side of sieges and such. Mozi set an example, he said he would walk for 10 days and 10 nights to try to talk rulers out of declaring war. He tore pieces off of his clothes to bind up his feet when his shoes wore out to keep going. All of that is in contrast with Yang Zhu, who is the philosopher associated with pure selfishness. It is said that Yang Zhu would not sacrifice one hair from his body even if it benefitted the whole world. You have these extremes of Yang Zhu being very selfish and Mozi being willing to sacrifice everything for the good of the people.

Mozi's school declined during the late Warring States period, though later Mohists made advances in the fields of logic, mathematics, optics, and mechanics. He was ignored for a long time and then in the 19th century, his ideas were rediscovered. Partly by Christian missionaries, who were very interested into this idea that there was an early Chinese philosopher whose principles were based on a universal love. That sounded a little like their religion. Then in the 20th century there have been some who look to his followers for the origins of science and logic in China

I'm going to move to our second great thinker of our course. His name is Huizi, Master Hui. He lived from 380–305 B.C. We'll categorize him as a Terminologist, a Logician He composes a series of paradoxes that point to the relativity of time and space. Unfortunately, we don't have a whole book from him we just have a list. It includes things like this though, and we have to try to figure out what he was talking about. He says, Mountains and marshes are the same height. How can that be? Though it is true from space, from enough distance, if the earth was the size of a billiard ball it would be about that smooth. The difference between the highest mountains and sea level are not that great compared to the circumference of the earth as a whole.

Huizi says when something is born it is also dying, those processes go together. He says the center of the world is north of Yen, the state of Yen, and south of Yueh. It would be like saying that the center of the world is north of Maine and south of Florida. How does that work? I think his idea is that if the world is infinite then the center can be anywhere or everywhere. One more, he says an egg has feathers. Somehow since chickens come from that there must be some proto feather something in an egg. Which kind of makes sense.

Huizi's paradoxes are often compared to those of the Greek philosopher Zeno, who lived a century earlier, especially his observation that if you take a foot-long stick and cut it in half every day, the next day you cut that half in half, and then what remains in half. In the end of ten thousand generations you'll still have something left, which is a little bit like Zeno's paradox. You'll remember that if Achilles is racing a tortoise. He gives the tortoise a 100 yards head start, then the quick runner can never overtake the slow one, since the pursuer, Achilles, must first reach the point where the tortoise started. By that time the tortoise has already moved a little bit, and by the time he gets to the place the tortoise has just moved from, it's moved a little bit more and so on and so on. He can never catch him; the slower must always hold a lead. It doesn't work that way in real life but there's this notion that infinite pieces and how that intersects with ordinary life.

Let me just tell you very quickly about one other philosopher in this Terminologist school who you may encounter sometime. His name is Gongsun Long. He's famous for saying a white horse is not a horse. By which he seems to mean, if you ask for a white horse then you have to have a white horse. But if you ask for a horse, somebody may bring you a brown horse or a grey horse and that still will fit the category. So the category of white horse is a subset, it's smaller, category of horse. A white horse is not a horse, people argue about that for a long time, lots of fun.

We'll move on to our next and last great thinker in this hundred schools period. His name is Zhuangzi. This is a name you might have seen before; it's spelled in more recent books, Z-h-u-a-n-g-z-i. In earlier transcriptions it will be C-h-u-a-n-g-z-i. Zhuangzi is born about 369 B.C. and dies maybe 286 B.C. He is the second great Daoist thinker after Laozi. I'm not sure that he would he have considered himself a follower of Laozi but there are commonalities in their approach to life. Once again, there's a man and a text that's also named *Zhuangzi*. The text that we have it today has 33 chapters, but the first 7 chapters seem to be the work of one person. It's called the inner chapters of *Zhuangzi* and the other chapters may have been added in later on in the text history.

Unlike Laozi, Zhuangzi seems to be a real person. In these stories, in his writings, he talks about conversations he has with friends, including his friend Huizi who was the Logician I just talked about. He talks about his reaction to the death of his wife. He sounds like a person. His ideas are similar to those found in the *Daodejing*, but he takes them to a more extreme position. He is also one of the most elegant, witty writers in all of Chinese philosophy and I think perhaps in philosophy period.

Laozi argued that ordinary distinctions were meaningless, but he generally had a preference for the less valued. Remember he pointed out the advantages of weakness, femaleness, and passivity. Zhuangzi, by contrast, really has no preference, even in such matters as life and death, or power and powerlessness, or dreams and reality. The most famous story about Zhuangzi is that he was one day taking a nap on the bank of a river, taking a nap is a good Daoist activity. He dreamed while he was napping that he was a butterfly, sort of flittering from here and there. Then he woke up and says, I'm not sure whether I am Zhuangzi who just had a dream that I was a butterfly, or if I am a butterfly who's now dreaming that I'm Zhuangzi. Who knows, dreams or reality.

Where Laozi offered advice to rulers, Zhuangzi is resolutely non-political. There's another story when Zhuangzi was out fishing one day, another great Daoist activity, and some ambassadors, representatives from the state of Chu, which is a huge state to the south come to him. They offer him the prime minister position there. Zhuangzi says to them, I've heard that in Chu you have a sacred tortoise that's been dead for 3,000 years dead that you keep in a box in ancestral temple. Every so often you bring it out and show it reverence and such. Do you think that tortoise would rather be dead and honored, or would it rather be alive and dragging its tail in the mud? They said maybe the latter. Zhuangzi said, I would rather be alive and dragging the mud so I'm not interested at all in your position. Just go back and tell the king no.

Zhuangzi argues for a radical skepticism that refuses to choose between contradictory positions. He suggests that all of our judgments are based on limited, partial perspectives. It's a little bit like Jain epistemology. Zhuangzi was very wary of language, which can't really do justice to fluid, complex realities though he used words in order to deconstruct language, it's an interesting paradox. The book, *Zhuangzi*, begins with a description of a fantastically large bird, miles long, whose wings cover the sky as he flies south, even though he is miles above the ground. As he passes way overhead, a cicada and a dove make fun of him. We can hardly get to the next tree, they say, how can anything fly thousands of miles? But, Zhuangzi points out, they have no idea what they're talking about.

Or take death as an example. Zhuangzi asks, How do we know that our love of life isn't a mistake? Perhaps it's like the daughter of the border guard who was sent to be a wife of the Duke. She cried and cried when she arrived at the palace, but after she had eaten the fine food and enjoyed the lifestyle at court, she regretted that she had wept. How do we know that the dead won't someday repent of clinging to life so tightly? Who knows.

Or to give you a better sense of how he writes, I'm going to give you a direct quotation. It's kind of long but stay with me here. When he talks about the creator, he actually is not talking about a monotheistic god he's talking about nature. He'll tell a story,

> [Master Yu] fell ill and [Master Si] went to see him. "Great is the Creator!" said the sick man. "See how he has made me crumpled up like this!" His back was hunched and his backbone was protruding. His internal organs were on the top of his body. His cheeks were level with his navel. His shoulders were higher than his head. The

hair on top of his head pointed up toward the sky. The yin and yang in him were out of order, but his mind was at ease as though nothing had happened. He limped and walked quickly to the well and looked at his reflection, and said, "Alas! The Creator has made me crumpled up like this!"

"Do you dislike it?" asked [Master Si].

"Why, no, what would I [dislike]? If the process continues, perhaps in time he'll transform my left arm into a rooster. In that case I'll keep watch on the night. Or perhaps in time he'll transform my right arm into a crossbow pellet and I'll shoot down an owl for roasting. Or perhaps in time he'll transform my buttocks into cartwheels. Then, with my spirit for a horse, I'll climb up and go for a ride. What need will I ever have for a carriage again?"

He continues, what a great attitude about physical discomfort he's got here:

"I obtained life because the time was right. I will lose life because it is time. Those who go quietly with the flow of nature are not worried by either joy or sorrow. People like these were considered in the past as having achieved freedom from bondage. Those who cannot free themselves are constrained by things. However nothing can overcome Heaven—it has always been so. So why should I dislike this?"

Charming story. It actually reminds me of another story in American history about Roger Williams. Do you remember the great defender of religious freedom and the founder of Rhode Island? He died in 1683 and was buried on his family ground next to his house. After a while that sort of fell into decay, 200 years later some people from the Rhode Island historical society, said we should dig up Roger Williams and we should make an appropriate memorial to such a great man. They started digging around, they found the spot where he had been buried, but what had happened was that an apple tree nearby had sent a root down and into the casket. It actually had grown right through Roger Williams. This root has sort of a straight part that grew down his spine and then it splits in half at his pelvis one goes down one leg and one goes down the other. You have this sort of man shaped root that Roger Williams has apparently turned into In addition people for hundreds of years have been walking by and grabbing the fruit off of the tree and eating it, so the question is who ate Roger Williams? Who knows what you'll be turned into one day as this body changes and is transformed into something else. If you're interested in seeing that Roger Williams shaped root that took his place you can see it at the John Brown House Museum in Providence, Rhode Island to this day.

Back to Zhuangzi. I want you to listen to this quote when he talks about language and how difficult it is to understand things through language. Don't try to follow the logic he's very quick here, but just get a sense for how he works. He says,

> Suppose here is a statement. We do not know whether it belongs to one category or whether it belongs to another category. [Remember he doesn't like to make categories.] But if we put the different categories in one, then the differences of category cease to exist. However, I must explain. If there was a beginning, then there was a time before that beginning, and a time before the time which was before the time of that beginning. If there is existence, there must have been non-existence. And if there was a time when nothing existed, then there must have been a time when even nothing did not exist. All of a sudden, nothing came into existence. Could one then really say whether it belongs to the category of existence or of non-existence? Even the very words I have just now uttered—I cannot say whether they say something or nothing at all.

This is that sort of humor that you sometimes get in Daoists hardly ever in Confucians. Zhuangzi was fond of intuitive knowledge, spontaneous action, logical puzzles, and humor. He sometimes told "knack stories," people who had a certain knack for something. One of the most famous of these is about Cook Ding, whose carving of an ox was like a dance. He had a big knife and the ox just fell apart into pieces. It was just so smooth and effortless that it seemed almost magical. It was spontaneous, but it wasn't random, it was the result of years of practice. He had the ability to size up an animal before he started carving. Then he just follows the natural form, he slides his knife between the joints, without ever hitting bones or hard sinews. He says a great cook changes his knife once a year, because he cuts. A mediocre cook has to change his knife once a month because he hacks. I haven't changed knives in 19 years, and it's as good as new. This sort of effortless action seems almost like the total absorption in a task and loss of self that we talked about in regard of the Bhagavad Gita. Success comes from letting go rather than from grasping. We'll see this sort of action, or this mode of living again when we talk about Zen Buddhism.

As you can see, Zhuangzi doesn't present reasoned, logical arguments. Instead, he illustrates his ideas in wonderful essays that feature fantastical language, and made-up dialogues between historical figures or imaginary creatures. He tells personal anecdotes and clever stories, some of which involve interactions with his good friend Huizi, the Logician. Let me give you an example. It says in the book of the *Zhuangzi*:

> Zhuangzi and Huizi were walking on a bridge over River Hao. Zhuangzi: Look at those fish darting about, such is the happiness of fish. Huizi: You're not a fish, how do you know what makes fish happy. Zhuangzi: You're not me; how do you know that I don't know the happiness of fish. Huizi: If I'm not you and so don't know what you know, then it follows that you, not being a fish, don't know the happiness of fish. Zhuangzi: Let's go back to original question, you asked *how* I knew the happiness of fish. Your very question shows that you knew that I knew. I knew it on this bridge.

For 2,000 years, the Chinese have looked back to the Warring States Period as a golden age in philosophy. Even in the 20th century, when Mao Zedong in 1956 proclaimed a new era of intellectual freedom, he referred to this ancient movement. He said, "Let a hundred flowers bloom and a hundred schools contend!" Those are the hundred schools of philosophy; this is the hundred flowers movement back then. As we'll see in Lecture 34, it didn't go well for those who stepped up to Mao's challenge.

In the next lecture, we'll discuss two more Confucian philosophers, Mencius and Xunzi, but I want to give the last word to Zhuangzi, who tried to get at a truth beyond language. Again, you can see how clever and engaging he is. Watch how he undercuts his own remarkable facility with words. He says,

> The fish trap exists because of the fish; once you've gotten the fish, you can forget the trap. The rabbit snare exists because of the rabbit; once you've gotten the rabbit, you can forget the snare. Words exist because of the meaning; once you've gotten the meaning, you can forget the words. Where can I find a man who has forgotten the words so I can have a word with him?

This notion that the utility of words comes to an end once you've gotten what's behind it, that's something you'll see later on in Buddhism and elsewhere. But it's that last line that's the real kicker, sort of this signature Zhuangzi twist at the end. "Where can I find a man who has forgotten the words so I can have a word with him?" And after that, there's not much to say. Thanks.

Mencius and Xunzi—Confucius's Successors
Lecture 9

Mencius's and Xunzi's relationships to Confucius have been compared to Plato's and Aristotle's to Socrates. Both philosophers had much in common with Confucius and each other, including beliefs in the importance of education, perfectibility of humans, moral responsibilities of rulers, and centrality of ritual. But Mencius was an idealist who believed human nature was essentially good, whereas Xunzi was a naturalist who believed it was essentially evil. Ultimately, Mencius's optimism had more appeal for the Chinese people.

Mencius lived during the 4th century B.C. and the time of the Hundred Schools, and his life story is quite similar to Confucius's. He served only briefly as a government official but was a fine teacher who had been taught by students of Confucius's grandson. His writings consist of extended arguments with his philosophical opponents, including followers of Mozi.

Mencius's most famous debate is with the philosopher Gaozi over whether human nature is good or evil. Gaozi says it is neither but can be channeled one way or another. Mencius contends that human nature is essentially good, "just as water naturally flows downhill." Evil is a consequence of not acting on our natural good impulses, which is why education is essential to moral development. Anyone can become a sage through proper moral cultivation, which involves both *qi* (vital energy) and *xin* (heart/mind).

Mencius refined Confucius's political ideas; for example, he said rebellion is justified when rulers neglect their responsibilities. He also performed some of the first economic analysis in Chinese history, arguing for a free market and encouraging trade, but he also said that rulers must put righteousness before profit.

Xunzi belonged to the next generation of Confucians. He was a prominent, respected political advisor and essayist, as well as a teacher, and lived to see most of China conquered by the rising state of Qin. Xunzi believed that direct observation and the historical record left no doubt that human nature is evil, or at least selfish, but that enlightened self-interest can motivate people to choose virtue and cooperation. Since morality must be learned, Xunzi agrees with Mencius and Confucius on the importance of education.

Xunzi's outlook is primarily secular. For him, morality is a human construct, not an inheritance from heaven. Rituals work, but they are the products of sages' minds, not revelation, and foster goodness through psychological satisfaction. Nor are natural disasters messages from the beyond; they are natural phenomena. If the government is good, it will be prepared for floods, droughts, and so on, and the people won't go hungry. But if the government is corrupt, when natural disaster strikes, the people will suffer. Disasters are natural, but the outcomes are man-made.

Also, if Mencius is one of the earliest economic thinkers, we can recognize Xunzi as one of the first environmentalists. He urges rulers to adopt laws that conserve plants and wildlife.

Since morality must be learned, Xunzi agrees with Mencius and Confucius on the importance of education.

Mencius's ideas eventually overshadowed Xunzi's, perhaps because their inherent optimism was better suited to the mood of China under the Qin dynasty. In the 12th century A.D., Mencius's writings were included alongside the *Analects* as the core texts of imperial civil servants' education for the next 800 years. ■

Suggested Reading

Chan, *A Source Book in Chinese Philosophy*.

De Bary and Bloom, eds., *Sources of Chinese Tradition*.

Graham, *Disputers of the Tao*.

Knoblock, *Xunzi*.

Mencius.

Nivison, *The Ways of Confucianism*.

Shun, *Mencius and Early Chinese Thought*.

Questions to Consider

1. Are humans by nature good or bad? Is this even the right question to ask?

2. Is education necessary to moral development?

3. Is a secular approach to nature and ritual compatible with morality?

4. Are ethics derived from nature or revelation, or are they human inventions? And if the latter, can they ever be seen as authoritative?

Mencius and Xunzi—Confucius's Successors
Lecture 9—Transcript

Hi, welcome back. In this lecture we're going to talk about Mencius and Xunzi, who were the two great successors to Confucius. That second name is a little tricky, Xunzi is X-u-n-z-i. The *x* makes a sort of *sh-* sound. Both Mencius and Xunzi accepted the main precepts of Confucianism but they disagreed on several issues, including most memorably whether human nature was basically good or basically bad. Mencius's ideas, and he takes the more optimistic position, eventually became dominant in the Confucian tradition. It's a quick way to tell them apart: Mencius thinks that human nature is good and Xunzi thinks that it's bad. But there's more to their thought than this one idea, as important as it may be.

We'll start with Mencius. He lived from about 372–289 B.C. He's a contemporary with Aristotle, and he lives during the time of the hundred schools philosophy, which we mentioned earlier. Mencius's life was in many ways parallel to that of Confucius. He was actually only born about 50 miles from where Confucius was born, also lost father at a young age, raised by a single mother, he devoted himself to scholarship, but times were even worse, remember this is the Warring States Era now. Mencius travelled for about 40 years seeking government employment. One story from those years is he had an interview with a king who he was hoping he could give him advice for military conquest. Mencius replied that gaining the empire through violence was a little bit like climbing a tree in order to look for a fish. It's just not going to happen that way. He didn't get that job of course. Mencius served briefly as an official but he was, again like Confucius, mostly a teacher He himself had been taught by students of Confucius's grandson. So there's a lineal connection there.

Mencius as I said, was raised by a single mother. In this course we can use all the women that we can find, so let me talk about Mencius's mother for a little bit. She's often thought of as a role model to Chinese mothers today. The story is that she was trying to find a place for her and her young son to live. She found a place next to a cemetery. Then when her son would be playing he would wail and pretend that he was a professional mourner. She said, "This isn't quite the environment I want for my son." She moved to a marketplace and the next thing she knew little Mencius was playing buying and selling and arranging goods as if he was a shopkeeper. She said that's not exactly what I want either for my son. So she moved a third time to a home next to a school. Then Mencius would play school, teacher and student and he would pretend to read books. She said this is the right sort of place for my son to grow up.

She was invested in his education and that continued. There's a story once that he came home from school and she said, "What did you learn today?" Mencius said, "Same as usual." His mother who was weaving at the time something that women in Chinese homes often did, took a knife and slashed through the cloth that was on the loom. Her son was quite shocked by that and said, "What are you doing?" She said, "If you neglect your studies, if you're not taking them seriously it's the same as me cutting cloth from the loom. Unless I weave, who is going to take care of me? Unless you study you're going to be dependent on others. In fact unless you get more serious about your studies you're going to end up a servant or thief." Mencius was taken aback by that and vowed to study even harder.

One more story from his mother. When Mencius was older and married, he once walked into his bedroom door and his wife was there not completely dressed, which is a sort of breach of etiquette. Remember how important ritual is for Confucian scholars? He left without saying anything but was a bit put off by that. His wife noticed that he had started treating her as a stranger. She went to her mother-in-law, they are living with the mother, and said, "Why don't you just send me back home to my family because this marriage isn't working out." Mencius's mother went to talk to her son and said, "It was impolite to barge into people. Next time before you enter a room why don't you make a little noise, like you could knock or you could say something but because you haven't behaved properly you blame other people. You blame your wife for not being appropriate, having the right sort of etiquette. Don't blame other people." Mencius of course took his mother's words to heart and became a great moralist as well. The moral of these three stories is that behind every great man in China is a mother.

Once again, with Mencius there's a man and a book. The man's name is Mencius and the book is known as the *Mencius*. It's a record of his conversations, but unlike the *Analects*, Mencius's text offers extended arguments where he debates back and forth with his philosophical opponents, including the followers of Mozi. Remember the philosopher who talked about universal love, or impartial caring. Mencius says that Mozi is wrong since morality should come from principle, not self-interest or from utility. Remember that Mozi said that if it doesn't contribute to food, clothing, or shelter than it just doesn't matter. Mencius said no there are things that matter like principle. He also says you can't love person's family as much as you love your own. Then he's going to argue with the followers of Yang Zhu, and say it's wrong to assert that self and pleasure are more important than duty and service. Yang Zhu is wrong because he's too much on the selfish side and Mozi is wrong too because it's too unrealistically generous. Both of those are wrong because they deny human nature. Mencius wants his morality to be grounded in human nature. Which is the subject of his most famous debate; this is with Gaozi, over whether people are naturally good or bad. Gaozi says human nature is neither one. It's sort of like water, people can be made to do good things or do bad things it depends, like water can be channeled one direction, to the left or to the right, it just doesn't matter. Mencius's reply was people are actually naturally good. I like your analogy but it's more like water goes downhill. That's its natural tendency. You can splash it up high or you can keep it up by a dam but it does have to a natural tendency.

Nice analogy, but what evidence would there be that people are naturally good? Mencius gives a famous example. He says, imagine that there's a child, a toddler, who's walking along and is about to fall into a well. Anyone who sees this situation will feel this momentary sense of panic as this happens. It's not anything thought out or calculated, it's not that you gasp because you want to please parents or enhance your reputation for being a moral person, or you say I just hate it when kids fall into wells they just cry and they cry, ruins your whole day. It's nothing like that; it just comes perfectly naturally and spontaneously. Everyone has the beginnings of morality within them.

He says there are four beginnings. There's benevolence, that's *ren*, this sort of human heartedness; righteousness; propriety, which is *li*; and wisdom. Those are as natural as having four limbs for everyone. When someone says that human nature is good, it's fair to ask why is there evil in the world then? Mencius's answer is people have good impulses but those can atrophy if they're not acted upon, which is why education is so important in moral development. Mencius once said, "The great man is one who does not lose his child's heart." You want to feel those impulses and then nurture them and cultivate them. Natural goodness is instilled in humans by Heaven and every person has the potential to become a sage through moral cultivation, which involves both *qi*, which is vital energy, we'll talk more about that when we talk about Neo-Confucianism, and *xin*, which is one's heart/mind. In Chinese there's just one word that refers to as both heart and mind. Those go together.

Mencius then offers some refinements to Confucius' political ideas. Confucius talked a little bit about the Mandate of Heaven. Here's the idea: Heaven gives its seal of approval to some sort of political regime as long as those rulers are taking care of the common people, are generous, are helping out, providing order. But when those rulers, actually their decedents become corrupt, Heaven will withdraw its seal of approval and give it to some other family. They'll lose it. We'll know when Heaven starts to withdraw its approval because there will be portents. There will be natural disasters, eclipses, floods, and droughts. Rulers need to pay attention to those kinds of things. I know that may sound a little bit superstitious and perhaps it is. We know that eclipses and earthquakes have nothing to do with the morality of the rulers but some of it kind of makes sense. In Chinese history the Yellow River often times broke through the dikes that kept it in. Sometimes in Chinese history, the bed of the river was many feet above the flood plain so when the dikes broke through it was just disastrous. That was thought of as a portent from Heaven. Of course sometimes that happens because the people in charge of the waterworks were ciphering off money and things weren't getting paid, there's corruption, and the dikes weren't actually being maintained. There might actually be a connection between flooding on the Yellow River and poor government. That kind of makes sense.

Mencius takes this idea of the Mandate of Heaven and he takes it a little further by talking about the other part of that, which is when Heaven gives its seal of approval to another family that new person or family is justified in rebellion. I should mention that Heaven is not a personal god that sees over things, in Confucian thought it's an impersonal moral force. The Mandate of Heaven is closely associated with the welfare of the common people. I'm going to give an example from Mencius. This is from the founding of the Zhou dynasty. The last dynasty, the Shang dynasty, had a ruler named Zhou, different character different pronunciation so a little confusing, but the last ruler was a very corrupt guy. He was cruel, oppressive, lost the mandate of heaven and then in the fighting that came he actually was killed. There's a king that's asking about that particular episode in history and he asked, "May a minister then put his sovereign to death?" Notice what a politically-loaded question this is. This is a king who's saying is it ever appropriate for a somebody else to kill a king? Mencius said,

> He who outrages the benevolence proper to his nature, is called a robber; he who outrages righteousness, is called a ruffian. The robber and ruffian we call a mere fellow. I have heard of the [punishment] of the fellow Zhou, [the last cruel king] but I have not heard of the putting a sovereign to death, in his case.

So he's saying that he lost the kingly seal of approval, and then yes those kinds of people can be killed.

This is dangerous stuff. The founder of the Ming dynasty in china, this is in the early 1400s so he's new into this empire and he doesn't want to hear any justifications for people rebelling against him. He disliked these ideas in *Mencius* and he halted the sacrifices at Mencius' ancestral temple and tried to get rid of about a third of the book, all of those passages that touched on the "right of rebellion."

Some of the earliest economic analysis in Chinese history comes from *Mencius* as well. This is as an important aspect of statecraft. A philosopher named Xuzi who suggested to Mencius in conversation that it would be beneficial if everything had a set price, so that no one would take advantage of even a child who went to the marketplace. You send a kid with some money, he can just read the prices, and he wouldn't be at a disadvantage in negotiating these prices haggling. Mencius replied that that didn't really make sense. If, for example, every shoe of the same size were sold at the same price, why would anyone work harder to make a better quality shoe?

He also encouraged trade, which is a little bit of a change from Confucius. Confucius once said that the superior man cares about doing what's right the inferior man cares about making a profit. There's a hesitancy about market values there. Mencius thought that trade was important.

He also thought that the division of labor was something that could be a good part of a well organized society. He came across a king who was proud that he farmed himself, right alongside his subjects. When he talked to him he asked this king, "You're growing your own grain that's great, but where did you get your cap? Where did you get the pots that you cook with? Or the plows that you use?" The king said, "Well I don't make those myself, I have to barter for those." Mencius says, "Why then would it be bad to barter for ruler ship? Some people might give food and clothing to a particular individual in return for good government, administration." Mencius says, "Some labor with their minds, others with their strength."

Then finally he encouraged a well-field system as a way to ensure limited, sustainable taxation. That needs more explanation. The Chinese character for a well it looks like a tic-tac-toe board, or maybe like the pound sign. The idea there is to divide up land in that shape, then have eight families all have land around the outside. Then there's one square in middle they all farm that together and the produce from that middle square pays the taxes for everyone. limited, sustainable taxation; that idea was talked about later on in Chinese history, it never really got off the ground. It was hard to implement.

Mencius is thinking along these lines of practical administration. Don't get me wrong, Mencius didn't exactly celebrate capitalism that would be pretty anachronistic. Indeed, the beginning of his book the *Mencius* starts with a famous story. I'll paraphrase it for you. He went to see King Hui of the state of Liang. King Hui says, "You've come all this distance, several hundred miles. You surely must have something to profit my kingdom." Mencius said,

> Why talk about "profit"? All I have is benevolence and righteousness. If you ask about profit for your kingdom, then ministers ask about profit for their family, commoners ask about profit for themselves. Everybody all down the line is going to follow your example and

say what's in it for me? In a kingdom with 10,000 chariots, the king is going to be killed by vassal who owns 1,000 chariots. Then in a smaller state, a 1,000-chariot state, the king is going to be killed by a vassal with 100 chariots. Even 100 chariots is a lot to have but when profit is put before righteousness, no amount can satisfy. Even if you have 100, even if you have 1,000, you'll always want more. Now do you see why I teach benevolence and righteousness? Why bother to mention profit?

Sima Qian, the great historian in about 100 B.C.—I talk about his in a lot of my lectures; I will have a whole lecture about him later—writes a biography of Mencius. He actually writes biographies of most of these early thinkers. Then he has a personal response at the end of that chapter. He says, "Whenever I read the book of *Mencius* and I come to the passage where King Hui of Liang asks, 'How can I profit my kingdom?' I cannot help but set my book aside and sigh, saying, 'Alas, desire for profit is surely the beginning of ruin.' " I always like that image because Sima Qian hasn't read more than the first page of *Mencius* before he sets it aside with a sigh. Alas, profit, self-interest let's say, is going to be the ruin of everything.

We're now going to move the second great mind of this lecture. This is Xiunzi. Xunzi lives from about 300–c. 210 B.C., so he belongs to the next generation of Confucians after Mencius. In contrast to Mencius, Xunzi was a prominent, respected political advisor whose writings are essays rather than records of conversations. He was a major figure in the Jixia Academy in the state of Qi, a fairly prominent state. He lived to see most of China conquered by the rising state of Qin—that's Q-i-n that's an important name we're going to pick up that story in the next lecture.

Xunzi believed that direct observation and a record of history left no doubt that human nature is evil. Okay, maybe not quite evil in the sense of cruel or depraved, but selfish. Nevertheless, enlightened self-interest can motivate people to choose virtue and cooperation. A follower of Mencius might say, Well if people want to do right where does that desire come from? Maybe that's innate. And Xunzi says, No, everybody wants what they don't have. Just as the poor want to be rich, people who are evil desire goodness. Goodness is not natural, but is the result of conscious effort. Morality doesn't come from innate impulses; it has to be learned and that's why education is the key. On this point Mencius and Xunzi are going to be in perfect agreement. This is why they're both Confucians they both care about education. For Mencius, you're innately good but those impulses have to be nurtured and paid attention to. For Xunzi, you are bad at the core but that can be changed and improved through education.

Xunzi's analogy is that people are like warped wood. Warped wood can be made straight by the application of steam, a straightening board, and pressure. What is needed are teachers; rituals, this is *li*, rituals that bring out positive in people; and laws to deter negative behaviors. The rules of conduct are an important part of ethics, but morality is, in the end, a human construct rather than an inheritance from Heaven. The sages in ancient times came up with the rules of ritual themselves. They work, they are valuable but they are not the product of revelation they don't come from god or heaven.

Xunzi actually takes a rather secular approach to life. Heaven is just nature—the Chinese word *tian* literally means sky. It's just the sky. It functions in a mechanical fashion with no concern for human society or for human values. Natural disasters, he says, are not messages, portents, or warnings, as in mandate of Heaven theories, they are simply natural phenomena. Xunzi makes sense in an age of science. He would see eclipses and earthquakes as just part of the way the world works. In his Essay on Heaven, so this is part of this book called the *Xunzi*, he makes the following sorts of observations. Heaven does not suspend winter just because people don't like the cold. Don't worry about eclipses or comets or trees that make strange sounds in the night and people say, what does that mean? It doesn't mean anything, it's just the transformation of yin and yang. Notice that even Confucians talk in means of yin and yang by this point, this is after the hundred schools and things are getting mixed up and people are debating each other in the Dao hotel. Rather than heavenly portents, it's human portents that matter. What are human portents? He says when you're travelling around and you see fields that are abandoned and untended, when you see high prices for basic commodities, when people are starving, when there are bodies on the roadside then you know that things are going wrong. Those are human portents.

I love what he says about natural disasters. If the government is good, if the rulers are practicing the Way and looking after the people, even if there are floods and droughts, people won't go hungry. But if the government is corrupt and oppressive, even if there are no floods and droughts, people will still suffer and they'll still starve. Ultimately, the worst disasters are manmade. It's how people react to what comes just mechanically by nature, through natural processes. Rituals are crucial in fostering goodness. They provide psychological satisfaction but they do not influence the workings of the cosmos.

Xunzi notes that when people pray for rain, it rains sometimes. Why is that? He says, Well actually, it will always rain eventually, whether people pray or not. Rulers can participate in ceremonies and sacrifices, but whereas the people believe in them superstitiously, rulers know that the most important function is to promote harmony and order. For instance, sacrifices to the ancestors give expression to feelings of remembrance and longing for the dead. Expectations of supernatural intervention by departed loved ones are rather beside the point. I have a friend who's an Atheist, who believes in the power of prayer. I remember asking him, "You don't even believer there's a god, why do you pray? It doesn't make any sense." He actually said, "There's something about prayer where you sit in a calm place, you focus on particular things, and when you do that that sort of concentration leads to ideas that you haven't had before. I think you can get answers to prayer, even though I don't think they come from god at all." Compare that to Xunzi talking about rituals, he says, "The gentleman understand them as the human way; the common people think of them as matters having to do with spirits."

Let me talk for just a minute about ancestral worship. When you're parents die you're still connected to them, you still have the same relationship. But it's not like they've gone into a completely transcended realm, it's more like they moved away—far away, let's say to Indonesia. They're never coming back, you're never going to see them again but you can still send care packages, send letters, this is prayers and sacrifices that you make to feed the ancestors who might be hungry on the other side. IN return they might pull some strings on your behalf to help you out, sort of like they did when you were alive to make you feel better in some ways. Now you worship three degrees of ancestors—actually this is all in your father's side—so it has to be your parents, your grandparents on your father's side, and then paternal great-grand parents. Just three levels of ancestors for ordinary sorts of people. When Christian missionaries, Jesuits, came into China originally they looked at what was going on with ancestral worship and they said, What are we going to do about this? Is it idolatry or not? The Jesuits said it's actually just respect, a very high degree of respect but it's just honoring your mother and father. Later on Dominican's came in and said no this idolatry, if we're not going to put up with Protestant Christianity why would we put up with Confucian Christianity? The issue got debated back in Rome, the Pope came down on the side of the Dominicans and said ancestor worship is inappropriate for Chinese Christians, which actually is going to pretty much end Christianity in China. It just pulls people too far out of civilized society the way that the Chinese had defined it. Eventually the emperor himself sided with the Jesuits and said I'm not going to accept any Dominican, who is this guy in Italy telling my people what they can and can't believe, and Christianity just falters away in china over the issue of ancestor worship.

Back to Mencius; early on Mencius gets credit for early economic thinking, we can recognize Xunzi as one of the first environmentalist philosophers. He urges rulers to adopt laws that conserve grasses, trees, fish, and turtles, so that they remain abundant. For instance, he suggests that mountain forests should not be cut down when they are flowering or putting forth new shoots and he wants nets and poisons prohibited from marshes during the times when fish and turtles are depositing their eggs. He says, "so as to not cut short their life, and not to break off their growth."

Finally, language is also a rather arbitrary human construct according to Xunzi so words should be used precisely. Xunzi talks about the rectification of names, which is basically matching names to reality, particularly in government offices where you want to make sure the person doing the office has the right title and the right description of what his responsibilities are. Xunzi's philosophy is very carefully articulated and it's very readable.

Where does this all go from here? Mencius and Xunzi as followers of Confucius have been compared to Plato and Aristotle who are followers of Socrates. They have a lot in common: Both of these thinkers like education, they think that people can be sages, they like moral government and ritual, but Mencius tends to be more idealist and Xunzi more realistic. Sort of like how Plato is thought of as more idealistic and Aristotle more down to earth.

Xunzi's unsentimental realism was a better fit for Warring States Era, a time of great violence and chaos. He was probably the more influential in early China, yet Mencius' ideas eventually overshadowed those of Xunzi. Why is that? It may be that Chinese culture basically optimistic, they like the idea the people are naturally good. Xunzi was more open to the role of laws in statecraft and some of his students were associated with the Legalism, which we'll talk about in the next lecture. Consequently, Xunzi's reputation suffered when the Legalist Qin dynasty was taken over and repudiated by its successors the Han dynasty. People blame all those bad things on the Legalists.

In the 12th century, the writings of Mencius, actually the book of *Mencius*, is going to be included in the Four Books along with the *Analects* and two chapters from the *Book of Rites*. This collection became the fundamental text of Neo-Confucianism, we'll see that in Lecture 23. Those four books will be the subject matter for the imperial civil service exams for the about 700 years. The prominence of Mencius in Chinese thought is the reason why he and Confucius are the only two Chinese philosophers who are known in English by Latinized names because they were first introduced to the West by Jesuit missionaries writing in Latin in the 17th century. Confucius and Mencius, that *-ius*; in Chinese it's Kongzi, there's that *-zi* that means master, and Mengzi.

In popular culture, Chinese is a challenging language. You have to learn a lot of words but also some four character phrases, slogans. Chinese are always putting these phrases in their discussion. The closest thing I can think of in English is "monkey see, monkey do," which would be hard to understand if you weren't a native English speaker but if you've heard that phrase you know what it means. Mencius writes fairly clear straightforward Chinese, it's a good place to start learning classical Chinese. He includes some memorable stories and illustrations. For example, A man from the state of Song was impatient for seedlings to grow, and he went out pulled them up a bit to help them out. Went home to his sons and he said, "I'm tired, I'm just exhausted." His son said, "What have you been doing?" He said, "I've been helping seedlings grow." His son went out to the field to see what was going on and already everything had started withering. Mencius says you can't force self-cultivation. There's this four character phrase, *bá míao zhù zhăng* that means "pulling at the sprouts to help them grow." People hear that and they know that means you can't rush a natural process otherwise you'll ruin things in the attempt.

Alright, two more, that you've already heard about. For hopeless, wrongheaded actions, someone Chinese might say *yuan mu qiu yu*, it's like "climbing a tree to look for a fish." Remember the king that Mencius was talking to that tried to gain the empire by violence?

Finally, in China a wise mother who is devoted to her children's education, might elicit the comment *meng mu san qian*: "Mencius' mother moved three times." What a lovely example of how a mothers sometimes can nurture, cultivate, and set an example for their children. Perhaps that's a good place to end here, with the question: What are you willing to do for your children?

Sunzi and Han Feizi—Strategy and Legalism
Lecture 10

> Out of the chaos of the Warring States era, China's Han dynasty (202 B.C.–A.D. 220) built a powerful empire. Legalism and military strategy emerged from the Hundred Schools to join Confucianism and Daoism as leading ideologies of the new Chinese state. Sunzi's militarist *Art of War* reflects the changing nature of warfare in the period and a Daoist-like approach to the world. The Legalists argued for the consolidation of state power through practical means and rejected almost all of earlier Chinese moral philosophy and statecraft.

The major military development of the Warring States period was a shift from one-on-one fighting between aristocrats driving chariots to massive battles between armies of peasant conscripts. This new kind of warfare demanded a new kind of military theory, which was supplied by thinkers like Sunzi.

Sunzi was said to have been a contemporary of Confucius, but the book attributed to him, *Art of War*, was probably written during the Warring States period in the 4th century B.C. It was likely written by one of his descendents, named Sun Bin. The principles espoused in the text seem akin to Daoism in many ways, advocating reversals, going with the flow, and defying conventional morality: A skilled general relies on deception, hiding his true power and intention from his foes; he takes advantage of weather and terrain; he expends the fewest resources to the greatest effect. The only thing a general can be certain of in war is change.

Legalism's basic tenet is that people can be made to do anything through reward and punishment.

But it was Legalism that consolidated the Chinese empire. Legalism was not a unified school but a loose group of thinkers who shared an interest in strengthening the state through rational, practical means. Legalism's basic tenet is that people can be made to do anything through reward and punishment. It rejects the Confucian idea that human nature is essentially good, as well as its reverence for tradition.

Legalists recommended the use of a code of law, punishments, and rewards as the best way to motivate citizens. This is not the same as a rule of law; law should be a tool for rulers, who are above the law. Ideally, laws should be objective, even quantifiable, and punishment should be harsh and public. Somewhat surprisingly, Legalism was also often associated with Daoism, because rulers could practice *wuwei*, or nonaction, while the state governed itself through laws.

Han Feizi represents the epitome of Legalist thought. His central argument was that a ruler must be careful not to allow his ministers too much power. Punishment and reward were the "handles" of government, which the leader must hold tightly. Rulers should watch their ministers carefully, hold them accountable for their failures, and take credit for their accomplishments. An ideal ruler is also mysterious, like a Daoist sage; even a weak ruler can control his ministers through keeping them guessing.

The Qin consolidation of China in 221 B.C. was the founding of the first truly Legalist state, but the dynasty barely outlasted its first emperor. The emperor's rule was too harsh, his power too centralized. The Qin dynasty was succeeded by the Han, which combined Legalist government structure with Confucian ideology. This proved a solid foundation for the government of the long Han Empire and beyond. ■

Suggested Reading

Chan, *A Source Book in Chinese Philosophy*.

De Bary and Bloom, eds., *Sources of Chinese Tradition*.

Ivanhoe and Van Norden, eds., *Readings in Classical Chinese Philosophy*.

Lieberthal, *Governing China*.

Sunzi. *Sun Tzu: The Art of War*.

Questions to Consider

1. How important are laws in ordering a society or governing a state?

2. Can techniques of management be separated from morality?

3. Why would the mystical, quietist ideas of Daoism come to be associated with militarism and Legalism?

4. Would you consider yourself more Confucian, more Daoist, or more Legalist? Why?

Sunzi and Han Feizi—Strategy and Legalism
Lecture 10—Transcript

Hello, thanks for joining me. With this lecture, we are going to start a new section of this course the age of empires. So far, we've had lectures about key thinkers in India and China at the beginning of those two traditions—the Darshana Hotel and the Dao Hotel in China—mostly in the historical context of competing, regional kingdoms, in both locations. Now, it's like the hotels are under new management, they've been taken over by maybe a very large multi-national corporations or to get back to the historical situation what happens is that powerful, unified highly centralized regimes are taking hold in India and in China. These are empires that are going to hold sway over many different ethnicities and languages.

By the end of this lecture we will see the emergence of a universal empire in China. That's the Han dynasty that lasts for about 400 years, from about 202 B.C.–A.D. 220. It's contemporary with the Roman Empire on the other side of the Eurasian land mass. It has about the same size of territory, the same number of people, it's fairly comparable. It's not the first of these universal empires that would be the Persian empire, then followed by Alexander's empire, then the Mauryan empire in India, but we are going to keep the story going in China before we go back and back track to pick up some of those other stories.

All of these universal empires have some basic similarities. I suppose because when you're governing over very large territories with large populations there are some administrative techniques that basically have to be in place. They divide the territory into smaller administrative units, provinces in the Roman empire, satrapies in the Persian empire, commandaries, they're called in the Chinese empire. These are more centralized then say the United States; it would be as if the governor of each state was appointed by the president. There are law codes in these empires. There's an ideology that gives some justification for why the people in charge are ruling. There's an elaborate bureaucracy; there are records that have to be kept. There's often a new title for the ruler, like before there were kings of all the small kingdoms, but now there's a king of kings in Persia or the emperor, as he's called in China. They build an impressive capital that intimidates visitors from afar.

There's propaganda. There's a common language so that people serving in the army can understand commands, even though they come from different areas, regions, and linguistic families. There are more trade that happens that uses a lingua franca. There are often good roads; standardized weights, measures, and coinage; often times tolerance for local beliefs and customs. All of this is pretty practical.

In China, how do we get from the Warring States Era, the time of the Hundred Schools, to a single, unified empire? The answer is going to lay with military strategists and Legalists. Legalism is the third great philosophy of China, along with Confucianism and Daoism. Let me start with a story from Sima Qian, seems like I mention him in about every lecture. This is about Zhang Liang, one of the great generals of the day about 200 B.C. When Zhang Liang was young, he met an old man on an embankment. The man was wearing rough clothes, wasn't that impressive, and he threw a shoe down the embankment and said, "Go fetch that for me." Zhang Liang was taken aback by that but he scrambled down, got the shoe and brought it up. The old man then held out his food and said, "Put it on for me." Zhang Liang was actually angry for being treated this way, but he did put it on the old man. The old man started to walk away and then he turns around and says, "You can be taught, young man. Why don't you meet me here in five days at dawn." Zhang Liang was just curious so five days later he shows up about sunrise and the old man's there who says, "Why are you late? I'll give you another chance come back five days from now but don't be late." Five days later, Zhang Liang went even before light. The old man was already there, "Once again, why are you late? One last chance, five days from now." Five days later, Zhang Liang gets up about midnight and goes over to this place. The old man wasn't there. Finally he shows up and says, "Ah this is the way things ought to be." Then he gives Zhang Liang a book and says, "Read this and you will be a teacher of kings." Then he disappeared never to be heard from again.

It turned out that this book was a secret handbook of military strategy called *Grand Duke's Art of War*—wait doesn't this sound like every kung fu movie you've ever seen? Wouldn't you like to know what was in that book? I'd actually like to know too but it was so secret that it was lost. Or perhaps it was just a legendary explanation for Zhang Liang's uncanny abilities on the battlefield. Fortunately there's another text, not so secret, that we still have: the *Art of War* by Sunzi. This is going to be a tricky name here, in the last lecture we talked about Xunzi, the Confucian philosopher, and this is Sunzi. The characters are different and the tones are different, actually the sounds are different that's why there's an *x* it's the *sh-* sound. I'll try to help you keep this straight.

In this lecture we'll be talking about Sunzi, Master Sun, the military strategist. According to tradition, there were two strategists named Sun, both from the same family line, and they both wrote books called the *Art of War*. Both of them are called Master Sun, Sunzi, so even the Chinese sometimes confuse them. Sun Wu, who was the older of the two, the ancestor, was supposed to have lived at the time of Confucius, but his book, and that's the one that is most familiar today, that *Art of War*, probably was written maybe in the 4th century B.C. in the Warring States Era. The work of the descendant, Sun Bin, was lost centuries ago, until ancient versions of both books were discovered in an archaeological excavation in 1972.

Sun Bin was said to have had his feet cut off as a punishment on a trumped-up charge brought by a rival. He couldn't even walk to the battlefield, but could control it like a chess game from afar. Warfare was changing from aristocrats fighting one-on-one from chariots, like in the *Iliad* or in the *Mahabharata* in India. This aristocratic virtue so they want to fight fairly, you don't want to attack your enemy until he's ready. Now they are losing that and going to massive armies, sometimes thousands or tens of thousands on the battlefield. These are made up of peasant conscripts The older book, the older *Art of War*, is more abstract while the newer one is based on specific battles, but both of them have the same sorts of principles. According to the *Art of War*, warfare is based on deception. The skilled general gives the impression that he is strong when he is actually weak, that he is weak when he is actually strong. That he is far away when he is actually near. He always hides his true intentions from his foes. He acts in surprising, unorthodox ways.

A good general will take advantage of weather and terrain. They use the term *shi*, which is translated as situational power. It's sort of like a rock sitting at the top of a mountain. There's a lot of potential there for the person who can see that that's there. There might be an unusual terrain to fight on. A good general attacks when the enemy is weak and he avoids battle when the enemy is strong. Protracted warfare, that just goes on and on, that is always a mistake.

The best victories are those that expend the least resources, without fighting at all, if possible. You should keep destruction to a minimum. It doesn't do you a lot of good to take over a territory that's been devastated, everything's been burned, everything torn apart. You can use spies, secret agents, and manipulative diplomacy, those can be almost as important as the number of soldiers you have

The principles espoused in this text seem like Daoism in some ways. There's reversal, paradoxes—pretend to be weak when you're strong, or strong when you're weak. They're following the natural flow of territory and weather patterns. It's against conventional wisdom, conventional morality sometimes. Let me give you some examples of things that sound almost Daoist from the *Art of War*: "The positioning of troops can be likened to water: Just as the flow of water avoids high ground and rushes to the lowest point, so on the path to victory avoid the enemy's strong points and strike where he is weak." Another quotation: "As the water shapes its flow in accordance with the ground, so an army manages its victory in accordance with the situation of the enemy." Remember how important the image of water was in the *Laozi*, the *Daodejing*. And one more: "War has no constant dynamic; water has no constant form."

The *Art of Warfare*, that's Sun Wu's ancient art of warfare, was studied by generals throughout Chinese history and was important in Mao Zedong's successes against the Japanese in World War II and then the Nationalists under Chiang Kai-shek in the 20th century shortly thereafter. The book is still read in military academies in China, Japan, and the United States, and it has lately been adapted for use in the world of business. There are several of these titles but one that I like particularly is Mark McNeilly, *Sun Tzu and the Art of Business*. He spells Sunzi in that old way so it's S-u-n T-z-u instead of -*zi* at the end. Chapters tend to follow the *Art of War*. They have titles like "Win All Without Fighting: Capturing your Market Without Destroying It," "Avoid Strength, Attack Weakness: Striking Where They Least Expect It," "Deception and Foreknowledge: Maximizing the Power of Market

Information," and then finally "Speed and Preparation: Moving Swiftly to Overcome Your Competitors."

What will eventually make the difference in the quest to create an empire, we're back in the ancient world now, is not just winning individual battles but organizing entire countries for war. That is the contribution of Legalism, a philosophy closely associated with the rise of the state of Qin, which in 221 B.C. united all of China under the First Emperor. The word *qin* is where we get our word China from. Chinese call their own country *Zhong guo*, that means the middle kingdom or the central states.

Traditionally when I talk about Legalism that would be your cue to boo and hiss because these are the bad guys of Chinese philosophy but they were remarkably effective. The basic idea of Legalism is that people can be made to do anything through rewards and punishments. Most rulers have somewhat questionable ambitions for power and glory. They can use Legalist tactics to make their people serve them in those ways. Moralists like Confucius and Mozi they said are hopelessly idealistic. What's realistic is that human nature is evil, sort of sounds like Xunzi, the philosopher from the last lecture. At least it's selfish; it's self-centered. The Legalists were not a unified school but were rather thinkers who shared an interest in strengthening the power of the state though rational, practical means. Sometimes they are compared with 20th-century totalitarians. Or one modern commentator referred to the movement as devoted to the "amoral science of statecraft."

They rejected the ways of the past including traditional forms of morality, culture, and aristocracy. Instead, they advocated for new laws, new administrative policies, and new methods of personnel management. As states get larger and more powerful, there was an increased need for more organization and centralization. But frequently, what rulers really wanted was to make their states more successful in war.

Legalists recommended the use of laws, along with punishments and rewards, as the best way to motivate people. This isn't law set up for rule of law something that even rulers have to submit to. It works the other way law is a tool, it's instrumental. Ideally, laws should be objective comprehensive, universal, harsh, and public. Let me go through that list again a little more slowly. They should be objective so if you want your people fight hard in battle, let's say you offer them a piece of gold for every enemy head that they bring in. The nice thing about this is that there isn't a lot of arguing, you can count: Two heads is two pieces of gold. It's fairly simple, kind of grisly I suppose.

The law should also be comprehensive. It should include both good and bad things. We're going to punish people for running away in war and we're going to reward people for successfully killing enemies. It should be universal, it applies to everyone equally. It doesn't matter if you're father was a shoemaker or your father was a great general, everyone gets the same reward: a head, a piece of gold. Actually heads are kind of gruesome, they ended up using ears—and it has to be a left ear. You can't get two for one in this case, so quantifiable standards if possible. We're on to the fourth standard: It should be harsh. If you get gold for killing the enemy, for running away from battle you get execution. We'll kill people who are cowards in battle. Finally the law should be public, everyone should know what's expected of them, punishments, and rewards and then they'll act in accordance with that.

Legalists taught that the government should promote agriculture, because that's important for feeding large armies out in the field, and they should discourage unproductive activities such as trade, scholarship, or the manufacture of luxury goods. They also argued that the king should rule over the peasants directly rather than through local aristocrats, or hereditary landowners.

Let me just return to one point quickly here, that's this idea of trade. In ancient China it was different from in our modern world where we know how important business and trade is for the growth of economy. Back then they thought merchants were suspect since they bought at a low point and sold at a higher prices, they're profits were directly correlated with the accessibility of good or to people's ignorance to how much things were actually worth. They tended to think of merchants as parasites. They're just making money off of other people's efforts, better to get rid of that class and have people just producing through agriculture.

Somewhat surprisingly, Legalism, like the military theories of Sunzi, was often times associated with Daoism. It seems strange that an assertive aggressive philosophy might be connected to something that talks about non-action. The idea was that legalist philosopher would go to a ruler and say, let me set up the laws for the country and I can make people do things with rewards and punishments. That will free up you to just do nothing, non-action in your palace, where you can enjoy wine, women, song, whatever it is your heart desires. Here's a quotation from a man named Han Feizi, speaking to a ruler, "Do not let your power be seen; be blank and actionless. The sage holds to the source and lets the four quarters come to serve him. In emptiness he awaits them, and they spontaneously do what is needed." That's a nice introduction for our second great mind of this lecture, who is none other than Han Feizi, the person I just quoted.

Han Feizi lived from about 280–233 B.C. He represents the epitome of Legalist thought. He was from an aristocratic family, which was unusual for wandering debaters of the time, and he was a student of the Confucian philosopher Xunzi. Because of a speech defect, Han Feizi was forced to put his ideas into essays, to write them down, he couldn't really hold forth orally in front of a ruler. His own ruler, unfortunately, was not much interested in these writings but they caught the attention of king of Qin. When his country was taken over by Qi, this is Han's country, he sent as envoy, maybe like a gift, to king of Qin. There was a prime minister in the state of Qin who was one of his fellow students. Long before he knew Han Feizi and he didn't want him around. He accused him of basically treason, he said to the First Emperor, this guy's always going to be looking out for his state's interest, he's not really going to be serving you. He manages to get him killed. This minister, Li Si, will someday himself be similarly executed on a trumped up charge. These are very deadly games, intrigues that these men are playing.

In the book, the *Han Feizi*, again the book's title is the same as the author. We see several themes; let me give you five of them, sort of advice for government. First: Punishments and rewards are the two handles of government. Think of it as a plow that you can move one way or another by two handles. He says rulers should hold these powers tightly, rewards and punishments. If he allows his ministers to give out rewards or punishments, then people will try to please the ministers instead of himself.

The second theme: There are three components to effective rule: law; situational power, which we talked about before remember the rock on top of the cliff; and methods, specifically methods of controlling the bureaucracy.

The third theme: Rulers need to keep a careful eye on their ministers, carefully assign them responsibilities and then hold them accountable. Sometimes ministers that do too much can be as dangerous as those who do too little. If good things happen the ruler should take credit for accomplishments; if bad things happen he should blame it on his subordinates. There's something kind of Machiavellian about this.

The fourth theme from Han Feizi: The ideal ruler should be transcendent and mysterious, like a Daoist sage. The state should be able to continue even a weak ruler, because men of talent are somewhat rare even in royal families. A ruler should hide his true desires and emotions in order to protect against flattery. If people know what he wants to happen, people will tell him what he wants to hear.

Han Feizi gives arguments for some of these ideas. For example, he says imagine that there's a bad young man who gets in all sorts of trouble. His parents try to deal with him, and his neighbors try to talk to him, his teachers try to do an intervention, and they all fail, but if the magistrate sends out soldiers ready to arrest him that young man is going to change his ways. The best punishments are those that are severe and inescapable. He gives an example of a famous villain in Chinese history named Robber Zhi. He says there's a way to make it so that Robber Zhi, even he wouldn't reach out and pick up some gold that was on the ground, even if it was right there and in reach. That is if the gold was molten, liquid gold. Even Robber Zhi wouldn't touch it because he would know he would get burned. That's what punishments should be like absolutely inescapable and immediate. Then you can motivate people.

Han Feizi says farming is hard and literature is easy by comparison. If the ruler rewards literary scholars then people are going to quit farming they're going to all go to school and start writing books. The state's going to be impoverished because there aren't going to be people doing agriculture. He tells a famous story about a man from the state of Sung who sat on stump. One day as he was sitting there, a rabbit came running through, hit the stump broke his neck and fell over dead. Then the man picked up the rabbit, went home, had some rabbit stew, and said this is pretty good. The man quit farming and sat on a stump waiting for a rabbit to come by again. He became a laughingstock of course because things that work in the past don't necessarily work now. Precedent doesn't help out; you need to focus on what's actually effective. Don't waste time on literature and trade focus on agriculture and what's going to work now. That story gets to be one of those chengyu, remember those four character phrases, *shǒu zhū dài tù*. To sit on a stump and wait on a rabbit to come by again.

As part of the *Han Feizi*, there's a chapter called the Five Vermin. These are people that Han Feizi thinks are dangerous—scholars spouting their own morals, conniving advisers of uncertain loyalty, these are the itinerant debaters from the hundred schools; private swordsmen; bribing draft dodgers; and merchants peddling useless luxury items.

Time for a quick review since we're going to leave China for next four lectures, let's make sure you've got things down. We're going to compare Legalism with some other schools. Compared with the Confucians there is some contrast. Confucians like the influence of parents, neighbors, and teachers, Legalists say that's not enough, you can't count on moral rulers setting an example and precedent doesn't matter—don't look at what worked in the past, look at what works now. But they do agree with at least some Confucianism in Xunzi that people are self-interested. They care about the rectification of names, making titles match up with responsibilities.

When we compare Legalists to the Mohists, remember the ones who care about impartial caring, Legalists are not religious and they don't care about morality but they do care about authority, mobilizing society, utilitarian ends, and uniform standards. They share all of that with Mohists.

When we compare Legalists to the Daoists, Legalists are competitive and aggressive that doesn't seem like the Daoists but they also value inaction at least for the ruler and laws should follow nature if at all possible. Now the grand questions: In a contest between a Confucian state, a Daoist state, and a Legalist state who is going to win? The answer might be obvious, Legalists are going to win, but that's only sort of true. The state of Qin takes over all of China in 221 B.C. The First Emperor's success was due in part to his adoption of Legalist techniques of governing. Qin was a newer state on the borders of the Chinese cultural region, there were fewer entrenched traditions and fewer aristocrats. He was able to remake it according to new laws. This is the same guy who built a tomb for himself with the terracotta soldiers near Xi'an that some of you may have visited. He built the fortifications that will eventually become the Great Wall. He takes a new title—he calls himself Shi Huangdi, which means emperor but he makes this up, we just call him the First Emperor. He divides China into 36 commandaries. He standardizes weights, measures, laws, and axle widths so that the same roads can be used everywhere. He standardizes the script, before this time Chinese was written in different ways in different places but now he says we're all going to write it the same way. The way that Chinese is written today goes back to reforms of the First Emperor.

But he's not interested in tolerance. Legalism says all of that scholarship is a bunch of nonsense. The First Emperor says I want history to begin with me, we're going to get rid of all literature and all history. We're going to get rid of all books except for those that are very practical—those that have to do with medicine, divination, maybe agricultural manuals. He managed to bring all china together but his dynasty only lasts for 14 years and then it collapses. What happened?

For one thing it looks like there was too much concentration of power, too much power at the top. Once the first emperor had gained all of China his next goal was to live as long as possible, to live forever if he could. He got advice from experts who would come in. Some of them said you should live like a Daoist; you should be hidden in your palace. If people see you they will think, he's just a guy we can take him on. But if you're a mysterious presence they will give you more reverence. This is sort of like the Wizard of Oz theory of government. Don't pay attention to the man behind the curtain, the great and powerful First Emperor in this case who was in control of everything. He was open to that because there had been several assassination attempts on his life already, including Zhang Liang—remember the guy who got the secret book from the guy who through his shoe down the embankment. If you've seen the movie *Hero*, Zhang Yimou's 2002 movie, that's about an assassination attempt on the First Emperor.

He's hidden away but he has these advisors who come and say, we can give you the secret to immortality, the elixir that will make you live forever but we need some money for research. He would give them some money, they'd bring in something, he'd try it out but it wouldn't work so he'd kill them, but somebody else would come. Finally there was a group that came and said, we're so close but the secret ingredient is on an island offshore, but the island floats around so it's hard to get to and there's also a big sea monster guarding it. The First Emperor is a real take charge kind of guide and says, well let's go down there and see what's happening. He goes down there and he shoots some sort of big fish, or something like that and then suddenly he dies.

When he died he was in a special imperial carriage, where no one saw him except for his chief eunuch and his prime minister. Those two men, when they found that the first emperor was dead, said to each other, Wow, he's dead and we're the only two people who know about it. The heir apparent is somebody that we can't really work with, let's just pretend that the first emperor is still alive and we'll forge some orders. Food kept coming into the imperial carriage, kept coming out apparently he'd lost his appetite. Some orders kept coming out—one to the heir apparent, a suicide order, the young man got this killed himself (a sort of tough family), another order to put a younger brother, who somebody that these two guys thought they could manipulate, on the throne. But in order to make this happen they had to get back to the capital as soon as they could. A strange unpleasant odor started to come from the imperial carriage, they put a cartload of salted fish behind it to cover this up. They get back to the capital and they manage to make this work, but they have somebody on the throne who's not very capable. Things start to fall apart pretty. quickly

Another problem that they have is that it's too harsh, rebellions start to happen all over the place. There's a man named, Chen She. He is required, with other men from his village, to go to a work detail to build a road a couple hundred miles away. They start on this journey to go there and they get behind schedule, some rain comes in and washes out the road, then comes the magic moment when they look at the map to see how far they've got left, they look at the calendar to see how far behind they are. They know that to arrive late for a work detail means execution, you're going to get killed. They look at each other and say, what the heck? We're going to die anyways, so they revolt. All over China there are these revolts that happen.

Messages start coming to the emperor, this is the second emperor now, who says, how could there possibly be a revolt? My father set up everything perfectly, you must be lying and he kills the messengers that come. The messengers stop coming with messages of revolt until it's too late. The rebels are actually right there, the Second Emperor is going to die, things are going to collapse, and the eunuch behind this is going to die as well—almost immediately China is going into a civil war between some of the old aristocratic families and a man named Liu Bang, who's going to win this four year war and found the Han dynasty.

Liu Bang is one of only two men in Chinese history who goes all the way from being a peasant to an emperor. When he comes to power he promises the people that the days of Legalism are over. He's going to run China with a law code of just 10 Chinese characters. It basically says murderers will be executed and those who injure or steal will be punished appropriately. You can't really run an empire on a two sentence law code. What happens is when he comes in he actually keeps a lot of the Legalist administrative tactics, government, and laws. It's a little bit like what happens in the Roman Empire when Caesar Augustus comes to power and promises to restore the Senate and the old way of doing things, but basically he's brought in a monarchy. Liu Bang promises to get rid of Legalism but he pretty much continues what's been going on before. He combines the Legalist government structure with Confucian ideology, actually not Liu Bang but a successor later on does that pretty quickly, and that's a very powerful combination. You've got these very practical, realistic ways of governing people and motivating people along with a layer of thought about concern for the common people and about acting in moral ways. That combination of Legalism and Confucianism is very powerful. It proved to be a solid foundation for stable, lasting government not just for 400 years of the Han dynasty but throughout Imperial China into the 20th century.

Zarathustra and Mani—Dualistic Religion
Lecture 11

The Persian Empire gave rise to two religious figures—Zarathustra and Mani—whose ideas spread along the Silk Road. Zarathustra preached dualism (not monism), with good and evil locked in cosmic conflict. Mani attempted to synthesize the faiths of Adam, Zoroaster, Buddha, and Jesus—all true prophets but with incomplete knowledge. Although Zoroastrianism and Manichaeism did not last as major world religions, they affected the lives of millions both directly and indirectly through their influence on other faiths.

The first Persian Empire, often called the Achaemenid Empire, controlled Iran, Iraq, Palestine, Turkey, Egypt, Afghanistan, and Pakistan—the entire western expanse of the Silk Road, which transported both goods and ideas across the Asian continent. Although usually considered a part of the Western world, Persia bridged East and West in several significant ways.

Zarathustra (in Greek, Zoroaster) was a Persian priest who lived sometime between 1400 and 1000 B.C. Little is known about his life; all that remains of his writings are 17 brief hymns, called the Gathas. They are composed in Old Avesta, which is related to the Sanskrit of the Vedas, and Zoroastrianism and Brahmanism have some deities in common.

Where Brahmanism is monistic, however, Zoroastrianism is dualistic: Good and evil, as represented by the great god Ahura Mazda and the minor deity Angra Mainyu, are locked in a perpetual struggle for control of the cosmos. Individual human beings are free to choose between good and evil, but Ahura Mazda's triumph is an article of the faith, so Zoroastrians worship him alone. Zoroastrians also believed in a Last Judgment after Ahura Mazda's victory and eternal paradise for the good. Zoroastrian

> **Zarathustra's teachings had a profound effect on the development of Greek thought, as well as on Judaism, Christianity, [and] Islam.**

practices include prayer five times a day, seven yearly feasts, purification rituals, and sacrifices.

Zoroastrianism was the official religion of the Sassanid Empire (A.D. 224–651), the last pre-Islamic regime in Iran. Under Muslim rulers, Zoroastrianism was tolerated but discouraged. There are fewer than 200,000 Zoroastrians left in the world today, and almost all of them live in India. Yet Zarathustra's teachings had a profound effect on the development of Greek thought, as well as on Judaism, Christianity, Islam, and even Western popular culture.

Mani was a 3rd-century A.D. successor to Zarathustra and one of the most influential figures you've never heard of. Manichaeism, now extinct, was once one of the most widespread, popular religions in the world, blending the ideas of East and West. Mani's ideas rested on Zoroastrian dualism but added concepts probably borrowed from Christian Gnosticism and Buddhism: Human beings were created by dark cosmic forces, but each person contained spiritual light, which could be released via asceticism. His followers were divided into hearers (ordinary believers) and the elect, who strove for purity through nonviolence, vegetarianism, and celibacy. Hearers might someday be reincarnated as one of the elect.

Manichaeans spread the faith westward to Spain and eastward to China. It thrived in China from the 7th to 12th centuries, where Mani was known as the Buddha of Light and

Marco Polo encountered Manichaeans in China.

was thought by some to be an avatar of Laozi. In the West, Mani was seen as a Christian heretic, yet one of Christianity's most influential theologians, Augustine of Hippo, was a Manichaean for nine years before converting to Christianity and may have been influenced by Mani's ideas.

Manichaeism died out in the Roman Empire and the Abbasid Caliphate around the 9th century A.D. and survived in China until at least the 14th;

scholars believe Marco Polo identified a group of Manicaeans living near the southern Chinese port of Fuzhou in 1292. ■

Suggested Reading

Boyce, *Zoroastrians*.

Questions to Consider

1. Why is dualism a natural way of making sense of the world?

2. How is it that a religion few have heard of has nevertheless managed to influence the lives of most of the people in the world today?

3. What makes the difference between religions that survive and grow and those that decline and eventually become extinct?

Zarathustra and Mani—Dualistic Religion
Lecture 11—Transcript

Hello, are you ready for a couple more great minds? In the lectures on China, we made it from Confucius about 500 B.C. to the establishment of the Han dynasty in about 200 B.C. Now we're going to return to India for Mauryan Empire but that's in the next lecture. First, let's take a detour through Persia, which was the site of the world's first universal empire. The Persian Empire, which is in present day Iran, set the pattern of strong, centralized government—remember it broke it into administrative units called satrapies, there's a bureaucracy, lots of records, they build roads including the royal highway, etc. The first Persian Empire, which is often called the Achaemenid Empire, was founded by Cyrus the Great and it lasted from about 550–330 B.C.

The Persian Empire is going to be part of Western history. You might remember that the Greek historian Herodotus wrote a history of the Persian Wars, stories about marathon and the Battle of Thermopylae, Darius and Xerxes as Persian rulers, but Persia is also part of Asian history. It controlled Iran, Iraq, Palestine, Turkey, and Egypt, but also Afghanistan and Pakistan. Persia is a bridge between East and West. In this lecture we're going to talk about religious figures whose influence spread from Persia in both directions: It's going to be influential in Western history and also influential in Asian history. The two are Zarathustra and Mani. Persia is going to be at the western part of the Silk Road, there are merchants, diplomats, and missionaries going across the Silk Road trade goods but also trading ideas, as well.

Zarathustra was a priest in Persia sometime between 1400 and 1000 B.C. In Greek his name is Zoroaster so his religion is sometimes called Zoroastrianism. Its sometimes called Mazdaism, after the god that he worshipped, the Ahura Mazda. Zarathustra seems to have been an actual person, but his dates are very much disputed—remember 1400–1000 B.C. is a big gap there. As with the Buddha, the first biographies were written many centuries after his death. It said that light shone from mother's womb, which would have been an unusual thing. When he was a child he was unusual as well, sparked a lot of hostile attention. When he left home at 20, he wandered for a decade until at the age of 30 he received a revelation at 30. He preached for many years, not a lot of success at first and he persecuted by established clergy. Finally he left home, left his native land, and fled to a neighboring state where he converted the ruler. The ruler's name was Vishtaspa, he converted him by healing his horse. A miracle for which the ruler was very grateful. He was allowed to preach there, gained a number of followers, and then he was assassinated at the age of 77 by a priest of another rival sect while Zarathustra was praying at an altar.

Of Zarathustra's writings, we have just 17 brief hymns. They are called the Gathas. Alexander the Great takes over Persia, and when he does that he is blamed for burning a lot of the Zoroastrian scriptures at the time. Today only about 20 percent of what was written still survives. The Zoroastrian scriptures included the Gathas by Zarathustra himself. They are difficult to understand, but we can see the outlines of his thought. Zoroastrianism is a sister religion to Brahmanism in India; remember the Indo-Iranians parted ways sometime around 1800 B.C. These Indo-European people start to migrate and some of them go West into Iran and Persia, and some of them go East down the Indus River valley into Pakistan and India today. The language of the Zoroastrian scriptures—the scriptures are called the Avesta—is called the Old Avesta is related to Sanskrit, the classic language of India, the language of the Vedas. Some of the divinities are common between the two texts, the two religious traditions.

Zarathustra's great insight is that the universe is characterized by dualism, not monism. It's not just one thing there are two things. Those two things are good and evil and they are locked in a cosmic conflict. In addition to various angels and demons that line up on both sides of that, there is a great god of goodness. His name is Ahura Mazda, which translates as the Wise Lord. Then there is a somewhat less powerful deity known as Angra Mainyu, the Liar, who brings suffering and evil into the world.

This may be new to you but you already know something about this because you probably know about Mazda automobiles. That company was named for Ahura Mazda. This isn't just an urban legend, if you go to the Mazda global website it explicitly says that the company name as derived from Ahura Mazda, who they describe as the ancient god of wisdom and intelligence.

They also describe him as the symbol of automobile culture, I'm not exactly sure how that works. But what happened was the founder of Mazda motors, his name was Jujiro Matsuda, in 1931 when he started the company, he wondered what he should name the company. He was tempted to name it after himself, Matsuda, but that was not appropriate in Confucian culture to bring yourself to the forefront. Zoroastrianism was just being rediscovered in the West, so he said the god Mazda that's who I'll name my company after—and it sort of sounds like Matsuda as well.

Both of these gods, Ahura Mazda and Angra Mainyu, the god of goodness and the god of evil, are uncreated and powerful but Ahura Mazda is going to be the one who is going to win out in the end, so worship is focused on him. Zoroastrianism is said to be "devotionally monotheistic, doctrinally dualistic." There are these two gods but all of the worship is focused on one. A modern scholar named Mary Boyce, calls this "perhaps the most rational solution to the problem of evil ever devised." Do you remember the problem with theodicy? It's a philosophical problem that has its own name, it is how can there be a god that's all powerful and perfectly good, but you still get a world that has so much evil in it? Zarathustra speaks of a supreme god who was wholly good, but not omnipotent, he's not all powerful, he didn't create everything. Zoroastrians don't struggle with that problem of theodicy the way that monotheistic religions in the West do.

Individual human beings are called upon to take up one side or the other in this conflict between good and evil, and they can choose which side they are going to be on. Here in Zarathustra's own words in the Gathas, he says:

> Now the two primal Spirits, who revealed themselves in vision as Twins, [this is going to be Ahura Mazda and Angra Mainyu] are the Better and the Bad in thought and word and action. [Remember that combination we'll see it again.] And between these two, the wise once chose aright, the foolish not so.

If you're wise you make the right choice as to whose side you're going to be on.

It matters because people will be judged according to their choices, actually choices that they make every day along the way. They're going to be judged on their thoughts, their words, and their actions—remember there was that trilogy I told you to hang on to for a bit. Eventually, everyone will be resurrected for a final judgment, after which each person will be sent either to heaven or hell. Zarathustra says, "In immortality shall the soul of the righteous be joyful, in perpetuity shall be the torments of the Liars." The liars are the people who joined Angra Mainyu, the great liar, and served on his side.

You've got dualism but worship is focused on Ahura Mazda with confidence that he will ultimately prove victorious. As I said, there are also some lesser divinities sort of lined up on both sides. They're kind of like angels and demons, they're not exactly gods but they're certainly not human either. There's ritual that involves them, calling on them for help, and to keep away from the bad side as well.

In addition to this theology there is also blessings that come in this life. I like this quotation from the Gathas, this is Zarathustra, who is a prophet, who's speaking to Ahura Mazda, "This I ask thee, tell me truly, Ahura—whether I shall indeed, O Right, [Right was a description of Ahura] earn that reward, even ten mares with a stallion and a camel, which was promised to me, O Mazda, as well as through thee the future gift of Welfare and Immortality." You've got to like a religion that in addition to promising you rewards on the other side, which may or may not happen, offers you something in this life. A religion that offers you 10 mares, a stallion, and a camel is a religion worth taking seriously.

The rituals of Zoroastrianism include prayer five times a day, seven yearly feasts, purification rituals, and sacrifices. The priests in this religion were known as Magi. Of key importance were fire temples, where sacred fires were kept burning perpetually. Zoroastrianism is going to survive to this day in India. There are Zoroastrianism temples there, called *parsi* temples. There is one temple there in particular at a place called Udvada, it's about 120 miles from Mumbai, which use to be called Bombay. There is a fire there that has been burning continuously since 1742.

Zoroastrianism is important in Persia, in the Achaemenid Empire started by Cyrus the Great in about 550–330 B.C., which was conquered by Alexander. Zoroastrianism is also in the Parthian Empire, which is about the time of the Romans, they fought with the Romans. That's from about 247 B.C.–A.D. 224, about 400 years. Later it became the official religion of the Sassanid Empire that goes from A.D. 224–651. That's the last pre-Islamic regime in Iran. Under Muslims when they came, Zoroastrianism was tolerated but discouraged. They considered Zoroastrians a people of the book, sort of like Christians and Jews—they were sort of right but they didn't accept Muhammad as a prophet. We can allow them to believe but we're not going to encourage it. The religion gradually declined and in the 10th century, a number of Zoroastrians immigrated to Gujarat, on the northwest coast of India. There they became known as the Parsis, which was the local pronunciation for Persian. There are not many Zoroastrians left in the world today, probably less than 200,000, and almost all of them live in India. They generally don't accept converts, which is why it's not spreading a great deal and many around Mumbai.

One of the most distinctive practices of Parsis, these Indian Zoroastrians, is the use of funerary towers. They are sometimes called "towers of silence." Because corpses were thought to be unclean, and the faithful did not want to pollute either the earth by burial or sacred fire by cremation, they laid out these bodies of their deceased loved ones on the top of large circular towers. There's a platform at the top and then they allow vultures to come down and eat the flesh. The bones that remain are dissolved in lime. Unfortunately, the population of vultures around Mumbai due to environmental problems has plummeted in recent years, and so this practice, which dates back millennia, is now under reconsideration. They're figuring out what they can do with their dead that would be appropriate for Zoroastrian beliefs.

Despite their miniscule numbers, there have been several prominent Parsis, including Dadabhai Naoroji, who in 1892 became the first Asian elected to the House of Commons, Parliament in England. At that time, he shocked people by refusing to take his oath of office on a Bible. He wasn't Christian. Instead he used his own scripture the Avesta, which included the Gathas, which were written by Zarathustra. Other prominent Parsis include Zubin

Mehta the classical conductor. He was born in Mumbai. As well as Freddie Mercury, who is the lead singer for the rock band Queen.

If you travel to India, you will see the roads filled with Tata trucks—Tata is a brand name of trucks. The Tatas are a Parsi family that has been at the forefront of Indian manufacturing for several generations. In fact, the Tata group is India's largest business group. That group includes the world's 5th largest steel company, the 18th largest automobile company, and the 2nd largest tea company, they own Tetley Tea.

Zoroastrianism is important in Asia in the East but it's also important in the West. The most significant influence of Zoroastrianism has probably that end of things. Zarathustra was known to the ancient Greeks, if only vaguely. The word magi, priest is going to be related to our word magic. Zarathustra was admired by philosophers such as Voltaire, Nietzsche—in fact Nietzsche wrote a book called *Thus Spake Zarathustra*, the classical composer Richard Strauss wrote an orchestral piece of that name that was used in *2001: A Space Odyssey*. Zarathustra is the only philosopher in this course, *Great Minds of Eastern Intellectual Tradition*, who was depicted in Raphael's 1511 fresco *The School of Athens*. You might remember that's the one that has Plato and Aristotle up front, with Plato pointing up to the heavens and Aristotle pointing out toward the world, a more realistic philosopher. He has a place in Western philosophy and he has a profound effect on many of the world's great religions. Think again about the teachings of Zarathustra, this cosmic conflict of good versus evil. People have to make a choice about who they're going to follow. There's a resurrection eventually, a judgment, and then people are assigned to heaven or hell. Does that sound familiar? Of course it does, it sounds like Christianity, it sounds like Islam, it sounds a little bit like Judaism. Why is that?

Do you remember the Babylonian exile? About 587, the southern kingdom of Judea was taken over by Nebuchadnezzar and the Babylonians. Thousands of thousands of Jews were taken back to Babylon. Then Babylon was taken over by Cyrus the Great, he's setting up the Persian Empire. The Jews at the time said can we go back to our homeland and rebuild our temple? And Cyrus said, sure. That's going to happen in about 538 B.C. but for those intervening years (587–538 B.C.) Jews were living in Babylon among the

Persians. There they encountered Zoroastrian ideas. Many scholars believe that Judaism started to pay more attention to various angels and demons as a result of conversations they would have had with Zoroastrians. They also developed clear ideas of the afterlife and resurrection. Those notions were rather vague in early Judaism because they don't show up in the Torah.

You may recall that even at the time of Jesus, there was a division between the Pharisees and the Sadducees; one of the things they disagreed about was the Sadducees didn't believe in the resurrection, they didn't believe in the afterlife. When I tell my students this, it always comes as something of a surprise because they don't understand why you would be religious if you believed in a god but you didn't believe there was an afterlife. I try to explain that many of these Sadducees, and actually some Jews today, believe there is a god, that god has requirements that he makes of human beings, there's a covenant, but when you die that's all there is. You still need to do that because that's what God wants you to but there's no expectation of eternal punishments or eternal rewards to do the right thing. My students are often puzzled by that; they say why would you do all those hard things—keeping kosher and keeping all those laws of Moses—if you don't get to enjoy the rewards eternally? Part of the problem that they have is they know this Zoroastrian story so well.

Christianity adapted many ideas from Judaism including ideas of the afterlife and resurrection that most Jews came to accept, and Zoroastrians even make a bit of an appearance in the Gospels. Remember the wise men who visited the newborn Jesus? They're called the Magi they would have been Zoroastrian priests, coming from Persia.

Islam also accepts these ideals of good versus bad, resurrection, and heaven and hell. Many Muslims regard Zarathustra as an early prophet from God. They have adopted the Zoroastrian practice of prayer five times a day.

Even for people who aren't necessarily religious this story shows up in popular culture. You may remember *Star Wars*, there's Luke Skywalker on the planet Tatooine, sort of in the middle of nowhere and nothing is happening. Then it turns out that there's this conflict between the Empire and between the Rebels, the Jedi and Lord Vader. He has to choose which side he's going to be on, he has a crucial role to play in this. He chooses the right side and goes with the force and is rewarded afterwards. Or you may remember Harry Potter, who's a young boy, maybe 11, living under the stairs with the Dursleys but he finds out that there's this cosmic conflict between Lord Voldemort and the wizardry world. He has this role to play and choose which side he's going to go on, he's tempted one way then the other. Finally makes the right choice and everything turns out ok in the last book, or the last movie. Or you may remember *The Lord of the Rings*. Frodo, the hobbit gets the ring and then he suddenly thrown into this cosmic conflict. There's Sauron on one side and Gandalf on the other, he has to make it to Mount Doom across all kinds of obstacles, finally he's going to do the right thing. I hope I'm getting the details right on these stories, some people know these stories really, really well—the point is that they all follow the same basic plot. This story, the Zoroastrian story about individual who find themselves in a conflict and have to choose and then are rewarded, that story has a great hold on our imaginations. Perhaps it's because so many of us hope that we have some role to play, that our individual choices and decisions, our individual lives make some difference in the conflict, the fight between good and evil, that we may play some role in the eventual triumph of good over evil.

This brings us to the second great thinker, Mani. He was a successor to Zarathustra. He was a prophet much later, in the 3rd century A.D. maybe from A.D. 216–276. Mani is one of the most influential figures you've never heard of. If Zoroastrianism is nearly extinct, Manichaeism certainly is, even though it was once one of the most popular, widespread religions in the world. Strikingly, Mani tried to bring together the religions of the East and the West.

Mani was born in Iraq, or what today is Iraq then it was part of Parthian Empire, a Persian Empire. At the age of 12, he saw a heavenly vision of a his twin who was his heavenly parallel up there. At the age of 24 he had another vision in which this twin ordained him to start preaching. Mani went to Northwest India, Pakistan or Afghanistan, and he had some success, converted a ruler, and then returned to Persia two years later, where he converted the brother of Shapur, who was the second king of the new

Sassanid Empire. There's been a shift from the Parthian Empire to the Sassanid Empire.

Mani traveled throughout Persia, preached and made many more converts, but after the death of the king, who was kind of his patron, he was persecuted by Zoroastrian priests and eventually was arrested, put in prison, and died a month in later. There was a Persian Muslim in the 11th century named Al-Biruni who is one of our main sources for Mani's biography. Remember that name, Al-Biruni will be a major figure in Lecture 21 when we talk about Islam in India.

Mani took over the basic Zoroastrian notion of dualism, of a grand conflict between good and evil, between the forces of light and the forces of darkness, but suggested that human beings had been created by the dark forces. Still, each person contains particles of light within him or herself that can be released through asceticism, remember those religious practices of self-denial and renunciation. Asceticism is not a part of Zarathustra's thought, it's sort of a more positive and life-affirming religion. In Mani's thought good versus evil becomes spirit versus matter. He was probably adopting these ideas from Christian Gnostics. Paul in his letters talks a little about how the spirit is willing but the body is weak. Some of that contrast becomes much more accentuated in later forms of Christianity.

Mani believed that Adam, Zoroaster, the Buddha, and Jesus were all true prophets, but that he had been sent to synthesize those faiths, to bring them all together. This is a very powerful religious argument, where you say to your opponents, your rivals, it's not that you're wrong, it's just that only partially right. You're on the right track but there's a greater truth that's going to bring all of that in, that's going to encompass what you believe. This is what Christianity does to Judaism—you worship the right god, you've got scriptures, you've got prophets there, it's just that there's this other part of it that you're missing that God actually came down to earth, he was incarnated, and that he sacrificed himself for the sins of man. Or that's actually what Islam does to Christianity. Muslims believe that Jews are right they worship the right god, that Christians are right they worship the right god, they just got a little bit off track when they thought that Jesus was the son of God or Jesus was God. Actually, according to Muslims, Jesus was a prophet and there's another prophet, Muhammad, that brings the full truth from Heaven and encompasses everything that's gone before. Then again, there's another religion coming out of Persia, called Baha'i, that does to Muslims what Muslims did to Christians, what Christians did to Jews. Baha'i say that Muhammad was a prophet but there's this other prophet who comes later, in the late 19th century, who brings it all together. Muslims try to get around that by saying the Muhammad was the seal of the prophets; he was the last one. You can see how this appeal to partial truth fits a lot of religious transitions.

Mani wrote scriptures in Syriac, it's a later related to Aramaic, which is the language that Jesus spoke. He also writes scriptures in Persian. He created a church complete with hymns, rituals, and liturgy. He's clearly the founder of this movement. Mani's followers were divided into two groups: Hearers, those are ordinary believers who tried to live good lives, and then the Elect, those who strive for purity through nonviolence, vegetarianism, strict celibacy, and abstaining from wine and from harvesting or preparing food. Their meals had to be prepared for them by Hearers. This sounds like the difference between the ordinary and extraordinary path that we saw in Jainism, where some people try to be born into a better life here, others try to go all the way to nirvana and escape this cycle of existence entirely. We saw the same thing in Buddhism as well between ordinary Buddhists and monks and nuns. The Hearers in Mani's religion might someday be reborn as the Elect. That idea of reincarnation probably derived from Buddhism. With reincarnation, they step a little bit off that basic story that Zarathustra has.

Manichaean missionaries traveled as far as Spain in the West and China in the East, and Manichaean merchants helped to spread the religion all along the Silk Road. We say Silk Road, but actually there are several routes. There's a north route and a southern route, both of which go across central Asia. There's also a maritime route which will travel through the Indian Ocean. It wasn't the case that a lot of people traveled from one end to the other, often times people would go a little ways, pass on goods, then go another way in sort of a relay kind of thing. That's especially early on where the Parathions tried to keep the Romans separate from the Chinese so that they could continue to be middle men and do business with silk that was going all the way across. But in Mani's time, people start moving further along the Silk Road and these ideas start to spread, especially from Persia into China.

There were Manichaeans in China from the 7th to the 12th century. Manichaeism became the official religion of a Uighur kingdom for a couple hundred years—the Uighurs are a minority people, a Turkic people, in China. Manichaean texts were translated into Chinese. When that happened they used a number of Buddhist terms, to explain these terms in ways that the Chinese would understand. The founder himself, Mani, was referred to as "Mani, the Buddha of Light" and was thought by some to be an avatar, an incarnation, of Laozi, which is sort of amazing.

In the West, however, Mani was seen as a Christian heretic, and Saint Augustine, for example, was outraged that he had signed some letters "Mani, An Apostle of Jesus Christ" and that Mani claimed to be the Comforter, or Paraclete, promised by Jesus in the Gospel of John. Until the discovery of some actual Manichaean texts in China in the early 20th century, what we knew of Mani came almost exclusively from his enemies, which included Augustine. It's possible that Augustine attacked the Manichaeans so ferociously out of a guilty conscience. Augustine himself had been a Manichaean Hearer for nine years before his conversion to Christianity, from the age of 19–28. Are you saying that Augustine believed in the Buddha for a decade? Not exactly, the doctrines don't quite go like that. But some have suggested that elements of Augustine's theology, which shaped Western civilization decisively, may have been derived from or at least colored by Mani's doctrines. Certainly his hostility to the flesh and sexual activity, as well as his deep sense of sinfulness would have echoed what he had learned in his years as a follower of Mani.

Manichaeism was once a serious rival to Christianity, but it was severely persecuted in the Roman Empire after Christianity became the state religion. It was treated just as harshly in Persia when Muslims established the Abbasid Caliphate in the 8th century. Eventually it died out in Central Asia and in China but it was an amazing attempt to bring together the major religions of the Mediterranean, Persia, India, and China.

Let me end with a story about a familiar figure. When Marco Polo and his uncle arrived in a southern Chinese port of Fuzhou in 1292, a foreigner told them that there was a strange sect that practiced a religion that no one could identify. They didn't worship fire so they weren't Zoroastrians, they didn't worship Christ, or the Buddha, or Muhammad. The Polos were asked to pay these people a visit. At first the believers were a little apprehensive, they didn't know what they were after, but after several more visits they warmed a bit and showed the Polos their holy books, which included what seemed to be a copy of the Psalms, or at least that's what the translator said. The Polos figured that they were an unknown group of Christians and they urged them to petition the great Khan, this is under the Mongols, to allow them the privileges of Christians, which they did. Marco Polo reported that the group included 700,000 families. That is an impossibly large number, but even conceding some exaggeration, there is no evidence of anywhere near that number of Chinese Christians under the Mongols. There are, however, accounts from both Confucians and Buddhists at the time of a significant Manichaean movement in China. Most scholars believe that the Polos had actually stumbled upon a good-sized group of secret Manichaeans.

One wonders how the world would be different today if political rulers had embraced Manichaeism rather than their religious competitors. Mani, along with Zarathustra, deserves a place among the great minds of the Eastern intellectual tradition. Though these two faiths haven't lived up to their potential as world religions, they still affected the course of history and influenced the lives of millions, both directly as believers and also indirectly, as their ideas were adopted and adapted by other religions. Thanks.

Kautilya and Ashoka—Buddhism and Empire
Lecture 12

> The Mauryan Empire's conquest of the Indian subcontinent gave rise to two of India's most renowned political thinkers: Kautilya and Ashoka. Kautilya was an advisor to the first Mauryan ruler and wrote on war, economics, administration, trade, and espionage; his cold pragmatism has been compared to Machiavelli's. Ashoka was the third Mauryan emperor and one of Buddhism's most famous converts. He defined Buddhist kingship by governing with compassion, ending military aggression, and proselytizing the faith.

Kautilya (c. 350–275 B.C.) was a Brahmin advisor and prime minister to Chandragupta Maurya, the founder of Mauryan Empire. His ideas can be found in the *Arthashastra* ("the science of politics" or "the science of material gain"). He advises on many matters, from agriculture and manufacturing to law and its enforcement, but about a third of the book concerns diplomacy and war. He was also a stickler for time management: The model king followed a schedule divided into 90-minute periods of meetings, audiences, inspections, prayer, eating, and sleeping.

Ashoka's role in Buddhism is similar to that of Constantine's in Christianity.

Kautilya identified seven elements of the state: king, ministers, lands, fortifications, treasure, army, and allies. Good statecraft involved strengthening these elements in one's own kingdom and weakening them the enemy's. He also identified six methods of foreign policy: peace, war, neutrality, preparing for war, seeking protection, and duplicity (pursuing peace and war with the same state at the same time). He writes openly of espionage and assassination, even fratricide, yet speaks of the dharma and moral duty of a king as well and says, "The happiness of the subjects is the happiness of the king." Like the Legalists in China, Kautilya attempted to combine ethics and pragmatism.

Two generations later, Chandragupta Maurya's grandson Ashoka became the third ruler of the Mauryan Empire. His rise to the throne was legendarily brutal, but in the eighth year of his reign, in the aftermath of the conquest of Kalinga, he took stock of the massive devastation caused by his war and converted to Buddhism.

Ashoka's role in Buddhism is similar to that of Constantine's in Christianity. He established monasteries, built 84,000 stupas (reliquaries), sent missionaries abroad, abolished animal sacrifice, and took up vegetarianism. He even traveled as a teacher throughout his empire. While Ashoka was committed to his faith, he practiced tolerance and was one of the first proponents of religious pluralism in world history. He considered "the welfare of the whole world" his mission.

Although there are few Buddhists in India today, you can see evidence of Ashoka everywhere. India's national emblem of four seated lions comes from Ashoka's court, as does the spoked wheel of dharma—the Ashoka chakra—that appears on the Indian flag. Despite Ashoka's influence, Buddhism virtually died out in India in the 13th century A.D. The Mauryan Empire lasted only 130 years, and both Ashoka's and Kautilya's works were lost for centuries as the subcontinent dissolved into smaller warring kingdoms. ∎

The quadruple lion, the national emblem of India, can be traced to Emperor Ashoka.

Suggested Reading

Embree, ed., *Sources of Indian Tradition*.

Mitchell, *Buddhism*.

Radhakrishnan and Moore, eds., *A Source Book in Indian Philosophy*.

Thapar, *Aśoka and the Decline of the Mauryas*.

Questions to Consider

1. When is ruthlessness in politics a virtue?

2. How might a person balance various aims in life that seem contradictory?

3. What is the role of political patronage in spreading new religions?

Kautilya and Ashoka—Buddhism and Empire
Lecture 12—Transcript

Hello. Congratulations, you've now made it to the 12th lecture and we've made it back to India. This might be a good time for a quick review. You've heard a lot of names and terms, I hope at least some of them are new to you but I don't want you feel overwhelmed. We've been looking at two traditions so far in India and China. Both of those traditions have answers to life's questions: What's the nature of reality? How do we know what we know? How should society be organized? What's the source of suffering? How can you find happiness? We've actually seen several different answers to those in each tradition. India and China come at those questions form slightly different perspectives.

In India there's slightly more of a focus on metaphysics, so you remember samsara, which is reincarnation; karma, cosmic justice; dharma, caste duty or the Buddhist teachings; moksha, which is liberation freedom from the cycle of existence; atman is inner most introspective reality; and Brahman is sort of the absolute reality that's outside of us. All of that has to do with metaphysics. In India we're dealing with sacred texts that are thought to have been revealed. There are many gods and there's a keen attention to suffering. Often times in India, people think that family can be an obstacle to spiritual progress. We saw that in the Jains and the Buddhists, though in the Bhagavad Gita they try to bring those together. We see the caste system everywhere. The great thinkers tend to transmit their messages orally, by word of mouth.

In China on the other hand, they tend to concentrate on politics and social interactions. We heard terms like *run*, which is benevolence; *li*, which means ceremony or ritual. Daoists do talk about the dao, yin, and yang that actually do seem to be cosmological but most of Chinese thinkers tend to be more this worldly. They tend to care about human nature. The key texts are derived from sages long ago, and in Chine they tend to look for history for guidance. The family is thought to be the solution to problems rather than a cause of problems. Ancestor worship is a basic component of religion. The literature is likely to have started in written form, with philosophers who are first writing down their ideas and then transmitting it through that written communication.

After Alexander the Great conquered the Persian Empire in 330 B.C., he marched west into India and past the Indus River, before returning to Babylon. After his death in 323 B.C.—when he was 33 years old, Alexander accomplished a lot in a very short lifespan—his eastern lands fell to his general Seleucus. Seleucus had his hands full on the western borders and Chandragupta Maurya, who was the ruler of a growing kingdom in northeast India, saw an opportunity so he launched an attack and captured a good chunk of what is today Pakistan and Afghanistan. He signed a treaty with Seleucus in 305 B.C. in which they established borders and traded Punjab, this area of what is today Pakistan for 500 war elephants.

Eventually Chandragupta gained control over northern India, and then his successors ruled over nearly all of the subcontinent. This is a time when India is united for the first time in history. The Mauryan Empire, which he founded lasted from 322–185 B.C. It was the setting for two of India's most renowned political thinkers: Kautilya and Ashoka. Those are the great minds that we're going to talk about in this lecture. Both of them lived in the same area and in both cases they're involved with military conquest and the creation of a universal empire. They're both part of the Mauryan Empire.

We'll start with Kautilya. He is sometimes known as Chanakya. He lives from about 350–275 B.C. He was a Brahmin, an advisor and prime minister to Chandragupta Maurya, the founder of the dynasty. Kautilya was trained in the Vedas and perhaps in Zoroastrians. His ideas can be found in a book called the *Arthashastra*, it's sometimes translated as the "Science of Material Gain," or the "Science of Politics." This book was lost for many centuries and then was rediscovered in 1904 in India written on palm leaves. That version includes some later additions. It probably dates from about A.D. 250, so it's quite a bit after Kautilya, but the basic ideas in that seem to go back to this great thinker at the beginning of the Mauryan Empire.

The *Arthashastra* offers detailed, practical advice on economics and politics, with discussions of fortifications, which are important in building an empire, laws, taxation, prisons, irrigation, agriculture, manufacturing, trade, coinage, and mining, as well as administration, spies, and diplomacy—as you can see it's a handbook, kind of an encyclopedia of everything you need to know to run an empire in India. About a third of the book is taken up with diplomacy and war, including military tactics. Kautilya's specific recommendations—and let me warn you here, we're going to do lists. Now remember that lists are not arbitrary they're rational, numerical analysis of giving a comprehensive view of how things ought to be.

We'll start with a list of the jobs for a hard working kings, what his daily schedule ought to be like. Kautilya says lets lay it out in 90 minute increments, so an hour and half. At sunrise, he spends the first hour and a half hours of receiving reports, then public audiences, then an hour and half for breakfast and bath, then 90 minutes for meeting with ministers, another 90 minutes for correspondence, then he gets 90 minutes for lunch, then an hour and half inspecting the military, then meeting with Chief of Defense, another period for interviewing secret agents, then he gets an hour and half for dinner, then 4 and half hours for sleep. He gets up in the middle of the night for a 90-minute period of meditation, then another 90 minutes for consult with counselors and spies, and then right before dawn some religious duties and palace affairs. Then he starts all over again. This just sounds exhausting to me if anyone could do this day after day.

Another list: Kautilya gives us the seven elements of the state: the king; the ministers; the country, by that he means geography, population, natural resources; fortifications; treasure; army; and allies. Following that list he gives detailed explanations of each component. The key ideas is that you want to strengthen these elements in one's own kingdom by focusing on them and concentrating, and you want to weaken them in the kingdoms of your enemies, often times though spies or secret agents you send to make trouble.

Kautilya presents the mandala theory of interstate relations. A mandala is a schematic representation of the world, sometimes square sometimes circular, in this case it's going to be circular. Kautilya says imagine your kingdom is in the middle, and circling around your kingdom are the territories of your enemies. You're going to have different interests then they do, you will be competing with each other. Then if you draw a circle around the circle of your enemies, they're going to be your enemies' enemies because they're right next to them. Your enemies' enemies are actually your allies. Then there's another circle around that which is going to be your enemies allies and you need to be careful with them. And so on it goes to 12 layers, or levels of concentric circles. He gives advice for dealing with each type of state depending on where it falls in that schematic representation.

Another list—I know the lists just keep coming here—he identifies six methods of foreign policy: peace, war, neutrality, preparing for war, seeking protection, and duplicity where you're pursing peace and war with the same state at the same time through different chains of communications.

Kautilya's unsentimental political analysis has sometimes been compared to that of Machiavelli, since Kautilya writes openly of secret agents and assassinations, he analyzes when it's useful to violate treaties, when you might have to kill your own family members, or spy on yours ministers. But he's not always ruthless. Kautilya also writes a lot about the dharma of a king, remember the dharma means duty or morality as well. The king has a particular moral duty, for example not to covet other men's property or not to covet other men's wives, that's just going to cause problems for the king. Kautilya's ideas about the dharma of the king can be summarized in this quotation. He says, "The happiness of the subjects is the happiness of the king; their welfare, is his; his own pleasure is not his good, but the pleasure of his subjects is his good." Antony Black, a professor at the University of Dundee, has observed "One might compare Kautilya's teaching with the almost exactly contemporary combination of Legalism and Confucianism in China, which was another attempt to combine ethics with political pragmatism." Strangely enough, Kautilya's employer, Chandragupta Maurya, is said to have ended his 20-year reign by retiring from the throne and become a Jain ascetic, and then eventually starving himself to death. But perhaps, and this is just my own idea, following all of Kautilya's recommendations about what a king should be doing from hour to hour was just too exhausting to keep going.

Our next great thinker is Ashoka. He's the grandson of Chandragupta and the third ruler of the Mauryan Empire. He reigns from 269–232 B.C. He was definitely religiously inclined, though not at first. There are two ways of spelling Ashoka; one is A-s-o-k-a the other is A-s-h-o-k-a but it's always pronounced with a -*sh*. He is one the most famous converts to Buddhism ever. As is typical, there are many legends about Ashoka, most dating from several centuries after his death. It is said that he was a younger son of the emperor. While serving away from the capital as the governor of a province, he fell in love with Devi, the Buddhist daughter of a merchant and then married her, much to the displeasure of his father.

Ashoka eventually killed several half-brothers in order to claim the throne. He was a brutal; he was a conquering ruler who expanded the borders of the empire. In the eighth year of his reign he gained a great victory over the state of Kalinga on the southeastern coast. But when he visited the battlefield the next day and saw the ground littered with corpses, he didn't feel ecstatic over his victory he felt sorrow. He wondered if it was worth it. Perhaps he remembered the Buddhist teachings he had encountered while he was a governor, or had listened to the words of his wife at some point and he decided to convert to Buddhism. The name Ashoka means "without sorrow." He established Buddhist monasteries, built 84,000 stupas, each with a relic of the Buddha inside (these are sort of memorials to the Buddha) and he put those throughout India. He sent missionaries abroad, including his own son and daughter to Sri Lanka, to take the good news of Buddhism. If you're interested, you can get the full Bollywood treatment of this story, complete with melodramatic acting and elaborate song-and-dance numbers, in the 2001 movie *Ashoka*, with the Bollywood superstars Shahrukh Khan and Kareena Kapoor.

These are Buddhist legends of course, preserved in Sri Lanka, whereas Buddhism became very popular. But in India, Ashoka was for the most part forgotten, even though he had left some remarkable relics of his reign. There are inscriptions on some 18 rocks and 30 pillars that he set up all over India, remember that propaganda is one of the universal things that these empires do. These inscriptions were written in a very early script that was related to Sanskrit. The language was deciphered in 1837 by a Western scholar James Prinsep, and these are the earliest inscriptions in India, certainly the first actual records of Buddhism. They offer a glimpse of an extraordinary mind.

The story of Ashoka's conversion seems to be accurate. According to the Rock Edict 13, the conquest of Kalinga resulted in 150,000 people taken captive, 100,000 people killed in battle, and many times that number in total deaths. There may be some exaggeration here but still a tremendous devastation and slaughter. Immediately thereafter according to his own record, Ashoka became devoted to the study of dharma. Remember in Hinduism it's caste duty, in Buddhism dharma means the teaching of the Buddha. Let me give you the quotation, this is so good that I really ought to read it here. Ashoka writes this on his inscription:

> On conquering Kalinga the Beloved of the Gods felt remorse, for, when an independent country is conquered, the slaughter, death, and deportation of the people is extremely grievous to the Beloved of the Gods and weighs heavily on his mind. What is even more deplorable to the Beloved of the Gods is that those who dwell there, whether brahmins, [ascetics], or those of other sects, or householders who show obedience to their teachers and behave well and devotedly toward their friends, acquaintances, colleagues, relatives, slaves, and servants—all suffer violence, murder, and separation from their loved ones.

He goes on to say that he now understands that moral conquest is the most important conquest of all, more important than military conquest. One would expect him at this point to give up the kingdom and become a monk. He doesn't do that. Instead, he vows to become a Buddhist ruler. He wants to govern with compassion, he wants to stop military campaigns and instead spread Buddhism throughout the empire, but he does warn rebels that he will punish them. He still has to maintain order, he has that responsibility. Is it possible to be a Buddhist ruler? A religion that's founded on kindness, how does that go with what actually has to take place to keep an empire going as far as spies, police, and armies and all of that? Isn't there a problem there? I guess you might ask the same question is Christian monarch an oxymoron? In Buddhism Ashoka finds a way, even though the Buddha himself had to choose. If you remember the prophesy when the Buddha was born that he could either become a great ruler, a Chakravartin that means wheel-turner in the sense that he launches chariot invasions into other territories, or he could become a holy man. The Buddha has to choose one way or the other, he chooses of course to go with spiritual progress and instead of turning the wheel of chariots, of invading armies, he turns the wheel of the law. That's how we describe his first sermon where he taught the Four Noble Truths to his old companions.

We learn from other inscriptions that Ashoka that he did away with animal sacrifices, became a vegetarian, and encouraged others to give up meat. Ashoka provided medicine for both people and animals, a compassion for even non-human beings. He had trees planted along the roads, along with rest stops and wells for travelers they could water both people and the beast that bore their burdens. He gave up hunting trips and instead toured his empire, interviewing and giving gifts to the aged, to holy men that including Hindus, Jains, and other non-Buddhists, and instructing the people in dharma. For this inscription he didn't describe it as the teachings of the Buddha, he's not trying to convert everybody to his particular religion. In his descriptions he defines dharma as obedience to parents and teachers, respect for the aged and for holy men, kindness to the poor and weak, and compassion for all creatures.

What's striking about this is the voice that comes through. Again let me read to you, Ashoka said, "For two and a half years I have been an open follower of the Buddha, though at first I did not make much progress. But for more than a year now I have drawn closer to the [Buddhist] Order, and I've made much progress." Whereas the earlier stuff that he does sort of fits into the category of propaganda, which is part of what happens in these universal empires. The part where I just read you that he was trying and didn't make progress at first, that part seems much more personal much more sincere in some ways. He says, "I am not satisfied simply with hard work or carrying out the affairs of state, for I consider my work to be the welfare of the whole world. ... There is no better deed than to work for the welfare of the whole world, and all my efforts are made that I may clear my debt to all beings."

Ashoka's role in Buddhism is similar to that of Constantine's in Christianity. They both are imperial sponsors of a new religion. It is even said that Ashoka convened the Third Buddhist Council in order to prevent schisms within the Sangha, much as Constantine convened the Council of Nicaea. In any event, without the support of Ashoka, and the weight of the Mauryan Empire behind it, it is very unlikely that Buddhism would have become a world religion.

You may ask, if Kautilya and Ashoka were so important, why were their works lost? Remember that the *Arthashastra* was only rediscovered in the early 20th century and Ashoka wasn't given a lot of prominence in India. In Ashoka's case, part of the problem is that Buddhism virtually died out in India about the 13th century, we'll talk a little more about that in a later lecture but for right now we'll just note that it did thrive in lands where Ashoka's missionaries had travelled—in Burma, Sri Lanka, and Afghanistan. For Kautilya, the political theorist, it is worth noting that India as a unified empire was probably the exception rather than the rule. The Mauryan Empire collapsed after 130 years, and then in the 4th century A.D. there was another empire, the Gupta, which lasted 220 years. But other than that, just warring kingdoms until the 16th century when the Mughal Empire is established. In that time period, maybe 350 years in which India is basically united; 350 years in India over that whole time period versus 400 years in the Han dynasty alone.

By contrast, once China was a unified empire—about the time of Ashoka—it stayed a single political entity until the present, with just a few centuries of civil war in the middle. In China the typical situation is a unified, centralized state; in India it happens but that's quite unusual in Indian history. For that reason perhaps Kautilya and his specific advice, the lists he gave about what the ruler of a large empire should do wasn't seen as quite relevant as it could have been otherwise.

In India, social order doesn't come from laws or a strong government, it comes instead from custom, particularly the cast system, which gave everyone guidelines for everyday behavior all the time and then there's enforcement as well as people look after what other people are doing within their caste, make sure that the rules and regulations are going. Rather than being opposed from a central government, this order in Indian society comes from social interactions among people of the same caste.

There's also some other traditions that fit into this. Kautilya mentions the Hindu ideals of the four stages and the three aims. Indians had long considered there to be four life-stages: student, householder, hermit, and ascetic right before you die. Each with their distinctive duties: when you're a student, you're leading a celibate life, you're being obedient to the teacher. Then eventually you marry and go into the householder time of life when you have family, children, and a profession. Then when you're a grandparent, when you can see your sons' sons, then it's time to retire and live a simpler life, get a smaller place and start to practice celibacy though you're spouse may go with you at this point but you break of marital relations. Then eventually you go into the ascetic at the end when it's complete renunciation; you give up all possessions and all family, devote yourself completely to spiritual matters.

There are four stages in life, there are also three aims in life. These re dharma, which is duty or piety; artha, which is prosperity like the *Arthashastra*; and kama, which is pleasure. Moksha, liberation is going to take one beyond ordinary life. All three goals in life have their place, but some are more appropriate for certain times of life. Kautilya, naturally, thinks that artha is the most important of these because it makes possible dharma and kama. If you want to remember those in an alliterative way it's piety, prosperity, and pleasure.

The acceptance of pleasure as a valid goal, a legitimate ambition in life at least for people in the householder stage, explains the existence of the *Kamasutra*, a text that is often misunderstood in the West. It is more than simply a catalog of sexual positions. It does talk about sex and sexual practices, but it also devotes chapters to courtship and marriage, to the lives of courtesans and the characteristics of extramarital affairs, which the author tells he disapproves of completely, but is providing information so that readers can detect other people's indiscretions. You have to wonder about that but he is writing in a tradition where dharma is still important in all of this. You have to harmonies all three of these aims in life.

I want to conclude with an observation and a question. It is amazing that while Ashoka was committed to a particular faith, he nevertheless urged tolerance, freedom of worship, and respect for all sects. He was, in fact, one of the first proponents of religious pluralism in world history. We saw how he gave gifts to holy men and clergy from other faiths, and he said this in one of his rock edicts: "Whoever praises his own religion, due to excessive devotion, and condemns others with the thought 'Let me glorify my own religion,' only harms his own religion. Therefore contact (between religions) is good. One should listen to and respect the doctrines professed by others."

He further adds that any criticisms of religions because they are different and had different beliefs, should be offered mildly.

Ashoka believed that religion in general was good for people and that identifying the positive aspects of other faiths could strengthen one's own religion. This was some 1900 years before John Locke's "Letter Concerning Toleration," written in 1689. Ashoka seems to have been going along similar lines of thought much, much earlier. In the two millennia since Ashoka, Asian governments have most often not been models of religious freedom and tolerance, but people who say that Asians are incapable of such ideals, simply because they are Asian, don't know much history and they certainly don't know anything about Ashoka. The principle of religious pluralism is at the heart of modern India, even though we think of it as a Hindu nation as opposed to Pakistan, which is a Muslim nation, there are still 150 million Muslims within India, about 15 percent of the population. The vision of India has always been a country that's open, accepting, and supportive of religion but also religious differences where there is freedom, tolerance, and pluralism. This is why, although there are few Buddhists in India, you can see evidence of Ashoka everywhere. The national emblem of India is four seated lions facing outward, which was originally at the top of some of Ashoka's pillars. This emblem, sort of like the U.S. bald eagle, is on passports, government letterhead, and all currency. There's also a spoked wheel signifying dharma was also part of Ashoka's pillar design, and this appears in the middle of the Indian flag, as the "Ashoka chakra," which is Ashoka's wheel.

And finally, a question. Western philosophy has long been interested in a universal morality, ethics that can apply to all people at all times. This is not exactly foreign to India—Buddhism says that everyone must eventually follow the path of the Buddha to gain enlightenment; there's one path. Yet in Hinduism, there is not one dharma for everyone, it depends on one's caste, or even on one's stage in life. And that's got me thinking. Might there be different standards of proper behavior for different times in life? Maybe there's some basic moral standards—don't kill, don't lie, don't steal, but in terms of day to day behavior is there a time to concentrate on career and building up wealth, and another time to focus more on family relationships or spiritual matters? Is it reasonable to expect different sorts of behaviors from single people, married couples, parents with children in the home, and grandparents? Maybe even in older people who still dress like a teenagers? Or even worse, there might be an older fellow out for a run without a shirt and you might say, that time in your life has probably passed, maybe there is a different standard for you right now. I don't want to wander too far into caste, that's going to be an uncomfortable subject, but people are born different. Do individuals with particular talents, social position, or inherited resources have heightened responsibilities to society? Does having unusual abilities, say musical abilities or business sense, mean that a person can be held to different standards, at least in some aspects of life? Does having a severe disability justify different standards? Or is there such a thing as universal moral principles that everyone must follow equally all through their lives? I'm not sure but I'll let you think about it. Until next time.

Ishvarakrishna and Patanjali—Yoga
Lecture 13

> The practices the West knows as yoga are a relatively modern development; in India, Yoga is a school of Hinduism based on dualist metaphysics. Two thinkers supplied the core of orthodox yogic philosophy: Ishvarakrishna codified its metaphysics, which divides the universe into prakriti (matter) and purusha (spirit), while Patanjali, the semi-legendary author of the *Yoga Sutra*, provided a sort of handbook to the meditative practices for disentangling spirit and matter.

Scholars divide Hinduism into six orthodox schools (Nyaya, Vaisheshika, Mimamsa, Vedanta, Samkhya, and Yoga) and three unorthodox schools (Jainism, Buddhism, and Carvaka). The six orthodox schools developed between the 3rd century B.C. and the 4th or 5th century A.D. All accept the authority of the Vedas and the Brahmin priests, along with samsara, karma, dharma, and moksha, but they have different ideas about the ultimate reality and engage in respectful debate.

The foremost proponent of Samkhya was Ishvarakrishna, a philosopher of the late 4th century A.D. His *Verses on the Samkhya* is the oldest surviving complete text of the Samkhya school. Ishvarakrishna believed that the entire universe can be divided into two entities: prakriti (primordial matter) and purusha (pure consciousness or spirit).

Prakriti is the source of the physical and psychological universe—everything we perceive both inside and outside our selves, but it cannot comprehend itself or the world. Purusha, on the other hand, cannot act; it simply observes prakriti. If purusha becomes entranced by what it sees, it can mistakenly identify with prakriti and become entangled in samsara and suffering. Liberation—which Ishvarakrishna calls kaivalya (isolation), rather

> **If purusha becomes entranced by what it sees, it can mistakenly identify with prakriti and become entangled in samsara and suffering.**

than moksha—comes from making a clear distinction between purusha and prakriti.

The Yoga school, in essence, is the practical response to Samkhya's metaphysics. Patanjali is known as the founder of the Yoga school, but scholars debate whether he lived in the 2nd century B.C. or the 3rd century A.D. His *Yoga Sutra* is the first systematic treatment of the topic. "Yoga" comes from a Sanskrit word meaning "to join" or "to yoke," here implying yoking body and mind to a spiritual discipline. According to Patajali, you cannot think your way out of suffering; thoughts are part of the buzzing, churning world of prakriti. Instead, one must use meditation to still the mind completely and detach the purusha self from the physical-mental world of prakriti.

Patanjali's *Yoga Sutra* consists of 195 aphorisms organized into four chapter-length books on meditation, yogic practices, psychic powers, and liberation. His ideas are drawn from several different traditions. He identifies five "turnings of thought"—valid judgment, error, conceptualization, sleep, and memory—along with various ways to stop these turnings. He describes eight stages, or limbs, of Yoga: restraint, observances, posture, breath control, withdrawing the senses, concentration, meditation, and absorption.

All Indian philosophical schools, both orthodox and heterodox, have adopted some form of yoga. In all cases, the program of improvements starts with ethical practices, then physical practices, and finally mental practices.

The purusha/prakriti dualism of Samkhya and Yoga is not exactly like Western mind/body dualism. Here, mind is a part of the body and prakriti, so the thinking self is not the real purusha self. Memory is acknowledged not simply as recollection of the past but a complex process that affects our perception. Even false or distorted memories are real because they have real effects in our lives. But still, our memories are not our true self. ∎

Suggested Reading

Embree, ed., *Sources of Indian Tradition.*

Miller, *Yoga.*

Puligandla, *Fundamentals of Indian Philosophy.*

Radhakrishnan and Moore, *A Source Book in Indian Philosophy.*

Questions to Consider

1. Is your thinking self your real self?

2. How did Yoga originally offer a method of liberation from the suffering brought about by the entanglement of consciousness and matter, as expounded in the Samkhya school?

3. Is it possible that insight can be acquired through a step-by-step process? Why does morality come before physical techniques, which are then followed by mental discipline?

Ishvarakrishna and Patanjali—Yoga
Lecture 13—Transcript

Hello, welcome back. Several lectures ago, we talked about the Bhagavad Gita and three ways to escape the cycle of samsara, reincarnation. There was Jnana Yoga, the way of knowledge, where you realize that Brahmin and Atman are the same thing; Bhakti Yoga, the way of devotion, and which you devote your actions and all the karmic consequences to a god, like Krishna; and then most importantly Karma Yoga, the way of works, and that means to act without thought of the consequences. All of those three yogas, and perhaps you thought at the time, "None of those sounds like what happens at the local yoga center in my town."

In this lecture, we're going to talk about the classical Indian school of Yoga. There's a connection with the modern Western practice, but the ancient version had somewhat different goals and methods. We'll be focusing on two major thinkers in this lecture, Ishvarakrishna and Patañjali. Once again, we don't know a whole lot about their lives (even their dates are somewhat in doubt), but their ideas are tremendously influential. And once again, metaphysics is going to lead to ethics. In this case, Ishvarakrishna provides the metaphysical theory, and then Patañjali explains the practice of Yoga, which is his answer, the practical answer, that will resolve the problems that are highlighted by Ishvarakrishna.

But we can start with some background. We're going to talk about the Six Orthodox Schools of Hinduism. And at last, we're going to get to the real darshanas. Remember that we are in that darshana hotel in India, and the darshanas are these six schools, and they developed during the time between India's two early empires between the Mauryan Empire that was in the 3rd century B.C. and then the Gupta Empire in the 4th to the 5th centuries A.D., so they're in between. The six schools are orthodox darshanas because they accept the authority of the Vedas and also the Brahmin priests who specialized in the Vedas and the Vedic rituals.

All six schools accept the ideas of samsara, karma, dharma, and moksha, but they have different ideas about how exactly ultimate reality and the self are related and what we can know about them. So, these philosophers, these schools, argue with each other, but they also respect each other and they adopt insights from other schools. As I did with the hundred schools of philosophy of early China, I'll give you a quick overview. Don't try to memorize this, but just get a sense of the whole, the kinds of issues that these schools address.

The six schools are usually grouped into three pairs so the first pair is going to start with the Nyaya School and this school concentrates on logic. They say that there are four sources of knowledge: perception, inference (like where there's smoke there's fire), analogy, and reliable testimony. I know it's a list, but that is a great list! Think again, how do you know what you know? They say there are four ways; you can directly perceive something, you can figure it out by inference, you can try to compare it to something else, or you can get some sort of reliable testimony from somebody else who isn't a direct observer of that. It's a great list!

The next school that it's paired with is the Vaisheshika School. This is the school of atomism. It says that the world, the universe, is made up of very small invisible, but so small you can't cut them anymore, bits of reality they're going to call atoms. They list the qualities and the substances that make up the universe. There are material atoms, but there are also some immaterial entities like space, and time, and mind. This school, the Vaisheshika School, merged with the Nyaya School in the 10th century. Both can be classified as pluralistic realism; that is there are many entities, not just one, not monism, not Brahmin, there are many entities and they actually exist independent of our perceptions. Those two schools, although important in history, are perhaps not so important today.

The next pair of schools are Samkhya and Yoga. Samkhya teaches a dualism between spirit and matter. It's not mind/body dualism; it's something a little bit different. We'll talk about this in a minute. Then the Yoga School is going to offer practical method for disentangling spirit and matter. These are the two schools that we'll be discussing in this lecture.

That leaves two more. One is the Mimamsa School, which is an interpretation of the Vedas, which they believed were uncreated and eternal and this school is concerned with trying to perform the Vedic rituals exactly correctly.

So, they want to say things with the right pronunciation and do things as precisely as possible. The last school that Mimamsa is oftentimes compared with its Vedanta, which means "the end of the Vedas." This is based on the Upanishads, which remember were texts that were added to the end of the Vedas, and this is a school that talks about the relationship of Brahman and atman and it comes in three flavors. There's non-dualism, monism, they're the same thing. There's qualified non-dualism, and then there's dualism. This is the most popular school, probably the most influential. We're going to give a whole lecture to this later on in Lecture 20.

So, if we were to add three non-orthodox traditions to those six schools and the non-orthodox traditions are Jainism, Buddhism, and Cārvāka—remember the one that was sort of atheistic, no afterlife, no gods, if you can't see it, it doesn't exist— that six orthodox schools, three non-orthodox school, that's classical Indian philosophy in a nutshell.

Now we can move to Ishvarakrishna. He lived in the latter half of the 4th century A.D. He was the foremost proponent of the Samkhya School of philosophy, though he's a relative latecomer. Samkhya is one of the oldest of the Hindu schools, but it didn't reach its classic form until Ishvarakrishna, whose *Verses on the Samkhya* is the first complete text of that school that survived. It was actually translated into Chinese in the 6th century, which is a rare non-Buddhist transmission of Indian ideas, at least one time when something got from the Darshana hotel to the Dao hotel, but not through Buddhists.

According to Ishvarakrishna, all of the entities that make up the universe can actually be reduced to just two, remember it's a form of dualism. There's prakriti, which is primordial matter, on the one hand, and purusha, which is pure consciousness or spirit. Purusha is an observer rather than an actor, so mental processes like thoughts and dreams are also part of prakriti. They're things that are happening that are changing. Let's talk about each of those parts of the dualism in a little more detail.

Prakriti is primordial matter and this is a single substance which is the source of the physical and psycho-mental universes, that is, everything that we perceive both outside and inside ourselves. This is what accounts for the changing, developing, diverse world is made up of three dispositions or gunas they're called. We mentioned these when we talked about the Bhagavad Gita. These can be thought of as three modes of nature. They're sort of like yin and yang in Daoism. They're not objects, but they're qualities within objects. The three gunas are sattva, which is bright and intelligent, raja, which is active and passionate, and tamas, which is heavy and lethargic. One or the other of those three may be dominant in some things or in some people and basically the effects of those three are pleasure, pain, and indifference, and then those get combined into different quantities in various things.

Everything in Nature is changing and transforming. The world is real, it's not an illusion, but it's in constant motion, and imbalance leads to interaction between things, particularly between prakriti, remember matter, and purusha, in spirit. When prakriti is in proximity to purusha it starts to become active. It may be something like children whose mother is on the telephone, she starts talking and then suddenly the kids start bouncing up and down trying to get her attention. It turns potentiality into actuality and then eventually prakriti might calm down in these interactions as well, things come and go. This ongoing process of coming together and then coming apart include our mental lives, so our ego is part of this process, our memories, our ideas, even our mind.

So what's left? What's the other side of this half of the dualistic system? The other side is purusha, pure consciousness. It can't act on its own, but it only watches the cosmos unfold. It's the eternal observer of prakriti, it's sort of moving out there. The problem is that purusha might be entranced by what it sees. It might mistakenly identify with prakriti and then become entangled in samsara, reincarnation right, which leads to suffering. It may be a little bit like watching sports on TV. You're watching your favorite team and as they start to win you get very excited or maybe you get depressed when it looks like they're behind, and you get emotionally involved with something that's actually quite separate from you. Or maybe even a better example is it's like watching The Weather Channel. You may see a huge blizzard coming in, but even though you're quite comfortable living in California or Florida, you start to feel a little bit chilly, maybe go put on a sweater.

Ishvarakrishna has a marvelous analogy for all this. He says it's like a blind person and a lame man who are trying to get somewhere together. The blind person has to carry the lame man on his back and the lame man is going to direct where he's going and the blind person is going to be the bottom part of that piggyback. So, prakriti can't see anything and purusha can't do anything. Back to this analogy, you can imagine the guy on the back saying be careful of that rock there, there's a step or to the left you're going to run into a tree and you just know somebody is going to get hurt in this and this is where sort of suffering in samsara comes from, from this uneasy, unnatural combination of prakriti and purusha.

Primordial Matter, prakriti, is unconscious both of itself and also of the difference between itself and Spirit. It has no idea what's going on. Consciousness is in the realm of spirit, and according to Ishvarakrishna, there are innumerable spirits or selves, each of which, in its pure state, is silent, peaceful, and inactive, but they become deluded. They've forgotten their true nature and now they're caught up in the world that they should be just observing.

Liberation, moksha, comes from making a clear distinction between purusha and prakriti. When one of these innumerable spirits is able to differentiate what's self from what's not-self, it can become isolated once again and thereby freed from the bondage of primordial matter and its attendant suffering.

How does one attain this kind of discriminative knowledge, one that can see the difference between the two? The answer is the other half of this pair of Indian philosophies, the school of Yoga. So, metaphysics is going to lead to ethics. This is the way the world is so this is how we should act.

The second great mind in this lecture is Patañjali. His life is even more obscure than Ishvarakrishna. Scholars debate whether he lived in the 2nd century B.C. or the 3rd century A.D., which is a big gap there, it depends on whether he's the same person named Patañjali, who wrote an early study of Sanskrit grammar. Non-scholars tell stories about how Patañjali was the incarnation of the mythical serpent Ananta. I don't know about that, but we do have a text that's ascribed to Patañjali—the Yoga Sutra. It's a little bit like the *Dao De Jing* in that we have a book, but the author is somewhat shadowy, or even legendary.

Yet the Yoga Sutra, unlike the rather eclectic *Dao De Jing*, is a much more coherent, integrated work, and it presents the first systematic treatment of the enormously important topic of Yoga. So just to make sure we're clear on this before we move on, Patañjali probably lived before Ishvarakrishna, but I spoke about the Samkhya philosopher first, because without the concepts of Primordial Matter and Spirit, Yoga is not going to make a lot of sense. So, Patañjali is responding to ideas that were already in existence, but were later put into their classical form by Ishvarakrishna. Samkhya is the theory and Yoga is the practice.

The term *Yoga* comes from the Sanskrit word that means "to join" or "to yoke." Yoke sounds like yoga because these are Indo-European cognates, the languages have similar roots. It also refers to actions such as taming horses or yoking them to a chariot. Here the idea is to tame one's body and mind, and yoke them to a spiritual discipline that will lead to liberation. When we think about yoga today, often the first thing that comes to mind are unusual, a little bit uncomfortable, body postures and breathing exercises. This modern form of yoga, which has developed in the last 150 years or so, is related to the ancient practice, but the goals are different.

Patañjali was not trying to help people reduce stress, or lose weight, or stay flexible, or realize their potential. Instead, he was describing a method for escaping the suffering that comes when purusha is entangled with prakriti. But it's not something that you can think your way to; remember that thoughts are part of the buzzing, churning world of prakriti. The key idea in Patañjali's yoga is meditation.

Let me make a quick clarification here. Meditation is not something mystical or exotic. Think of it more like learning to play a musical instrument. It's a skill that can be developed. It might feel awkward at first, but if you put in a concentrated effort and practice diligently, you're thinking of music here, under the direction of an accomplished teacher, over the course of many years, you can train your body and your mind to do things that will amaze your friends when you sit down at the piano.

When I was an adult, after I'd already become a professor, I started taking cello lessons. I'd never played a stringed instrument before. I actually played the piano and could read music, but still I found the cello very difficult. Learning to do vibrato is tricky, and intonation is hard. With a stringed instrument that doesn't have frets you have to listen really carefully to get your fingers in exactly the right position. It's not like the piano where you just hit a key and then whatever sound comes up is what you get. I will never learn to play like Yo-Yo Ma, but just attempting it, trying it out, gave me a much better appreciation for what he has accomplished. It also helped me to hear music in a different way. I now love string quartets and I can listen to what they're doing and I have a great appreciation. It's very difficult to even start and stop at the same time with three other people.

Similarly, when I teach the history of Buddhism, I ask my students to meditate. I'm not an expert. I can't give them a lot of guidance here, but I think that unless you've actually tried to sit still and think of nothing, you have no idea how fast your mind is racing, all the time. That incessant internal chatter is not the real you according to Patañjali. Now let's turn to the Yoga Sutra, but first we need an explanation of the term sutra, which is a particular sort of literary composition.

We've seen the foundations of Indian thought in hymns, those are the Vedas, and in dialogues as in the Upanishads and the Bhagavad Gita, between Krishna and Arjuna, but the disputes of the classic Indian philosophers were presented in a different type of writing—in sutras. These are collections of short, almost cryptic sayings or aphorisms, one right after another. The word sutra literally means, "The thread that holds things together." It's related to our word "suture." That's Hindu philosophy. In Buddhism a sutra is going to be a text that's ascribed to the Buddha himself, something he said while he was alive.

These sutras in Hinduism are different from the *Analects* in Confucianism, certainly different from later Confucian philosophical writings which sort of allow for more extended arguments and they're completely different from Western philosophy. Sutras may sound like just one list after another, but this form of writing allowed Indian thinkers to arrange their ideas into comprehensive, systematic, and rational order. They made the texts easier to memorize and then oftentimes, the real interpretive work is done by later commentators or teachers when they're passing this on to their students.

Patañjali's Yoga Sutra consists of 195 aphorisms and then they're organized into four books, each is about a chapter-length and the four chapters, we'll call them, are on meditation, yogic practices, psychic powers, and liberation. These short sayings seem to be drawn from several different traditions, but together they form a general handbook of meditation.

If you were to read just one book of Indian philosophy, it probably should be the Bhagavad Gita, but after that, I would recommend Patañjali's Yoga Sutra, particularly in Barbara Stoler Miller's translation. This was the last book she did before she died tragically of cancer at the age of 52. She was finishing it up from her hospital bed so she has a clear translation and then some very concise explanations. The Yoga Sutra is short and it's pretty engaging.

Let me give you an example. I'll just start with the first section which starts with four aphorisms. These are actually just going to be sayings, or in this case they're just sentences. So, here it is. Number one: "This is the teaching of yoga." Next sentence: "Yoga is the cessation of the turnings of thought." Three: "When thought ceases, the spirit stands in its true identity as observer to the world." And fourth, "Otherwise, the observer identifies with the turnings of thought." There are only 94 to go. The key terms and ideas in that, remember like being an observer, should be recognizable to you from our discussion of Samkhya philosophy.

Patañjali goes on to enumerate the various "turnings of thought." There are five of them that include valid judgment, error, conceptualization, sleep, and memory. Then he continues by listing the ways that one can stop these turnings, the obstacles that must be overcome, and so forth until purusha can become disentangled from prakriti, that includes these turnings of thought.

Patañjali's yoga includes eight stages, which are referred to as the "eight limbs." It sounds a little like the Buddhist eight-fold path; it's probably not a coincidence; people are talking and arguing with each other. In the path of yoga, this can be a long journey and it progresses from outer strengths to inner capacities. So, the first two stages involve moral discipline and then the next three are physical discipline, and then the last three are mental discipline.

Moral discipline starts with—here's the first of eight—restraint, and this list is borrowed from Jainism, the basic morality, no violence, no lying, no stealing, no lust, no greed or attachment. The second stage of yoga, again from morality, are the observances. We have the thou shalt nots and now the thou shalts, and they're going to be recommended positive habits of body and mind, things like purity, contentment, asceticism (austerity), study, devotion. Unlike Samkhya, which sees no need for God, the Yoga school has a role for a divinity; a supreme purusha that has never been intertwined with prakriti.

Then we move to the three stages of physical discipline starting with posture so you can keep your body healthy and under control with these because your body affects your mind. Actually your body and your mind are made of the same stuff, they're both prakriti. He doesn't give you specific postures, but he probably has in mind the lotus position; remember that famous sort of cross-legged sitting position that's used in meditation. Then later, this was elaborated into Hatha yoga, which is a whole system of hundreds of bodily postures.

The fourth stage is breath control—deliberate inhalation, and retention, and exhalation of breath and often while counting. The fifth stage is withdrawing the senses and they describe this as being like a turtle that sort of brings in its head and its limbs. This is complete control of the body freed from desires and distractions. You're going to isolate sense organs from their objects. So, when you meditate you don't exactly close your eyes, you sort of half close them, but you just don't pay attention to what's coming in through your eyeballs, and the mind is thought of as an internal sense-organ that can reach out and grab on to ideas, and concepts, and memories. You want to keep that still as well.

We've moved from moral discipline to bodily discipline and now we're into mental discipline for our last three stages. Number six is concentration, focusing one's attention on a single object, maybe on your navel, on the tip of your nose, or some internally visualized image, or being completely aware of the present moment. There's a steadiness, and a calmness, and stability. So, you bring wandering attention back to a focal point. When you try to meditate, just sort of counting your breath from one to 10 over and over, it's amazing how often you lose count because you get distracted by thoughts that are fleeting in and out.

The seventh stage, we're almost done, is meditation. It's dhyana, which is the parent word in Sanskrit, the Chinese word Chan, which is the parent word of the Japanese word Zen, if you've heard of Zen Buddhism. This is unwavering attention on a particular object, and then objectless attentiveness; so the agitations of the mind-stuff are quieted and pure consciousness can start to shine through. Then last, is absorption. The spirit is absorbed or immersed in meditation, but may still be aware of objects outside of itself and then the highest level of absorption that the consciousness is no longer conscious of anything outside itself. It's not even self-conscious; it's described as being like a "sleepless sleep."

Through this discipline of yoga then, thinking is stilled and consciousness is freed. Remember, "When thought ceases, the spirit stands in its true identity as observer to the world," remember that quote from the opening of the Yoga Sutra.

According to Patañjali, as a byproduct of this long and arduous moral, and physical, and mental training, individuals can sometimes gain supernatural powers and knowledge of the past, and the present, and the future where they have the ability for their minds to enter into the bodies of others or they can become large or small, or heavy, or light. This is the origin of the Indian practice of lying on a bed of nails without being hurt. Yogic masters might even learn to levitate, but those are all hindrances to progress. They're distractions. The true goal is to escape bondage to primordial matter.

Now let's think for a minute about practical applications. For its own practitioners, for believers, yoga offers liberation; freedom from the world of pain and suffering. Yoga is very influential in India; all of the six philosophical schools, actually including Buddhism and Jainism, they all adopt some form of yoga, some form of meditation, and it's interesting that the path of yoga that Patañjali teaches, with its eight limbs, has always been open to women; there are some famous female yogis. For outsiders who are interested in the practice of yoga, but they don't really care about the metaphysics of Samkhya, yoga can offer calmness, and mental stability, heightened perceptions, and higher states of awareness and consciousness. The program of improvement starts with morality, and then goes to the body, and then to the mind, which is an interesting sequence. I can imagine one that starts with your thoughts and then that comes to your body and then you act them out, manifest them in your morality.

For the philosophically inclined, it offers an astute analysis of mind, which is not quite like the mind/body dualism in Western philosophy. Patañjali sees this keen awareness of a connection between the mental processes and the body; and indeed, the mind is part of the body; so the thinking self is not your real self. Do you remember that the Western philosopher Descartes once said, "I think therefore I am," that wouldn't quite work in Samkhya or Yogic philosophy.

Then there's a psychological acuity here as they examine the processes of thought and mental action. For example, memory is one of the five "turnings of the mind," and it's not a simple recollection of past experiences, rather it's a complex process by which the mind perceives certain mental objects, which may be true or false, but which nevertheless have some reality because even false memories can cause behaviors and have other concrete effects. If you've ever struggled to recall something, you know how complicated and elusive memory can be. The potential is even richer from an Indian perspective that includes reincarnation.

Barbara Stoler Miller, in her introduction to the Yoga Sutra, cites a marvelous verse from Kalidasa's famous play *Shakuntala*. Kalidasa lived somewhere around the 4th or the 5th century A.D., during the Gupta Empire, and he's oftentimes thought of as the Indian equivalent of Shakespeare. In this play there's a king who goes on a hunting trip and he meets a young woman who has been adopted by a sage living in a forest hermitage. They fall in love, he marries her, and suddenly he's called back to the court. But, he leaves her with a ring so that when she follows him and comes to the palace she can produce this ring and claim her place as queen. Unfortunately, she inadvertently offends a wandering holy man who puts a curse on her that her husband will completely forget her until he sees the ring again. She's traveling to the court, she's crossing a river, she's in a boat, she leans down to touch the water and the ring falls off, she loses it. She still goes to court and alas when she sees her husband he doesn't remember her at all. She goes away broken hearted, rejected, but then a fisherman finds the ring and brings it to court, gives it to the king, the king suddenly remembers his wife. He goes out in search of her and the story goes on from there.

This play was translated into English in 1789, one of the first works of Sanskrit to come into Europe. The great German poet, Goethe read it and exclaimed, "If you want heaven and earth contained in one name, I say Shakuntala and all is spoken." So let's go back to the puzzle of memory. The king has been cursed to forget the woman that he loves, but when he overhears music (and what a powerful effect music can have on memory!), he says, this is so good I just want to quote this directly here, "Why did hearing the song's words fill me with such desire? I'm not parted from anyone I love. Seeing rare beauty, hearing lovely sounds, even a happy man becomes strangely uneasy … perhaps he remembers, without knowing why, loves of another life buried deep in his being."

How do we account for those vague, yet overwhelming longings that we all experience from time to time? There may be answers in science and psychology, but I sort of like this poetic, deep introspection that we see in this play. Memories of other lives buried deep in our being; what is the role of memory in forming our minds and our sense of self. They're crucial right, which is why Alzheimer's disease can be so terrifying. When a person loses his or her memories, does he or she also lose herself? But, that might be the goal of Patañjali's Yoga by which we can stop the painful turnings of thought and memory.

So we've got a lot to think about, about spirit, and about primordial matter, about metaphysics, and ethics, about the connection between memory, and identity. I'll see you next time.

Nagarjuna and Vasubandhu—Buddhist Theories
Lecture 14

Mahayana (or "greater vehicle") Buddhism arose in the 1st century A.D., driven by new scriptures said to be secret teachings of the Buddha. Two major figures in Mahayana's development were Nagarjuna and Vasubandhu. Nagarjuna's commentaries on the Perfection of Wisdom Sutras propose a metaphysical middle way between existence and nonexistence. Vasubandhu taught that the only things that exist are mental constructs. Both schools teach that meditation is the best way to understand reality.

The Buddha discouraged philosophy, yet in the four centuries following his death, 18 Buddhist schools developed, only one of which survives today: Theravada (the way of the elders). Theravada teaches that the Buddha is not a savior, only an example of beneficial behavior, and that enlightenment requires the sort of extensive study and meditation only available to monks and nuns. Today, Theravada is the main Buddhist school of Southeast Asia and Sri Lanka.

Mahayana Buddhism developed later than Theravada and diverges from it in significant ways. Based on sutras compiled in the 1st century A.D. (but likely transmitted orally for some time before), Mahayana holds that the Buddha is a god and in some sense still exists to worship and pray to. Mahayana Buddhists believe lay people can achieve enlightenment, becoming bodhisattvas, and emphasize the role of compassionate service. This is the Buddhism of East Asia.

The Buddha taught the theory of dependent origination, or conditioned arising. In brief, this means that nothing exists independently; every "thing" in nature is an event, and every event has a cause. The human problem is rebirth, which is caused by existence, which is caused by attachment, which is caused by ignorance of no-self, so for the Buddha, this doctrine is a tool for liberation. For Nagarjuna, it was a tool for understanding reality.

Nagarjuna's Madhyamaka ("middle way") school of Mahayana Buddhism explained how the world around us is ultimately empty but that "empty" is not the same as "nonexistent." Rather, between the notions of permanent external reality and total nonexistence is the idea that everything that exists is temporary. He also concluded that there is no real difference between samsara and nirvana, since neither can exist unconditionally. The ultimate truth, he suggested, is beyond all logical analysis. By exposing these contradictions, Nagarjuna hoped to free us to experience emptiness through meditation.

"Empty" is not the same as "nonexistent."

Vasubandhu was a 4th-century writer who lived in present-day Pakistan. His Yogacara school teaches a form of metaphysical idealism—that the only things that exist are mental constructs. Other Buddhists had argued that we have no direct access to the external world, only to our perceptions; Vasubandhu further argued that our perceptions could exist entirely within our own minds. The world we think we observe is simply a projection of our desires and habits of thought.

In Yogacara, karma is also a sort of mental construct; our suffering is created by our own mind out of guilt. There are eight levels of consciousness, of which the storehouse consciousness is the most basic: a collective subconscious where the seeds of your previous experiences are stored to later sprout and ripen into perceptions. Nirvana comes when no more seeds are deposited. Mental processes, such as yoga and meditation, allow us to "wake up" from our perceptions and stop planting those seeds, thus attaining enlightenment.

Buddhism died out in India by the 13th century A.D. due to a combination of social and political forces, yet it grew and flourished in other lands. For Buddhism, like everything else in existence, the only constant is change. ∎

Suggested Reading

Embree, ed., *Sources of Indian Tradition*.

Harvey, *An Introduction to Buddhism*.

Kasulis, *Zen Action, Zen Person.*

Mitchell, *Buddhism.*

Nagarjuna, *The Fundamental Wisdom of the Middle Way.*

Radhakrishnan and Moore, *A Source Book in Indian Philosophy.*

Williams, *Mahayana Buddhism.*

Questions to Consider

1. If everything in the world is caused by something else, which is in turn the result of earlier factors, what sort of reality does the world have?

2. How dependent are we on our senses for our knowledge of the world? Is there any form of knowledge that comes apart from our perceptions?

3. Are there limits to what we can know? Are some things beyond language and logical analysis?

Nagarjuna and Vasubandhu—Buddhist Theories
Lecture 14—Transcript

Hi, are you ready for a couple more great minds? This lecture is about early Buddhist philosophy, but we're going to start with a word of caution: The Buddha himself discouraged philosophy. In an early sutra one of his philosophically-minded disciples asked him several specific questions about the nature of reality. He asked, Is the world eternal or not eternal? Is the world finite or infinite? Are the soul and the body the same thing or are they two different things? Does an enlightened person exist after death or not? Rather than answering those questions, the Buddha instead offered a parable. He said, imagine a man who has been wounded by a poisoned arrow. Friends run to go get a doctor. They bring back the man who can heal him, but the person who has been injured refuses to have the arrow removed until he knows the caste of the archer, his name, how tall he was, his complexion, and what exactly the bow and arrow were made of. The Buddha says, that man is going to die before he gets all his answers. For the Buddha enlightenment is a matter of life and death; what's really important are the Four Noble Truths—remember he's identified the disease and the treatment that you need to escape from suffering and sorrow.

But some of the Buddha's disciples couldn't help themselves: They wanted to explore the ambiguous elements; they argued with Hindu philosophers from the six Darshanas; they argued with each other. In the four centuries after the Buddha's death, we're talking about 400–100 B.C., there were 18 Buddhist schools which emerged. Only one of them survives to this day, and that is the Theravada school—the Way of the Elders. This school of Buddhism is fairly strict: The Buddha is not a savior, he only set an example and then he went into nirvana. So he is no longer around to pray to or to answer our petitions. Enlightenment, in Theravada thinking, requires intensive study and meditation, the kind that is only possible for monks and nuns who are able to spend full time at this. The scriptures in Theravada Buddhism are written in the Pali language, which is an early vernacular. This is the Buddhism that become prominent in Southeast Asia—in Thailand, Cambodia, as well as in Sri Lanka.

Starting in about the 1st century A.D., there was another type of Buddhism arose called Mahayana Buddhism. Mahayana means greater vehicle, it's sort of like a comparison between a raft, which can just save a few people as it takes them across the ocean of trouble and turmoil, versus a cruise ship where you can get lots of people on board. In this type of Buddhism salvation, enlightenment just doesn't come to monks and nuns, but it's available to all people, lay persons as well. There are new scriptures, which are part of the tradition, that are written in Sanskrit. Remember Sanskrit is the classical holy language that the Vedas were written in. Now you may ask, how is it that 500 years after the Buddha's death, suddenly now we're getting new scriptures? The answer the Mahayana Buddhists gave was that the Buddha gave more of his advanced secret teachings to his more capable disciples. It sounds a little suspicious but remember that all Buddhist scriptures were originally passed on orally, so who knows? Maybe there were a few that were transmitted via a separate channel, from advanced disciple to advanced disciple.

In Mahayana Buddhism the Buddha is god and in some sense he exists still so that we can worship and pray to him. Remember in Theravada Buddhism the Buddha isn't a god he's just a man who figured out the truth about the universe and went on to nirvana, but he's clearly a deity in Mahayana Buddhism. There's a new emphasis on compassionate service, especially on Bodhisattvas. Bodhisattvas are men or women who achieve enlightenment and thus are enlightened and able to go into nirvana when they die but they chose not to. Instead they stick around in this world system to help out other people. In fact they make a vow saying, I myself am not going into nirvana until every other sentient being has also become enlightened. You can pray to them, and they can help you in very concrete, specific ways. This Buddhism—Mahayana Buddhism—is the Buddhism of East Asia, of China, Korea, and Japan. There is a third form of Buddhism, that of Tibet, we'll talk about that in another lecture, Lecture 28.

In this lecture, I want to introduce you to two major figures in the development of Mahayana Buddhism: Nagarjuna and Vasubandhu. But first, we need to go back and pick up one more significant concept from the earliest teachings of the Buddha. This is one of the more difficult concepts. It's called the 12 Links of Dependent Origination. The basic idea is that nothing exists independently; everything is caused by something else, which in turn has its own cause, and so on and so on in an infinite regression. Indeed, everything is actually an event, it's something that's in transition. So my tie for example, looks like a thing but it's actually changing, it's fading, it's fraying over time. (This particular tie I will probably throw out after I give this lecture series.) That idea that everything is changing and is dependent on earlier things is formalized in 12 stages. We'll start with suffering, aging, and death—that's the first stage and that's the problem. That's caused by birth, if you were never born, you'd never grow older and die. Makes sense, right? Birth—though in Buddhism this is always going to be rebirth—is caused by existence, which in turn comes from attachment; attachment comes from desire; desire comes from sensations—you perceive things coming in and then you want them; sensations come from contact with sense-objects; that comes from and is dependent on your six senses. You have six senses—remember it's the five regular senses plus your mind is a sense organ—because you have a mind and body. Your mind and your body are the result of conscious thought, which is conditioned, influenced, or caused by psychic dispositions—those include impulses, emotions, and mental habits. Those are all caused by ignorance, which itself is derived from suffering and death. We're back to the beginning of the cycle, and around and around it goes.

That can be a bit confusing; don't worry about all the details of that. I want to make just two points about this. The first is this comprehensive scheme includes the five aggregates—remember that from earlier Buddhism that you have a body, sensations coming in through your senses, perceptions (that's part of your mind that's talked about in these 12 stages); you also have psychic dispositions and conscious thought. These are seen in this cycle as processes, not things. The second thing to notice about all this is the weak link in this cycle is ignorance. The root human problem is not pride or disobedience, but it's ignorance—particularly the ignorance of no-self. We think that there is some eternal concrete permanent self and that's a mistake of our thinking. Through the concept of dependent origination, we can understand the Buddha's teaching of the three characteristics of existence: Everything is impermanent; everything is unsatisfactory, remember all life is suffering or is unsatisfactory; and third, everything is not-self, there's no permanent entities that continue forever. Dependent origination is also known as conditioned arising, that is everything is conditional, it's dependent on something else. For the Buddha, the concept of dependent origination is a tool for liberation; you can pinpoint the link in the cycle, ignorance, you can deal with that by learning the Four Noble Truths, and then you can move on from there. For Nagarjuna, this concept of dependent origination is a tool for understanding the nature of reality.

Nagarjuna is one of the most important thinkers you've never heard of. He was the founder of the Madhyamaka school, it means the school of the Middle Way. This is part of Mahayana Buddhism. Nagarjuna was born in Southern India, probably in the Brahmin caste, lived during the 2nd century A.D. He converted to Buddhism and came to prominence at the University of Nalanda, where he was a professor. The University of Nalanda is a Buddhist institution in northern India.

There are lots of legends about this guy. In India, they say that he was something of a playboy as a young man—he was once caught in an indiscretion with some palace ladies, felt bitter remorse at that, and then became a monk. In Tibet, there is a quite different tradition, that at his birth astrologers predicted that Nagarjuna would die at the age of seven, but he managed to escape that fate by entering a monastery as a young child. Even more fantastic is the stories they tell in Tibet about how he traveled to the depths of the ocean and taught Buddhism to the Naga king. A Naga is an underwater serpent-like or dragon-like creature. The Naga king was so impressed that he gave Nagarjuna a book called the *Perfection of Wisdom Sutra*, which he had kept safe in his underwater lair since the death of the Buddha, just waiting for someone who would truly appreciate it. Nagarjuna's name actually is a combination of Naga, these serpent beings, and Arjuna, the great hero from the Bhagavad Gita.

Actually, it's this last tale about the ocean, the serpent king, and the secret scriptures that we will follow, because Nagarjuna is closely associated with the Perfection of Wisdom Sutras, wherever they came from. He wrote several commentaries on them. The original works were long works in Sanskrit because they're Mahayana scriptures. They are attributed to the Buddha, but they only appeared in the 1st century. They explain how the world around us is, in some ultimate sense, void or empty. Some of these are huge texts, with 100,000 verses to them. There are some shorter, more pocket-sized versions, one called the Diamond Sutra that's quite famous and the Heart Sutra that's about a page. Many Buddhists recite the Heart Sutra every morning. These Perfection of Wisdom Sutras are somewhat cryptic and a little bit hard to understand. Fortunately, we have Nagarjuna's explanations. "Emptiness," he says, is not the same thing as not existing. Indeed, he taught a metaphysical middle way, which mirrors the Buddha's ethical middle way between extreme asceticism—like the Jains on one side—and selfish indulgence of regular life on the other. Nagarjuna finds a middle way between Eternalism (that there is some permanent external reality) and Annihilationism (which is total non-existence). Things exist, but in a conditioned, temporary, changing way. Notice that he's drawing on that concept of dependent origination—things are conditioned, they're influenced, they're caused by other things. Without those other things they wouldn't have existence.

Maybe we need a more concrete example. Think about going to the beach sometime, enjoying an afternoon watching the waves come in and saying, I just love waves at the beach. I would like to take home a wave in a bucket. You go out there, you grab a bucket of wave, and then you take it back. Of course it's not a wave, it's just water because a wave isn't really a thing, it's a happening. Or another example, and I'm going to borrow this from Ainslie Embree's *Sources of Indian Tradition*, which is a great book. It's like a monk with poor eyesight who squints and thinks that he sees flies in his begging bowl. The flies aren't real, but the illusion of the flies is real, real enough to the monk who's perceiving this that it may have real consequences. He's going to try to brush aside these flies that he thinks he sees, or maybe he'll drop the bowl in surprise. Whatever arises is dependent on something else which is neither identical to it, nor entirely different, which means that things don't ever perish completely, but they aren't everlasting either. Nothing has an independent, eternal self-nature. Everything is empty, at least in this sense.

Nagarjuna explores the idea of identity and difference with a four-part logical analysis. We're going to call this a tetralemma, as opposed to a dilemma (remember that's a problem that has two solutions, neither of which are really acceptable or practical). So instead of just two solutions, neither of which works, Nagarjuna says there are four possible solutions to things and none of those really work as well. There will be an affirmation, a negation, and then both affirmation and negation, and then neither; you'll see several of these in the lecture. There are four kinds of statements that one can make about things, think of the flies in the begging bowl: 1) They exist; 2) they do not exist; 3) they both exist and do not exist, in some sense at the same time; and 4) they neither exist nor do they not exist. That's pretty much all the logical possibilities there are. According to Nagarjuna, all four options are inadequate; they all sort of entail logical inconsistencies, they're all wrong in some way. Or as he summarizes the matter in his opening lines of his book, *Fundamental Verses of the Middle Way*, when he is undermining all notions of causation: "Nowhere and in no way do any entities exist which originate from themselves, from something, from both themselves and something else, or spontaneously."

There are some interesting implications. As Nagarjuna used this four-fold negation he applies it to Buddhist principles like the Five Aggregates and the Four Noble Truths. Do the Four Noble Truths exist or don't they? He finds that they do, and they don't, and both they do and they don't, and neither they do or they don't. He discovered through this logical analysis that there is no real difference between samsara (reincarnation) and nirvana, no real difference between being enlightened and unenlightened beings, since each is ultimately emptiness—neither has any independent existence—which means that in some sense, all people are already buddhas, even if they don't realize it yet. Nirvana isn't some other place or other time; there's no difference between that and the life we live now. Also, if nothing is ultimately real in the sense that it is self-existent, then I suppose Nagarjuna has offered us a theory about an unreal world, which was developed by an unreal thinker with unreal thoughts. Thus he could claim that he had no philosophical position, even as he demonstrated the impossibility of all positions. It's like he says, "I can't tell you what reality really is, I can just show you that every possible argument that you can come up with is flawed in some way." Any assertion about reality will naturally lead to contradictions. He did his critics a favor by pointing out himself that if what he taught was correct, then his theory of emptiness was itself empty. But it's still useful; it's a little bit like a raft: Once you use a raft to get to other side of a river or pond, then you can get rid of the raft and move on. His logical analysis is something that is empty but it's useful and after you've gotten to the other side, after you've gotten to enlightenment, you can sort of scrap all of this philosophy that he's been engaged in.

By exposing the contradictions in ordinary thinking, and negating opposites, Nagarjuna dismantles arguments of existence and causation, and thereby hopes to free us to experience emptiness directly through meditation. This is in accordance with the Perfection of Wisdom Sutras, which teach a non-thinking sort of knowledge, saying that enlightenment is beyond all description and categories. In the end there are two levels of truth: the ordinary, conventional type which we describe with words and arguments—there's a wave; and a higher, ultimate truth which is beyond all language and logical analysis—a wave isn't really a thing, though it's also really not nothing either.

The difference between conventional and ultimate truth is similar to the way that the regular teachings in the Theravada texts could be transcended by the higher understanding of the Mahayana scriptures. Theravada Buddhists will teach people the Four Noble Truths, and then Mahayana Buddhists will say that's true in an ordinary way but there's another level of truth by which even the noble truths are empty.

A quick summary of Nagarjuna's thought appears in the preface to his *Fundamental Verses*: "No production nor destruction; no annihilation nor persistence; no unity nor plurality; no coming in nor going out." In the end, perhaps Nagarjuna's philosophy, which shows the pointlessness of philosophical analysis and reason, that it's always limited and doesn't really get to ultimate answers, actually supports the Buddha's original aversion to answering philosophical questions. In any case, Nagarjuna's logic and his spirituality have been enormously influential in India, China, Tibet, Japan, and Korea for nearly 2,000 years. We will see Nagarjuna again in future lectures.

Now we'll talk about Vasubandhu, who's the founder of Yogacara School. This is also Mahayana). Fourth century, raised in northwestern India (present day Pakistan). Wrote a major philosophical summary of the doctrines of one of the now defunct schools of early Buddhism, but then changed his mind. Converted to Mahayana by his younger half-brother, Asanga, who was himself converted by a vision of the Maitreya Buddha. He had tried to gain a vision for years, he'd nearly given up in despair. Then one day he was on the road and he stopped to help a suffering dog who was on the side there, and that dog turned out to be an incarnation of Maitreya—always there and all sorts of things, but only now could he see it through the eyes of compassion. Isn't it amazing how different people can have very different perceptions of the same things? It's colored by our moods, our emotional tendencies, our memories, unique associations that we have, and so forth.

Vasubandhu takes that idea of how much our own mental processes add to our perceptions and he writes the key texts of the Yogacara School. "Yogacara" means "yoga practitioners" and has to do with meditation, but the school is also known as the mind-only or consciousness-only school. As you might guess, this type of Buddhism teaches a form of metaphysical idealism—that the only things that exist are mental constructs, that it's literally all in your mind. Other Buddhists had argued that we have no direct access to the external world; that we only perceive our perceptions only, and that seems to be true, even by modern science. You may think that you're hearing a lecture now, but actually, there are sound waves that are going into your ear and there's the mechanism with the anvil, the stirrup, and the eardrum, and that gets changed into electro interactions through the neurons in your brain. You have no direct access to me. Your brain is creating images or sounds based on these electrochemical reactions.

Vasubandhu doesn't quite go that way, but he has this idea that we're all dependent on perception, and he further argues that perceptions are not necessarily derived from the outside world; they could exist entirely within our minds, sort of like our perceptions in dreams do. In other words, because the existence of the external world is impossible to prove, and it's an unnecessary explanation, by Occam's Razor—which means the simplest explanation would most likely be true—it is quite reasonable to accept that everything is an illusion, created by our minds. Occam's Razor is a Western concept, but Vasubandhu uses it, and he's about a thousand years earlier than William of Occam. This is a philosophy of Idealism; something like the 18th century British philosopher George Berkeley. The world we think we observe is simply a projection of our desires and habits of thought. This is an extreme version of the Madhyamaka doctrine of emptiness.

There are several obvious problems with thinking like this. The first is that ordinary life seems much more coherent and consistent than dreams; it seems like we can make a distinction. Also, if everything exists only in one's mind, why do different people seem to have the same perceptions? A car backfires and lots of people turn at the same time. Why does the world seem impervious to our thoughts and desires? In other words, why can't we perceive what we want to perceive, as in daydreams? And then, from the Buddhist perspective, how does karma work mentally?

Vasubandhu is going to give a couple explanations to explain these sorts of problems. The first solution is shared karma. Karma affects similar people in similar ways, so their experience is inter-subjective. The example that he gives is: Think about poor souls in hell. (Buddhists do have hells that you're born into, and then you die in that hell and can be reborn someplace else—so they're just temporary, but they're awful places of torment and suffering, sort of like Dante's hell.) So imagine the guards in those hells. Those torturing guards are not real beings, because otherwise they would suffer themselves from the heat and from the stench, but they are mental projections of guilty souls by which they torture themselves. By bad deeds you can create your own mental hell, which you can share with other people who have committed the same sins that you have.

His second solution is something called the storehouse consciousness. This is a pervasive collective subconscious, but it's more like a river rather than a building. The seeds of previous experiences and actions are stored subliminally, in a consciousness stream that rolls on and on, and then later they sprout and ripen into sense perceptions. Nirvana comes when there are no more seeds put into that consciousness storehouse. It's kind of a complicated idea, but that should give you a general idea.

Some implications of his thought: The path to enlightenment comes by focusing on mental processes—yoga, meditation, conjuring visions. There are eight levels of consciousness, of which storehouse consciousness is the most basic, and then it sort of works up from there. But in general, just as when we wake up, we realize that our dreams didn't make much sense, so also it is possible to wake up from the unreal, mentally constructed "dream" that we call life. That's what it means to become enlightened, according to

Vasubandhu. Madhyamaka and Yogacara philosophers will argue will each other for centuries, and they will greatly refine Buddhist philosophy and logic in the process. And both schools taught that meditation offered the best way to understand the reality beyond words and beyond perceptions.

Now we're coming to the end of the story. And remember, according to the Buddha, everything is constantly changing and eventually everything will come to an end sooner or later. Let's go back to that idea of Nalanda University, which is as famous in India as the Library of Alexandria is in the west—this sort of wondrous, legendary institution of higher learning. It was an actual institution of higher learning that now has become legendary in retrospect. It was located in northeast India, and it was prominent from the 5th to the 12th centuries. At that time—as I said it's one of the world's great universities it had perhaps 10,000 students and 2000 teachers who came to Nalanda from all over India, but also from Korea, Japan, China, Tibet, Indonesia, Persia, and Turkey. It had a real international student body and staff.

There were dormitories, classrooms, temples, meditation halls, parks, lakes, and a huge nine-story library that had a phenomenal collection of not just Buddhist texts, but texts from the Hindu philosophies, and texts having to do with science. Every field of learning was taught in this institution, from medicine, astronomy, and other sciences to philosophy, grammar, and logic. But Nalanda was first and foremost a Buddhist institution. Nagarjuna taught there in the 2nd century, and 500 years later, the Chinese monk Xuanzang, who had traveled all the way to India in search of the true Buddhism, studied Vasubandhu's writings on Yogacara school in his two years at Nalanda. (We'll hear more about Xuanzang in Lecture 18). The Yogacara scriptures that Xuanzang took from India back to China and translated were extremely influential in East Asian Buddhism.

And then it came to an end; Buddhism virtually died out in India. Now, we're not exactly sure why, but it seems that it has something to do with Hindu tolerance, because Hindu said that the Buddha is actually an avatar of Vishnu (it's a very generous sort of thing). So when you worship the Buddha, you're actually worshipping our Hindu god, just in a different manifestation. You can still be Hindu, and all the good things that you enjoy in Buddhism you don't have to leave Hinduism to get. So, there's Hindu tolerance and accommodation. On the other hand, there's some Hindu hostility because Buddhists were very critical of the caste system that was so integral to Hinduism. There was also a lack of royal patronage for Buddhists; there was a sense that Hinduism was a national religion whereas Buddhism was more universal in scope—it was for everyone, and perhaps wasn't as important or relevant to Indian life. Then perhaps most significantly, the coming of Muslims took a great toll on Buddhism. In 1198, Turkish invaders destroyed the university of Nalanda, burnt the libraries there, and killed thousands of monks.

All over India, monks and monasteries also made inviting, easily identifiable targets for political opponents or for marauding troops. Without monks and nuns, Buddhism couldn't survive. Well, Buddhism did flourish elsewhere in Asia (and we'll pick up that story later in these lectures), but not in the land of its birth.

A few years ago I had an opportunity to visit Nalanda. I walked around through the ruins there and thought about Nagarjuna and Vasubandhu. But the university is gone. It no longer exists. Well, it sort of does—there are a few brick foundations, mounds, courtyards, and even some of the small dormitories where monks once lived (I would peek in and sort of imagine people living and teaching there). And of course the philosophies that were once taught at Nalanda University still live on. So the university doesn't exist anymore, but in another sense it sort of does. (Are you ready for another tetralemma?) It exists, but it doesn't exist, but in some ways it both exists and doesn't exist now. Or perhaps it doesn't exist and doesn't not exist. Or maybe Nalanda University is now just a projection of my mind. I was once there actually, but now it's just a memory, or even an imagined community of what it would have been like at a time when there were eager teachers and students there. Although ultimately, Nalanda University's emptiness still has a capacity to inspire me—to be a cause for my own teaching and learning; to condition and influence what happens in my life, which may in turn lead me to teach others, may lead to changes to me, in my students, perhaps even in you. Thanks.

Sima Qian and Ban Zhao—History and Women
Lecture 15

Sima Qian and Ban Zhao were the first thinkers in Chinese thought to deal systematically with history and women, respectively. Neither would be part of a traditional course on Asian philosophy, but their ideas have profoundly shaped the lives of millions of people. Sima Qian's *Shiji* is a breathtakingly comprehensive, exquisitely edited treatment of China's history from its legendary beginnings to his own day. Ban Zhao's most famous piece is the brief "Lessons for Women," the first work to pay specific attention to women and women's issues from a Confucian perspective.

In Chinese culture, where history writing is a crucial part of cultural identity, all history writing follows Sima Qian's *Shiji* ("the Grand Scribe's records"), the first systematically composed work of Chinese history by a named author. The project was started by his father, Sima Tan, and taken up by Sima Qian on Sima Tan's death in 110 B.C. A decade later, faced with a choice between death and castration as punishment for his unfortunate political loyalties, Sima Qian chose castration, seen as a shameful option, out of duty to his father and the work.

On its completion, the *Shiji* was comparable in length to the Bible. It covered the history of the entire world as Sima Qian knew it, beginning with China's legendary Yellow Emperor. It is not a linear narrative but is organized into five sections: 12 basic annals, each devoted to a dynasty; 10 chronological tables; 8 treatises on ritual, music, the calendar, astronomy, economics, and so forth; 30 "hereditary houses," which recount state histories of the late Zhou dynasty and family histories from the Han dynasty; and 70 biographies of significant people or groups, from poets and philosophers to doctors and politicians. It also includes chapters on the nomadic border peoples and Sima Qian's autobiography.

Several characteristics mark the *Shiji* as a breakthrough in world historiography. It is a masterpiece of literary style, demonstrates meticulous devotion to accuracy and critical historiography, and offers multiple perspectives on events and people. Later dynastic histories—of which there were dozens—all followed Sima Qian's model; the *Shiji* is the first of the 24 so-called standard histories that cover 18 centuries of Chinese civilization.

Ban Zhao, like Sima Qian, began her career in history writing by taking over the work of a late relative, her brother, the 1st-century historian Ban Gu. Born into a prominent family, Ban Zhou was probably the most educated woman of her time, and she trained several important male scholars. Widowed at an early age, she devoted her remaining life to scholarship, becoming a teacher, poet, tutor to the royal family, advisor to the Dowager Empress, and historian.

In light of such a biography, readers are often surprised by how reactionary and anti-woman the advice in her "Lessons for Women" seems. Full of references to Confucian classics, it advises young women about marriage and family—namely, that wives should always be humble and submissive to an extent that most modern Western readers would find extreme.

The *Shiji* is the first of the 24 so-called standard histories that cover 18 centuries of Chinese civilization.

So was this remarkably independent woman a hypocrite? Not exactly. Ban Zhao is giving practical advice for a very particular time, place, and kind of family. Chinese marriage is patrilocal, meaning brides always join their husbands' families and worship their husbands' ancestors. Having sons is the only form of social security, and a daughter-in-law, by definition, comes between a mother and son. Ban Zhao's advice is geared toward smoothing the mother-in-law/daughter-in-law relationship for the benefit of both. Ban Zhao is also trying to give attention to women's issues from a Confucian perspective—a daunting task, since Confucius more or less ignored women altogether. Finally, the true purpose of her essay may have been subversive: She argues that girls should be given the same education as boys—to make them better wives, of course. In any case, she is a fascinating early female voice in Chinese history and an influential one. ■

Suggested Reading

De Bary and Bloom, eds., *Sources of Chinese Tradition*.

Durrant, *The Cloudy Mirror*.

Hardy, *Worlds of Bronze and Bamboo*.

Sima Qian, *The First Emperor*.

Swann, *Pan Chao*.

Questions to Consider

1. What makes history an important source of values and understanding? If cultures have little interest in history, what other genres might provide these ideas?

2. Is the presentation of multiple perspectives truer to history itself, or just to our perceptions of it?

3. Would Ban Zhao be a role model for women today? What sorts of constraints did she have to deal with, and how did those influence her advice to her daughters?

Sima Qian and Ban Zhao—History and Women
Lecture 15—Transcript

Hello! I'm so glad you're here. I've been looking forward to this lecture for awhile. I wrote a whole book on Sima Qian, and Ban Zhao is the first woman among the great minds of the Eastern intellectual tradition. I wanted to subtitle this lecture: *The Discovery of History and Women.* Of course the Chinese were already aware of both history and women, but these two thinkers, Sima Qian and Ban Zhao, are the first people to deal with these subjects in a careful, systematic way.

Neither Sima Qian nor Ban Zhao would be part of a traditional course on Asian philosophy, but their ideas have profoundly shaped the lives of millions of people. When I was working on a dissertation on Sima Qian in graduate school, I was sometimes asked by family or friends, "We've never heard of this guy, who would he be comparable to in Western history?" I would say, "Maybe Plato." Sima Qian is absolutely central to Chinese thought and culture.

In the West, there were great traditions of Greece and Rome, like Herodotus and Thucydides, Livy, Tacitus, but then in the Middle Ages that historiographical tradition sort of dried up for awhile. In China, by contrast, Sima Qian starts a tradition of writing history that keeps on going. Remember, Alfred North Whitehead said that, "Western philosophy is a series of footnotes to Plato?" In China, histories are generally a continuation of Sima Qian's *Shiji.* It means the Grand Scribe's Records, and history writing itself is a crucial part of the Chinese cultural identity. So, it's appropriate to start with some historical context alright.

We're going to go from 4th century A.D. India and then we're going to jump back to China where we'll continue the story from where we left off in Lecture 10. Remember the First Emperor took over all of China and started the Qin dynasty, which didn't last for very long and then was followed by the 400 years of the Han dynasty from 202 B.C. to 220 A.D. Not every civilization has seen the study of history as an indispensible method for understanding the world or understanding our place within it, but that's certainly the case with China. This is in part due to the tradition of ancestor worship and also the early development of writing, which happened during the Shang dynasty (about 1500 B.C.).

The Five Confucian Classics were collections of ancient writings and two of them were specifically historical in nature. There was the *Venerated Documents*, which were supposedly speeches or announcements that were given by some of the early kings in the Shang and Zhao dynasties. Then another of the classics was the *Spring and Autumn Annals*; that was a history of the state of Lu, which was Confucius' native state.

During the Warring States Era, philosophers often cited historical precedents. Confucians and the Mohists looked back to the reigns of the Kings Wen and Wu and then the legendary sage kings Yao, Shun, and Yu. Daoists went even further back to the mythological Yellow Emperor, sort of a one-ups-manship right, our guy is even older than your guy, and that's marketing strategy in Chinese history and Chinese philosophical discourse. The strategists and the political advisors of the hundred schools era offered countless examples from more recent centuries of interstate diplomacy, and administration, and warfare and then they could use those historical art examples to illustrate various arguments.

The Legalists, though, dismissed history. They said it's all going to start with us; it doesn't matter, but not exactly. An early Legalist philosopher named Shang Yang said, "As rulers, King Tang and King Wu did not follow the ancients and yet they came into power. ... Therefore you need have no doubts: turning from the ancients is not necessarily bad." Can you spot the logical fallacy in that? There's a precedent for ignoring precedence. So, why should I ignore precedence then? You can figure this out.

Eventually exemplary stories from history were compiled into handy anthologies or even debaters handbooks. The first real history, however, with a named author and a systematic approach, was the *Shiji*, remember The Grand Scribe's Records that was written by Sima Qian.

Sima Qian lived from about 145 to 86 B.C. He was the Grand Scribe at the court of the Emperor Wu who lived during the Han dynasty. Sima Qian was a Minor official, the Grand Scribe. It sounds like a big title, but it's actually not all that prestigious. His responsibilities included recording astronomical phenomena, interpreting portents, supervising the calendar, and all of this gave him access to the imperial archives, which is really important for somebody who wants these primary sources to write history.

Sima Qian's father, Sima Tan, had had the same position, but on the side Sima Tan had started writing a private history. He probably just got a few chapters into it. Then when Sima Tan died, in 110 B.C., Sima Qian was there at his deathbed and he said to his son you need to finish this work that I started. Sima Qian, with tears in his eyes, said I'll do that for you. Sima Qian worked on this for about a decade and then there was political disaster. A general named Li Ling had been sent to fight against the nomadic tribes up in the north. He found himself outnumbered and surrounded. Reinforcements didn't come in time. It was just hopeless and this General Li Ling had surrendered.

The Emperor was furious at this and Sima Qian was the only person at court to stand up for the General and say he was kind of in an impossible situation. That made the Emperor even angrier and he sentenced Sima Qian to death. He thought that he was criticizing him, also the General who was supposed to bring the reinforcements were the Emperors brother-in-law, it all gets very complicated, but Sima Qian you're going to be executed. Now, for some reason that was commuted, he was offered an opportunity to buy his way out of execution, but Sima Qian doesn't have any money. Then another alternative is offered, which is okay you can be castrated rather than executed. Sima Qian accepts that offer so that he can finish his history that he's still working on. He survived that ordeal of mutilation and then he later served as a Palace Secretary. Eunuchs were accepted in the Chinese Court, but they were looked down upon, despised by everyone.

Later on, Sima Qin wrote a letter in which he explained his decision, and he said, "If I concealed my feelings and clung to life, burying myself in filth without protest, it was because I could not bear to leave unfinished my deeply cherished project, because I rejected the idea of dying without leaving to posterity my literary work." The implicit question is why didn't you commit suicide rather than suffer this humiliation? His answer is I wanted to finish my work, that of filial piety, out of respect for my father.

How could I face my father in the next life if I didn't accept and bring his history to completion? Sima Qian concludes, and this is so good I can't wait to read this,

> This is the thought that wrenches my bowels nine times each day. Sitting at home, I'm befuddled as though I have lost something. I go out, and then realize I don't know where I'm going. Each time I think of this shame, the sweat pours from my back and soaks my robe. I am now no more than a servant in the harem. How could I leave of my own accord and hide far away in some mountain cave? Therefore, I follow along with the vulgar, floating and sinking, bobbing up and down with the times, sharing their delusion and madness.

What does this book look like, this book that he sacrificed so much for? It's long; it has over half a million Chinese characters that it's written in. In English, it takes several English words to represent on character sometimes. A translation would probably be about the length of the Bible, I mean from Genesis to Revelation, but written by a single person. It was written on bamboo slips, so little thin strips of bamboo that were then tied together with cords and then you could roll it up like a window shade. This is the reason that the Chinese write from top to bottom as they started writing on these bamboo slips, and then from right to left.

If you have a whole copy, an entire copy of the *Shiji*, it would've been 130 of these bamboo bundles and it would've filled an entire a cart. It would just be very inconvenient to take around, but a huge work. The *Shiji* is also quite comprehensive. It's a history of the entire world, as Sima Qian knew it, from legendary beginnings to his own day. Just as the Han dynasty had consolidated the empire, so also Sima Qian's work consolidated and brought together knowledge of everything in the past and in the present and everything under heaven, from China to border areas and natural phenomena and history, everything found its proper place within this book.

But, the truly amazing thing is the book's unusual organization. It's not a simple narrative from beginning to end. Instead, the 130 chapters were divided into five sections. There are 12 Basic Annals, so each of those chapters is devoted to an early dynasty or, during the Han dynasty, to a specific ruler, and then in those chapters the events were arranged like chronicles, sometimes nearly year by year. That's followed by 10 Chronological Tables, which coordinate events across various kingdoms or feudal domains and then become more detailed as you get closer they get to Sima Qian's own time. He's got these charts that show years and events and how everything is happening at the same time.

That's followed by 8 Treatises and those are essays on ritual, on music, on the pitch pipes, which had to do with cosmology and also military strategy, the calendar, astronomy, state sacrifices, water control, particularly of the Yellow River, and the economy. Then there are 30 Hereditary Houses. These recount the histories of important states or kingdoms in the late Zhou dynasty, remember in the warring states era, and then once we get to the Han dynasty, it follows some powerful families; they get chapters of their own.

Then the largest section are 70 Memoirs. These are biographies of significant people, sometimes combining within a single chapter several individuals who might be connected by family relationships, or they had held the same government position, or they had similar temperaments, or they had the same occupations, so there's a chapter devoted to diviners, to famous doctors, some chapters about poets, a chapter about successful businessmen, a chapter about harsh officials, a chapter about local bosses or sort of like mafia like figures, a chapter on assassins, and several chapters on philosophers, which is why we've been mentioning them sort of all the way through, as oftentimes our first biographies of philosophers come from Sima Qian's work.

There are also chapters devoted to the nomadic peoples on the borders of China, and then the last memoir is Sima Qian's own autobiography. We know more about his life than we do about other early figures and a little bit about his thinking and he tells us something about his ambitions and something about how he deliberately organized this history.

At the end of most sections, Sima Qian adds a brief comment, beginning with the phrase "His honor, the Grand Scribe says …" and then he gives some sort of reflection or response or explanation. I want to interrupt for a quick point that I think is significant in Chinese civilization. Sima Qian starts his comprehensive universal history not with the creation of the world, but with a legendary ruler, the Yellow Emperor. Unlike the Indians, in India, and unlike the Hebrews, creation is not a central issue in Chinese thought. What really matters is civilization.

When Christian missionaries arrived in China with a Bible and they asked the Chinese here's our creation story from Genesis, what's your creation story? The Chinese couldn't really think of one. They dug around in some of their texts and they came up with a story from the 3rd century A.D. about a figure named Pangu; this is a legend, and this fellow grew ten feet taller every day and then he kept the earth and the sky separate for 18,000 years until he died and then his body became the world that we know with the mountains and the rivers and such and the fleas and lice on his body became living creatures, including human beings. It's kind of an interesting point. This story is very late and it's not all that important in Chinese tradition.

Sometimes Sima Qian has been accused of simply being a "cut-and-paste" historian. He just took some passages from text that he had access to and just put them all together. But, the way that he rewrites some of these narratives and especially the way he organizes his material shows him to be a very discriminating editor. He does some surprising things. For example, he puts Confucius in the hereditary houses sections, even though Confucius was not a feudal lord, Confucius didn't control territory, but what he started intellectually is something that's passed down and is incredibly significant. So, he puts them in this section with more significance than just the biographies. Similarly Empress Lü gets a basic annal herself. Even though she didn't directly govern China she was a regent for a couple of young boy kings, but Sima Qian recognized that this woman was the one who was really in charge of things so he gives her her own biography. That was actually criticized later on by some people who were a little stricter about Confucian separations of the genders.

There are several characteristics that mark the *Shiji* as a breakthrough in world historiography. I'm going to give you five of them. The first one is the *Shiji* is a masterpiece of literary style in classical Chinese. It narrates the Civil War that happened at the end of the Qin dynasty. Remember Liu Bang, the peasant, is going to win and become the emperor, the first emperor of the

Han. His rival is named Xiang Yu, and Xiang Yu gets in a position where he is outnumbered, he's surrounded, it looks like it's all over.

Shang Yu is an aristocrat from the state of Chu, a huge state down in the south. That evening before the last battle, he heard songs coming from the surrounding troops and they were songs from his native state of Chu and he realized that all was over because Rio Bon had taken over Chu, he had constricted soldiers from there and his own people were now against him. Sima Qian conveys that in a four character phrase, "Sì mìan Chǔ gē," which means all around, the songs of Chu and the Chinese sometimes use that phrase to express when you're in an impossible situation when you come to the end of the road.

The second characteristic is Sima Qian's attention to accuracy, which is manifest in many things, but especially in the careful way that he correlates the different calendars of various states. Each of those states have their own calendar system and he puts them all together in this comprehensive chart. In the west, the great Christian historian Exiguous does a little bit of this, but it's not really until Joseph Justus Scaliger, in the 16th century, when relative chronology is finally worked out, when they figure out how to match up the history of the Greeks and the Romans with the histories of the Egyptians and the Babylonians and the Persians and the Hebrews.

The third breakthrough in historiography is Sima Qian chose the emergence of a critical historiographical attitude as he evaluates his material based on rational principles, observation, and primary sources. Fourth, because information about a single person or single event is scattered across several chapters, readers have to take into account multiple perspectives, so do you remember I told you the story about Zhang Liang, he was the guy who got the secret book of military strategy from the old man who threw a shoe down the embankment. If you want to read about Zhang Liang you start with his biography, but you also have to read 16 other chapters that all mention him and reveal some more information about this man. Those chapters include three basic annals, two chronological tables, and several biographies of other generals and statesman. Oftentimes the negative aspects of a person's life are put in other people's biographies so that in their own biography they can look pretty good. It's sort of one of those Confucian politeness things that Sima Qian gives.

When you read the *Shiji* it's not like you're just listening to Sima Qian tell you these stories, he's inviting you to *do* history along with him. You have to put things together to figure out how they're related, look at these multiple perspectives. Sima Qian has sometimes been accused of having secret Daoist sympathies. Certainly his primary focus is his Confucian; I mean he's writing a history after all. There's something in these multiple perspectives that each give you a partial glimpse at truth that accords with Daoist sensibilities.

Then last, Sima Qian presents a holistic view of history that represents multiple sources and perspectives. I've argued in a book that I've written that the *Shiji* is a model of the world. It's like a microcosm and that's a concept that interested several Han dynasty thinkers, as we'll see in the next lecture. It's sort of a textual model of how the world works.

Let me give you an example that illustrates some of these points. It is the chapter on assassins. Sima Qian tells the story of Jing Ke who tried to assassinate the First Emperor of Qin, remember he was paranoid about this because of these bad experiences. Sima Qian ends this chapter by saying His Honor the Grand Scribe says: "People of the world say that when Jing Ke undertook the mission of Crown Prince Dan, heaven rained grain and horses sprouted horns. These are great errors." I'm taking you right in the middle, it's sort of nitty-gritty Chinese history so there are going to be lots of names, but I'll point out what's important. The first thing is he says there are some superstitions; those are errors. I'm not going to accept those.

Let me continue with Sima Qian's words, "They also say that Jing Ke wounded the king of Qin," the First Emperor. "This is all wrong. Gongsun Jigong and Dong Sheng," those are two names, "were at one time associates of Xia Wuju, and they both knew about the matter. They have told it to me as it is here." Okay Xia Wuju was an eyewitness, Sima Qian didn't have access to him, but he did interview people who had heard this story from someone who was actually there at the time. "As for the five men from Cao Mo down to Jing Ke," these are the stories that he's told in the chapter, "sometimes they succeeded in their intentions and sometimes they did not, but the ideas which they based themselves on are clear. They did not betray their resolve, and their names have come down to later generations. How can they have been in vain!" Now notice what he is saying there, that even if they're disgraced, even if they failed some of these, they were still true to their principles and so should be remembered for it.

Sima Qian saw himself in a similar light. He believed that he was the latest in a long line of thinkers who wrote books when they were misunderstood or even mistreated by their contemporaries, and that includes Confucius, remember who had a hard time getting a job, Sunzi, the military strategist who had his feet chopped off, Han Feizi, the Legalist who died in prison. Each of these men, Sima Qian said, wrote about the past in order to pass on their thoughts to future generations. He hoped that the sages and scholars of later ages would someday come to appreciate his work as well.

That indeed turned out to be the case. The *Shiji* is one of the most influential books ever written in China, and later dynastic histories, and there are dozens of those, followed the model set forth by Sima Qian with a few modifications. In particular, the *Shiji* became the first of the so-called Standard Histories, many of which were official projects sponsored by emperors. You claim a mandate of heaven, you stage a coup, you kick out the old dynasty, and then you write history of the preceding dynasty.

There are now twenty-four works in this series—one for each legitimate dynasty—and they comprise some 40 million words written over the course of eighteen centuries; together they constitute our most important source for the history of imperial China. It's one of the most complete records for any civilization in the world.

Now we come to the great mind Ban Zhao. The second history in those standard histories, dynastic histories, was written in the first century A.D. by Ban Gu, another great historian, but he was imprisoned and executed before he could finish the project. The Emperor asked Ban's younger sister, that's Ban Zhao to come to court and finish the book, which she did. She contributed to some of the more technical chapters on astronomy and chronology, and then she edited the book into its final form. She was probably the most educated woman of her time, and she trained several important male scholars.

Ban Zhao lived from about 45 to 116 A.D. She was born into a prominent family. Her father was an important scholar and she had two older brothers who were twins, one of them was Ban Gu, the great historian, and the other was a great general. Ban Zhao was educated at home and then she married at the age of fourteen, which is pretty typical at the time.

Her husband died young and rather than remarry, Ban Zhao devoted her life to scholarship. She eventually went to live in her brother's household in the capital and there she became a teacher, and a poet, and a tutor to the royal family, an advisor to the Dowager Empress, and, of course, a historian. But, she's most famous for a short work she wrote entitled "Lessons for Women." In her mid-50s, Ban Zhao wrote this essay as practical advice for the younger women in her extended family as they prepared to marry. It's quite erudite. It's full of references to Confucius and quotations from the Confucian classics. Sounds pretty interesting, right?

Actually, it's hard to know what to do with this essay in the 21st century. My students are invariably shocked by the opening words: "I, the unworthy writer, am unsophisticated, unenlightened, and by nature unintelligent," and they say wow does she have a self-esteem problem? No, everybody writes like this. This is this Confucian self-deprecating politeness. Even Sima Qian wrote of his "poor talents" and his "useless writings," completely conventional. But the contents don't seem to get much better. Ban Zhao's advice to young women is that wives should always be humble and submissive. Don't claim credit for good things and don't deny blame for the bad things that happen, she says. You should be up early, you should go to bed late, and you should fill your day with doing household tasks. Don't laugh, don't joke around, don't chatter. She says husbands should control their wives, and wives should serve their husbands, of course that might be easy for her to say because she wasn't married and hadn't had a husband for some time.

She says husbands and wives shouldn't spend all their time together, following each other around the house, otherwise they may begin to take liberties and "lust after each other," heaven forbid' I've heard lots of sermons in church, hardly any about the dangers of husbands and wives lusting after each other. Ban Zhao says a wife should, above all, strive to serve her in-laws, even if it requires sacrificing her personal opinions, and she should live in harmony with her husband's brothers and her sisters-in-law. Does this sound like repression of women? Is she complicit with the patriarchy? What's going on here? It's that last item, living in harmony with brothers and sisters-in-law, that provides a clue as to how to interpret all this.

Ban Zhao is giving practical advice for a very particular kind of family. You may have heard that Chinese prefer boys to girls. That's true, but it's not just misogyny, not just hatred of women. There're two key elements of Chinese culture from very early on that influence this. It's ancestor worship and patrilocal marriage. We've already talked about ancestor worship. Patrilocal marriage means that a bride always moves in with her husband's family and she worships her husband's ancestors. If you have all daughters, let's say five daughters, you are a loser in this life because you'll raise those girls and each of them will be married into other people's families and will take care of other people's parents in their old age. You will have no one and you will be a loser in the next life as well because when you die no one will give you offerings and ancestor worship and you will be a hungry ghost. There's no social security in ancient China; you have to have a son in order to take care of you in your old age, a daughter won't do it.

In China, the primary male/female relationship is mother to son; it's not husband and wife. If you've got, imagine you're female now, if you've got a son who you're very happy is going to take care of you, who is likely to come between you and your son? Right, it's going to be his wife, your daughter-in-law. Traditionally, mother-in-law/daughter-in-law relationships have been pretty tense in China, at least until that younger woman can get a son of her own and then now she's got some social security for her old age and beyond. Now remember, this is a society that does arranged marriages so these women, and they're not even women, these are girls, these are teenagers, go into a family all by themselves, their husbands, they haven't fallen in love. Their husbands may have only met them at the wedding so their husband is not going to stand up for them or be a protector. These girls are very vulnerable and Ban Zhao's advise is serve your in-laws, don't make a lot of waves, be obedient and deferent and things will be okay, at least until you can get a son seems to be the implication.

Now remember, in-laws, if your mother-in-law doesn't like you she can force her son, your husband to divorce you, like parents can break up marriages. So living in harmony with the husband's brothers, who are all still there, and sisters-in-law, all these women who've been married in, is a key to family harmony and romance, remember don't follow each other around or you may lust after each other, romance is an emotion that may disrupt the regular, harmonious workings of a family.

There are other ways in which Ban Zhao's essay isn't quite as reactionary as it may seem. First of all, at least she's giving specific attention to women and women's issues from a Confucian point of view and that's a new thing. Confucius himself mostly ignored women. He mentions a couple of famous women in the Analects, but otherwise, he speaks about women in general just once, when he says that women and subordinates are hard to deal with, if you're friendly to them they take advantage of you and if you keep your distance, they resent it. Ouch.

But I remember the first time I ever read that quotation. It was actually in a letter that was written to me by my girlfriend when I was living in Taiwan, and clearly the message there was you need to pay more attention to me, start writing more frequently. I took that hint, I went back home, I married that woman, and we're going to have our 28th anniversary next month. In some ways, perhaps I owe my happy marriage to Confucius. Ban Zhao is also treating women as people with specific responsibilities and standards of behavior. She's treating them as moral agents and that's an important new thing in Chinese history. She combines Confucian hierarchy with the Daoist principles of yin and yang (we'll see much more of this in the next lecture).

She says that husbands who hit their wives destroy the matrimonial relationship—I agree—and most strikingly, she says that girls should get the same education as boys. That's going to be a radical suggestion, which she makes palatable by arguing that if you educate girls you'll be able to make them better wives to help them fit traditional roles. But, I wonder if that isn't potentially subversive? I mean once women can read, who knows what they might do or what they might think. Unfortunately, that piece of advice was never really put into practice in China. Ban Zhao applied Confucian principles to women's lives, but recent scholars have suggested that, like Sima Qian, she may have had some covert Daoist tendencies. There's an emphasis there on taking a low position, maybe for self-preservation, for survival.

In any case, Ban Zhao represents a fascinating early female voice—influential in traditional China and then, in a different way, in modern China as women started to become more educated. They look back at Ban Zhao's example. Today, there's a crater on the planet Venus that's named after Ban Zhao. According to a proverb that was preserved in Sima Qian's *Shiji*, "He who does not forget the past will become the teacher of those who come afterwards." Or in the case of Ban Zhao, we might say, "She who does not forget the past will be the teacher of those who come afterwards."

Dong Zhongshu and Ge Hong—Eclecticism
Lecture 16

Confucianism became the official ideology of Imperial China during the Han dynasty, transformed from a movement about culture and ethics into one including cosmological speculation, thanks to Dong Zhongshu, prime minister to Emperor Wu. When the Han dynasty fell, many scholars turned toward Daoism. In this chaotic time between empires, an alchemist named Ge Hong brought together several strands of Neo-Daoism and reconciled them with Confucianism.

By the founding of the Han dynasty around 200 B.C., Daoism was the prominent school of Chinese thought. The Naturalists saw the world as composed of two complementary forces in ever-shifting balance and saw the *Yijing* ("classic of change"), a book of divination, as not only a predictor of the future but a guide for the present. Other thinkers tried to categorize natural and human phenomena in terms of the five phases of existence: fire, metal, wood, earth, and water, trying to fit phenomena into categories rather than establish cause and effect.

The fifth Han emperor, Wu, enacted educational reforms that returned Confucian thought to the fore on the advice of Dong Zhongshu, a minister, philosopher, and one of Sima Qian's teachers. Dong's ideas stressed synthesis and unity. He argued that heaven, earth, and humankind were intimately connected and proposed a macrocosmic/microcosmic model of the universe—the human body is a model of the cosmos—supported by numerology (i.e., your four limbs correspond to the four seasons, and so forth).

Emperor Wu's government returned China to Confucianism.

Dong's arguments may seem silly from a modern, scientific perspective, but his point was that morality is based in the natural world. Heaven provided a model for human action and (Confucian) human relationships: Emperors rule ministers, fathers rule sons, and husbands rule wives. His philosophy offered a rationale for strong, centralized rule and synthesized Daoism, Legalism, the Naturalism, and Confucianism.

Later thinkers reined in the wilder speculations of the Han Confucians. Wang Chong offered an early Chinese example of rational skepticism and suggested that heaven has no consciousness, no will, and no perception; everything happens spontaneously and naturally. On the other hand, New Text philosophers virtually deified Confucius.

Four forms of Neo-Daoism
- Confucian commentaries on the Daodejing and Zhuangzi.
- A life of hedonism and disregard for social convention.
- Several organized religious Daoism movements.
- A search for immortality through yoga-like practices and alchemy. (Incidentally, this alchemy movement led to the invention of gunpowder.)

Ge Hong, the most famous of China's medieval alchemists, fused several strands of Neo-Daoism and reconciled them with Confucianism. His book, the *Baopuzi* ("master who embraces simplicity") is divided into two parts: one about the quest for Daoist immortality and the other a Confucian perspective on government and social issues.

Ge Hong describes a Daoist immortal as someone so spiritually pure that they can fly, subsist on air and dew, walk on water, and live forever. To attain this rarified state, Ge Hong recommends living in harmony with nature and avoiding excess, along with incantations and alchemical elixirs to re-create within one's body the longer-term processes of the natural world.

Confucianism was somewhat discredited when the Han dynasty fell, and many 3rd-century scholars turned to Daoism.

Although he was a Daoist, Ge Hong did not entirely withdraw from the world. He was a successful militia commander, and he alternated between periods of government service and Daoist reclusion throughout his life. In fact, he saw Confucian morality as the foundation for Daoist immortality, saying, "Those who seek to become immortals must regard loyalty, filiality, peacefulness, obedience, benevolence, and trustworthiness as fundamental." Thinkers like Ge Hong showed the Chinese that it is possible to be both Daoist and Confucian at the same time. ■

Suggested Reading

Chan, *A Source Book in Chinese Philosophy*.

De Bary and Bloom, eds., *Sources of Chinese Tradition*.

Graham, *Disputers of the Tao*.

Kohn, *Daoism and Chinese Culture*.

Questions to Consider

1. What is the role of synthesis in the development of philosophy?

2. Can ethics be rooted in natural processes? Should they be?

3. What is the connection between political circumstances and intellectual movements? Must a thinker fit his or her times to be successful? What is the relationship between intellectuals and the state?

Dong Zhongshu and Ge Hong—Eclecticism
Lecture 16—Transcript

Hello again. In this lecture we'll once again be talking about the convergence of empire and thought. How political situations shape philosophy, and then what happens when the political foundation that gave rise to a philosophy or supported a philosophy collapses. Confucianism became the official ideology of Imperial China during the Han dynasty from 202 B.C. to 220 A.D. During this time, it was transformed from a movement that was focused on traditional culture and ethics to one that included cosmological speculations.

Many of these ideas originated in the "Hundred Schools," so you may be familiar with them from that lecture. Do you remember the Naturalists? In Chinese, this is known as the Yin-yang School. These theorists, sometimes allied with the Daoists, saw the world as composed of two complementary, opposite forces, which are ever-shifting in an ebb and flow manner like yin and yang.

The *Yijing*, or the Classic of Change, one of the five Confucian classics, was actually a divination text anciently. It used 64 hexagrams, so those are all the possible combinations of six broken or unbroken lines, and that eventually came to be understood in the Han Dynasty as representing a comprehensive model of being and change. It's not just a predictor of the future, but it's actually a guide for the present, as you try to understand what the present situation is like and then what it's likely to turn into and how you should behave in appropriate ways to that.

Other thinkers tried to categorize natural and human phenomena in terms of the Five Phases. That's fire, metal, wood, earth, and water. That sounds a little bit like the five elements in ancient Greek thought, but these aren't elements because they transform into each other. It was thought that these Five Phases succeeded each other in a regular pattern of conquest, and once again, these aren't things, but they're sort of aspects within things. The conquest cycle is water is conquered by earth, so you could build dikes or dams to control water. Earth is conquered by wood, and here you have to think of like a wooden plow that's cutting through the soil.

Wood, in turn is conquered by metal, as an axe cuts down a tree, and then fire conquers metal, as it melts it. Then finally, fire is conquered by water and then you're back again to the beginning of the cycle. It goes around and around.

Eventually, each of these Five Phases came to be associated with a particular season, or color, or a planet, or a compass direction, but there's only four of those so one of them doesn't quite match up, or they were associated with a particular number, or an internal organ of the body, or some type of animal. For example, fire was connected with summer and with the color red, okay that sort of makes sense. It was also associated with the direction south and with the planet Mars (maybe). It was also connected with the number seven, with the heart, and with feathered creatures, and here it gets sort of speculative, I guess. It was also associated with the Zhou dynasty; each of the dynasties is associated with a phase that seemed to be dominant at that time. This is where it really gets interesting.

The Qin dynasty, under the First Emperor had conquered the Zhou, so the First Emperor of Qin, proclaimed that his new dynasty ruled by the power of water, which had overcome fire. Water was correlated with winter, with the color black, and with the number six. Therefore, the First Emperor changed the date when New Year occurred to the 10th month, so it's at the beginning of winter. He ruled harshly, which was a characteristic associated with those terms. He dressed his officials in black; he put black flags and black banners around his court. He rode a carriage with six horses, and he divided his empire into 36 commanderies, remember those are like provinces and 36, of course, is 6 by 6! He's got all of this numerological stuff going.

Notice that he bases his claim to legitimacy on natural processes rather than on morality or the mandate of Heaven. He says I'm ruling because I'm in a court with disciples of the heavens and the earth. Later, philosophers argued for a different cycle called the production cycle that fire gave rise to earth in ash, and earth produces metal, because you have to dig metal out of the ground. Metal produces water; I think what they were thinking of was the way if you lay a piece of metal out overnight dew forms on it from condensation. Then, water produces wood, right, and then wood produces fire and then it goes around and it all gets sort of confusing and there are different ways of figuring out how all of this interacts.

But, it does extend itself to careful observation of nature and natural processes, but it's not exactly modern science. The goal is to fit phenomena into these preexisting categories, into these sort of pigeonholes, rather than establishing direct cause and effect.

When Liu Bang overthrew the Qin and founded his own Han dynasty about 200 B.C., Daoism enjoyed prominence and the people were pretty tired of the activist harsh government of the Legalists. They were looking for something a little more laid back and relaxed. But, Confucianism still made some progress. The banning of the books that the First Emperor had put into place was lifted. Some Confucian scholars were employed at court, including Lu Jia, who famously told Liu Bang that although he had won the empire on horseback, he couldn't rule it on horseback. There's a different skill set from being a conqueror and being a ruler.

There was also a Confucian scholar named Shusun Tong, who set up the court rituals for him. The story is that after Liu Bang had combined all of China into one rule, his old generals who now don't have much to do, sit around the palace, they're drinking and causing problems, they're hacking up pillars with their swords, and Shusun Tong goes to Liu Bang and says, I could set up a court ritual for you and Liu Bang says okay, but don't make it too complicated, not too hard, I hate that sort of stuff.

But, Shusun Tong gives everybody ranks. He lines everybody up and according to ranks they all have to go in and pay their respects to the emperor in order and back out in regular manner, and Liu Bang says ah, now I know what it's really like to be an Emperor. Confucians were useful after all, even if Liu Bang had shown his disdain for them previously, the stories are that when Liu Bang would meet a Confucian scholar he was a man of war and action. He thought the Confucians were sort of wimps and bookish kind of things. The Confucians scholars wore these very distinctive hats and Liu Bang would grab up the hat of a Confucian scholar and then urinate into it to show how much he respected Confucianism. But, things start to change.

It was the Emperor Wu, however, and he lives from 156 to 87 B.C. He's the one who really makes Confucianism official by putting in place some educational reforms; this is actually the same guy that Sima Qian ran into problems with. Emperor Wu is harsh. He has an aggressive rule, but he appoints Erudite Scholars in each of the Five Confucian Classics; they're like professorships. That happens in 136 B.C., and then twelve years later Emperor Wu founded an imperial academy that's devoted to the study of those Confucian classics and that enrolls some 3,000 students eventually. These policies that Emperor Wu put into place were undertaken on the recommendation from Dong Zhongshu, who was also one of Sima Qian's teachers. Dong Zhongshu is the one who combines traditional Confucian moralism with cosmological speculations and he's going to be our first great mind for this lecture.

He lived from 195 to 105 B.C. Dong Zhongshu was an advisor and a prime minister to Emperor Wu. He was probably the greatest of the Han dynasty Confucian philosophers. He wrote a book called the *Luxuriant Dew of the Spring and Autumn Annals*; it has something to do with that Confucian classic. This text tended toward comprehensiveness, and synthesis, and unity; he's bringing all sorts of ideas together, which was appropriate for a vigorous, expanding empire that's putting all kinds of things together.

Dong Zhongshu found hidden meaning in texts like the *Spring and Autumn Annals*. I mean he thought that heaven worked through historical events, so you can study those and learn something about the cosmos. Dong Zhongshu was famous for how diligently he studied. Sima Qian reports that Dong, this is his old teacher, for three years he didn't even take time to look out at his garden, so engrossed, engaged in this study. Dong Zhongshu argued that Heaven, Earth, and Man were intimately connected through correlative resonances, so this is based on numbers and Yin-yang, and the Five Phases, and he also proposed a microcosmic/macrocosmic model of the universe. For example, he says that the human body is a miniature cosmos.

According to Dong Zhongshu, your 366 smaller joints match the days of the year, the 12 larger joints correspond to the months, the five major internal organs that are also associated with the Five Phases, those reflect, as I said, the Five Phases, and then the four limbs are like the four seasons. Your front is yang, your back is yin, but also the upper-half of your body is yang and the lower half is yin. There's some overlapping in these categories, but that last one is kind of interesting because round is the shape of heaven and square is the shape of earth, which is why people alone, among animals, walk upright because your head it kind of round and it matches heaven and your feet are kind of square and they match earth. There're also carriages in Han dynasty China that had sort of a square carriage body and then a round canopy over the top, and you may have seen Chinese coins that are round coins with square holes in the middle. The holes are really convenient because you can string a cord through them and you won't lose loose change, but also those round coins with the square holes are going to represent heaven and earth together.

Is all of this kind of silly? It's not exactly. His idea is that everything is related to everything else, so that the universe becomes one organic entity. He looks at some evidence that almost seems scientific. He is really impressed by the phenomena of musical resonance. For example, if you've got a violin and you play a D string on the violin, make that sound, if there's another violin in the room, even if no one's around there, when you play that D string the D string on that other violin will start to vibrate. We know it's because of sound waves and stuff, but for Dong Zhongshu he just noticed that things that are similar, of a similar nature, tend to be connected even though there's no direct connection that you can see visibly.

In the same way, he said that portents and omens, like eclipses, and heat waves, and floods, and earthquakes, those are all natural rather than supernatural, that behaviors and actions in the human world will have a natural resonance with things in nature. He's trying to provide a rational, scientific basis for morality. Watch how Dong Zhongshu gets back to Confucian principles from cosmological theories. I'll give you a quote here,

> The greatest aspect of Heaven's Way lies in yin and yang. Yang constitutes virtue and yin constitutes punishment. Punishment presides over death and virtue presides over life.
>
> Therefore yang always occupies the vast summer and devotes itself to matters of birth, growth, nourishment, and maturation. Yin

always occupies the vast winter and accumulates in vacant and useless places. So far you're probably dosing off here, but here's the kicker, here's what I want. From this, one can see that Heaven relies on virtue and does not rely on punishment.

Because heaven is associated with yang—he's back to Confucius' ideas, remember that Confucius didn't like government by law so much as government by moral example and that's the example that heaven is showing. It relies on virtue and does not rely on punishment. The ruler is like Heaven and his ministers are like Earth, there's a connection.

An effective emperor, ruling in accordance with natural processes, can bridge the divide between Heaven and Earth. The Chinese character for king, it's *wang*, it's actually the same "wang" that occurs in so many Chinese surnames, that's written with three horizontal lines and then a vertical line that joins them. When Dong Zhongshu looks at that character he add his own sort of moralistic interpretation, cosmological interpretation, he says it's like heaven on the top and earth on the bottom, and man in the middle and the ruler, the king, is the one that's going to join those all together, heaven, earth, and man.

He also developed some ideas from Mencius, now do you remember Mencius talked about how goodness was innate in people, human nature was good. Dong Zhongshu also believed that moral principles came from nature, that heaven provides a model for human action. Dong believed that this heaven and earth model should be operative in three key relationships. Emperors rule over ministers, as heaven sort of looks over earth, fathers over sons, and husbands over wives. Dong Zhongshu's philosophy fit the times because it offered a rationale for strong, centralized rule, and like the empire, it brings together diverse traditions: Daoism finds a place with yin and yang, Legalism finds a place, the Naturalists' philosophies of the Five Phases all find a place, and of course, the one philosophy that's dominant in this mix is Confucianism.

As the political situation changed, later thinkers reacted against the speculations of the Han Confucians, which tended to get somewhat wild. There was something called the New Text School where those thinkers talked a lot about portents. They tended to write about Confucius as an uncrowned king; they almost deified him as a savior figure. In a reaction against that one of the key figures is named Wang Chong. He lives from 27 to 100 A.D. He gives us an early Chinese example of rational skepticism. He was orphaned early on. He started school at the age of eight, however; but he was so poor that he couldn't afford to buy books, he had to read them in a bookstore. Eventually, he was given an opportunity to study at the Imperial Academy; he had a disappointing career though as a teacher and as a minor official. He wrote a book called the *Balanced Inquiries*.

This is a fascinating text, it goes far beyond anything that Xunzi said. Remember Xunzi said that Heaven worked sort of mechanically and was against supernatural explanations. Also Wang Chong says Heaven does not reward the good or punish the bad. In fact, Heaven has no consciousness, no will, no perception. Even if it did, Heaven wouldn't bother with people, who are no more important in the big scheme of things than, and these are his words, than "fleas in the garments of the universe." Everything just happens spontaneously and naturally. Wang Chong is against what we view as superstition. He rejects the Yin-yang correspondences and the Five Phases cosmology. He doesn't believe in mythical animals like dragons or unicorns; he doesn't accept the significance of portents, or divination, or ghosts. He does accept reports of strange happenings, I mean people see things, they hear things that are weird, and he says that's true, people do see and hear strange things, but he thinks that those things have natural causes. I don't know that he's one of the great thinkers in this course; he's not quite influential enough, but he's just an interesting guy.

Let me share with you the arguments that he makes against the existence of ghosts. He says when people see ghosts, they tend to see one at a time, but if all dead people became ghosts, when you're able to see into that realm, wouldn't you see millions of ghosts, I mean wouldn't the halls and the rooms be full of ghosts everywhere. What about animals? Do animals have ghosts and if so how many animals have there been? He says when people claim that they see ghosts, they seem to recognize them, it's a departed father or mother or a friend. He said, but there's no reason why ghosts should look like people since a spirit in a body is something like rice in bag. When the rice is let out of the bag it just goes everywhere so ghosts should actually be sort of amorphous, they shouldn't look like people.

The last argument, which seems to me the strongest is he says why is when people see ghosts, those ghosts have clothes on because even if spirits existed and survived in the next life, there's no reason to think that clothes have spirits that would go along with those deceased people. Hu Shi, and he's a 20th century philosopher, we're going to see much more of him in a later lecture, Hu Shi said that Wang Chong had a "critical, scientific spirit" unique in Chinese intellectual history, unique is sort of a code word for "not particularly influential." He has been an inspiration in modern China. Wang Chong was one of the first Chinese philosophers, aside from Mencius and Confucius, of course, to have his works translated into English and that happened in 1907.

Because Confucianism was so closely associated with centralized rule, it was to some extent discredited when the Han dynasty fell. Many scholars consequently turned to Daoism to make sense of the politically fragmented society in which they found themselves. We call this movement Neo-Daoism and it takes four forms and all of these are found in the 3rd century A.D. First, there were important commentaries written by Confucian scholars on the Dao De Jing and on the Zhuangzi, which explored key concepts. They said that "non-action" is not just doing nothing but it's rather action that's natural and spontaneous. They said "non-being" is not just an absence of anything, but it's nothingness, which is actually something, it's the void from which the cosmos emerged. Those kinds of ideas are going to make possible later Buddhist/Daoist dialogue.

The second form of Neo-Daoism came from some educated men who withdrew from government service, remember the story about Zhuangzi saying that he would rather wag his tail in the mud than go be Prime Minister of the state of Chu. They're going to copy that behavior and they're going to withdraw from society, from government especially, and spend their time in witty conversation and poetry and music, and disregarding social convention. The most famous of these was a group of men called the Seven Sages of the Bamboo Grove. One of them is famous for having a servant follow him around all the time, and this servant had a jug of wine in one hand and a shovel in the other so that whatever happened to this guy he could drink when he wanted to and if he felt bad he would just dig a hole right there and throw him in to it. That's going to be shocking maybe to you; to Confucians who care so much about ritual and especially funerals, that is just beyond the pail

There was another one of these Seven Sages who was famous for drinking stark naked in his home, sort his private entertainment. Once a visitor came and was shocked by what he saw and this sage said, heaven is my roof, earth is my walls, and my house is my pants; what are you doing in my pants? Think what Mencius would've thought about this, Mencius was so offended when he accidentally walked in and his wife wasn't completely dressed. One modern scholar has described these Seven Sages as "drinking themselves into a state of spiritual communion with the Dao." That makes it sound like hedonism perhaps, but they're also rejecting Confucian ritual; they're deliberately trying to find another way, another path.

There's another third kind of Neo-Daoism which is religious Daoism. There were some men called Celestial Masters who organized actually several competing movements with scriptures, like the Dao De Jing became scripture. They said that it was revealed by Lord Lao. They believe in many gods; they arranged these gods into a celestial bureaucracy. There are priests and liturgy and rules of behavior for believers, and rituals for healing and for forgiveness of sins through confession and good works. Sometimes this sort of Daoist church, these religious Daoists are involved in peasant uprisings, the government wants to keep close tabs on them.

Finally, the fourth kind of Neo-Daoism is a search for immortality. People tried breathing exercises, yoga-like gymnastics, sexual practices, meditation, and alchemy. The alchemy is going to be similar to what we've seen in the west; they try to produce gold. They actually thought that artificial gold was more effective and powerful than natural gold. They try to find the elixir of immortality; now they didn't discover the secret of immortality, but they did discover some medicines, some dyes and glazes, and perhaps ironically gunpowder, so people who are looking to live a long time end up inventing gunpowder.

The second great mind of this lecture is going to be medieval China's most famous alchemist. His name is Ge Hong and he lives from 283 to 343 and he brings together several of these strands of Neo-Daoism and then reconciles them with Confucianism. In fact, he almost sounds like two different people when you read his book. This book is called the *Baopuzi* and it means the Master Who Embraces Simplicity; it's a quote from the Dao De Jing, and it's split into two parts. There are the Inner chapters, there are 20 of those, and they are about the quest for Daoist immortality, and then there are 50 Outer chapters, which are essays on government and contemporary social problems from a Confucian perspective.

In the first section, Ge Hong describes a Daoist immortal. He says, "He is so high that no one can reach him, so deep that no one can penetrate to his depth; he rides the fluid light, and whips space in the six directions, he crosses the watery expanses … he crosses the threshold of vastness," He's speaking about people who are so spiritually pure that they've been transformed so that they can fly, so that they can subsist on just air and dew, they can walk on water, and most importantly they can live forever. Such perfected beings were mentioned by Laozi and Zhuangzi in passing, but Ge Hong takes them quite literally. He says we've seen how caterpillars can turn into butterflies, tadpoles turn into frogs, people can turn into animals or trees, and that's a little more questionable, but there are lots of stories of that, why can't people turn into immortals? I mean, just because you haven't seen them doesn't mean they don't exist. I realize that that's an argument that you could use for unicorns and UFOs and all sorts of things, but Ge Hong is pretty serious about this. He offers practical advice for those, like him, who want to attain the rarified state of a Daoist immortal.

Do you remember Cook Ding? He was from the Zhuangzi, that guy who could sort of look at an ox carcass and then cut it up so smoothly and spontaneously. If you combine that sort of naturalness with the Five Phases theories of how the cosmos works then you get something that's going to lead into what Ge Hong is talking about. He says living in harmony with nature will lead to a long life. You should reduce stress, you should be content, maybe practice some breathing exercises, and calisthenics, nothing like jumping jacks or vigorous, more like slow, sort of controlled motions like Taijiquan. Avoid excess, he says, don't eat or drink too much, don't get overtired, don't sleep too long, don't abstain from sexual relations, but don't overindulge either.

Was this good advice for living longer? Perhaps, but then he's going to take it to the next level. He says natural processes can sometimes be speeded along, sort of like dyeing fabric, that you can make this permanent change with a little help from chemistry. He's going to recommend herbs and incantations, and then some drugs as well. He gives detailed alchemical recipes of 27 elixirs that involve cinnabar, which was witching mercury, and liquefied gold as well. Many alchemists, at the time, actually poisoned themselves as they were trying these things out. What he's trying to do is recreate, within his own body, the longer-term processes of the natural world.

Let's talk about his life now. Ge Hong is the only major Daoist who left us a personal point of view. The last chapter in his book is an autobiography, something like Sima Qian's last chapter, and somewhat surprising. For a Daoist, he's a pretty hard-working guy. He reads voraciously, he walks long distances to borrow books. He tells us that when he was young he cut and sold firewood in order to buy paper and writing brushes. Ge Hong was living in the 4th century, during this chaotic period between unified Empires, between the Han dynasty and then the Sui dynasty that's going to come at the end of the 6th century. During this time of social disorder, he's looking for control and security and stability.

Ge Hong is a southerner. He was born south of the Yangtze River into a prominent, aristocratic family. His father died when Ge Hong was 12, but he was still able to get a good education in both Confucianism and esoteric Daoism. At the age of 20, he was called on to organize and lead a militia against rebels, which he did quite successfully. That's actually pretty assertive for a Daoist. He belongs to these aristocratic families and that was part of their responsibility was to help keep order. For the next few decades, Ge Hong alternated between holding civil and military positions and then turning down such offices in favor of Daoist reclusion, like the Seven Sages. It was a time of political turmoil, kingdoms came and went, dangerous times where people got killed who were involved in politics.

In the second half, second part of his book are Confucian essays and in those he recommends that officials study widely, that they are appointed by examinations in the Confucian classics rather than by recommendations because that's too subject to political connections. He wrote about the importance of laws and punishments with a touch of Legalism in there, and then a remarkable autobiography in which he describes how unsuited he was to his times. He doesn't play politics, he doesn't visit officials, he doesn't try to cultivate useful friendships, he's unconcerned about his reputation, when he helps others he tries to keep it secret rather than trying to parlay that into some sort of political clout. He's unwilling to participate in corrupt dealings.

In this autobiography, he writes this,

> Honor, position, power, and wealth are like visitors, since they are not eternal things, and once they go they cannot be retained. ... It's like the case of flowers in the spring, which necessarily die and fall to the ground. In attaining them, one is not delighted. Losing them, what sadness is there? ... Now I know that I am lazy by nature and extremely short on talent. Even if I were to be respectful and to go about on my duties, proceeding as quickly as the dust on the wind, I would not necessarily be able to achieve great fame and position or avoid sorrows and encumberments. How much more so is such the case since I cannot do even this!

He combines Confucianism and Daoism. He doesn't entirely withdraw from worldly concerns. The Confucian ideal is to hold office when times are good and then retire when government is corrupt. He says that Confucian morality is the foundation for Daoist immortality and you may have noticed in that last quote there's sort of this humility, self-deprecation that's characteristic of Confucian virtues. One last quote, "Those who seek to become immortals must regard loyalty, filiality, peacefulness, obedience, benevolence and trustworthiness as fundamental. If one does not cultivate his moral behavior, and merely instead devotes oneself to esoteric methods, he will never obtain an extended lifespan."

Did you notice benevolence and filiality, those Confucian virtues. Along with other Daoists, Ge Hong believed that one's moral actions had a direct

235

effect on lifespan, so if you did something wrong you would get three days taken off of your lifespan and a major transgression would cost you 300 days. Again, he gives very practical advice. He lists 64 possible sins, mostly Confucian vices that you ought to beware of. Chinese have often been Daoist in private and Confucian in public and in part that's possible because thinkers like Ge Hong showed that it's possible to be both Confucian and Daoist at the same time with the Outer and the Inner chapters. It's not like being either Jewish or Christian or Catholic or Protestant. In a similar manner, Dong Zhongshu showed how Confucian ethics could be compatible with cosmological speculations. When China is unified again in 581, we'll see how Daoism, Confucianism, and Legalism all find a place within an imperial ideology, though with a new addition–Buddhism.

Strangely enough, even though the quest of Daoist immortality, right to live as long as you can, and Buddhist enlightenment to escape from this existence, they seem like they're almost opposite, it turns out that Daoists and Buddhists in China have a lot in common, as we'll see in the next lecture.

Xuanzang and Chinese Buddhism
Lecture 17

In some ways, Buddhism's success in China is surprising, with its foreign origins and abandonment of political and familial obligations. Its rise can be attributed to its arrival during a period of turmoil, its parallels with Daoism, and Xuanzang's program to translate Buddhist texts. Four Mahayana schools dominated Chinese Buddhism, including Chan, or Zen. By the 9th century, Confucianism had shifted to accommodate Buddhist insights, and Buddhism declined among the elite but remained popular among common people.

Introduced in the 1st century A.D. by foreign merchants, Buddhism became popular in the tumultuous period after the fall of the Han dynasty. Although it got off to a slow start, by the mid-6th century, there were some 2 million Buddhists in China and 30,000 monasteries. The first bridges for Buddhism in China were laid by Daoists, who were attracted to Buddhist cosmology, meditation, and yoga but ignored a lot of differences between themselves and Buddhists.

The Buddhist conquest of China involved dozens of important figures, but a great deal of credit can be given to Xuanzang, a Buddhist monk living under China's late Sui and early Tang dynasties. Frustrated by the lack of complete Buddhist texts available in China, he went to India in 629 A.D. and discovered just how much Buddhist thought the Chinese were missing. After 16 years traveling and studying, he returned to China with 657 texts and, with the emperor's patronage, set up one of the most ambitious translation projects in Chinese history.

Xuanzang's preferred school of Buddhism, Yogacara, had little appeal in China. Instead, four schools came to prominence: Tiantai, Huayan ("flower garland"), Pure Land, and Chan (Zen). Tintai and Huayan focus on doctrine and are related to Nagarjuna's middle way between existence and nonexistence, as well as a sort of monism that appealed to the Chinese intellectual tradition of synthesis. These doctrines were also attractive to the

Chinese because they are optimistic, like Mencius's belief that all people can become sages (or, in this case, can achieve enlightenment).

Pure Land and Chan Buddhism are more focused on practice than doctrine. Pure Land says the world is hopelessly corrupt and enlightenment in this life is impossible. Adherents practice bhakti (devotional) yoga and chanting to ensure rebirth into the Western Paradise, or Pure Land. Although there is scant evidence, some scholars think Pure Land Buddhism shows Zoroastrian influence. Chan emphasizes the importance of direct transmission of knowledge and eschews ritual and scholasticism. In the 7th century, Chan split into Northern and Southern schools, which disagreed on the speed of enlightenment. The Northern took the position that it was always gradual; the Southern claimed sudden enlightenment was possible. The contrast here is between Confucian-like self-cultivation and Daoist-like sudden transformation.

The Southern school was led by Huineng, probably the most important figure in Chan Buddhism.

The Southern school was led by Huineng, probably the most important figure in Chan Buddhism. He used unconventional teaching methods, such as shouting at or striking students and teaching through koans. He taught that enlightenment is beyond ordinary thought and meditation is the crucial method.

Buddhism's prominence among the political and cultural elite faded throughout the Tang dynasty, although it was influential in the formation of Neo-Confucian thought. It remained popular among the common people, however. By that time, it was a truly Chinese faith, with Chinese texts, Chinese heroes, and even Chinese bodhisattvas: Avalokitesvara, known as the bodhisattva of compassion in Indian Buddhism, was transformed into the female Guanyin in the Chinese tradition. The Maitreya Buddha, the future Buddha, became the laughing, fat Buddha, the antithesis of the notion that all life is suffering, but perhaps a better fit for Chinese culture. ■

Suggested Reading

Aldiss, *Zen Sourcebook*.

Chan, *A Source Book in Chinese Philosophy*.

De Bary and Bloom, eds., *Sources of Chinese Tradition*.

Harvey, *An Introduction to Buddhism*.

Kasulis, *Zen Action, Zen Person*.

Mitchell, *Buddhism*.

Wriggins, *The Silk Road Journey with Xuanzang*.

Questions to Consider

1. What made Buddhism attractive in China, despite its obvious foreign origins?

2. Why did the Buddhist tradition in China fragment into different schools? What did they have in common, and what were their underlying differences?

3. What are some of the difficulties faced by religions or philosophies as they cross national and cultural borders?

4. How far would you go to find the truth?

Xuanzang and Chinese Buddhism
Lecture 17—Transcript

Hello again. With this lecture, we're going to complete what's traditionally referred to as the "Three Teachings of China:" Confucianism, Daoism, and Buddhism. We've already discussed the origins of Buddhism and its later division into two major movements. There was the Theravada School, the School of the Elders, and then Mahayana, the Great Vehicle. Mahayana itself developed into competing schools, including the Madhyamaka School, the school of the Middle Way of Nagarjuna in the 2nd century, and the Yogācāra School, remember that's the Consciousness-only that Vasubandhu developed in the 4th century, and then there were lots of other schools.

The story from India is already complicated when it gets to China and there it gets even more confusing. There are dozens of schools and scriptures and major figures. In this lecture, I'll provide an overview of how Buddhism became widely accepted in China, with a few sketches of some key thinkers and especially a monk named Xuanzang.

We'll start with the big picture. Buddhism was first introduced into China in the 1st century A.D. In the beginning though, it didn't attract a lot of attention. It was mostly a religion for foreign merchants who were living in China. It became very popular, however, after the collapse of the Han dynasty in 220 A.D. As we saw in the last lecture, that was a time when a lot of people were looking for new answers. In some ways, the success of Buddhism is surprising. There were many cultural obstacles.

There were suspicions about its foreign origins, Confucius never talked about Buddhism, it's not mentioned in the Confucian classics, the fact that monks and nuns abandoned their political and family obligations, that they didn't pay taxes, that monks weren't conscripted into the army. They didn't give labor service, which was an important part of the taxation burden on peasants. Monks and nuns don't do ancestor worship so it was a concern about filial piety, and some people said well perhaps by their self-sacrifice they can earn merit that they can then transfer to their parents. There were also problems with translations in a lot of competing schools; they just kept everyone guessing.

Buddhism does succeed, in China, kind of amazingly. By the middle of the 6th century, it's reported that there were some 2 million Buddhists in China, and 30,000 monasteries. Now another list about what went right for Buddhism. First it came in a time of political turmoil. Do you remember the chaos and warfare after the fall of the Han dynasty? When Buddhist missionaries knock on people's doors, just sort of imagine this analogy, and said we have a message for you. Our message is the first noble truth, all life is suffering. Some Chinese people said wow that's what I've always about my life, so there's an openness to new ideas.

Confucianism had been discredited with the fall of the Han dynasty and its close association with the Imperial rule and now there came new rulers into China. Oftentimes nomadic peoples who invaded China and then settled down there and some of their kings were very interested in Buddhism, partly because these are non-Chinese rulers, and Buddhism was a non-Chinese religion and it stressed sort of a universality of human beings. Some of those rulers also claimed to be bodhisattvas.

Some Chinese people like the ethical standards of Buddhism as opposed to say the flaunting of conventional morality that we saw in the Six Stages of the Bamboo Grow. Then there were parallels with Daoism in terms of the kinds of questions they asked and the way they spoke about things. There are new forms of philosophy and art that come from India. For the first time in China, we see giant statues and cave temples and there are new ideas of the afterlife, very specific ideas of heavens and hells and there are miracles that are done by Buddhist monks and by missionaries.

Let's talk a little bit more on the Daoist connections. There are always considerable difficulties when a religion or philosophy crosses cultural barriers, and in China the first bridges for Buddhism were laid by Daoists. They were talking about cosmology, about being and non-being. They both had meditative practices and yoga. You could imagine Buddhist missionaries coming in and Daoists saying well we do it sort of like this and then they talk back and forth, but you need a common language to do that, which means you need translations.

The first translations just grab the closest Daoist term they can think of. For example, for the word dharma, which in Buddhism means the teachings of the Buddha, the word that they get from Chinese is Dao. For nirvana, they translate that as wu-wei, which is non-action or effortless action. Even though non-action, it seems like a very different idea than the liberation from suffering that we call nirvana. The Sanskrit term for enlightened ones, they translate as Daoist immortals. For the Sanskrit term for morality they're going to be more specific and they just translate it as "filial piety and obedience." They're conversing, but only because Daoists and Buddhists are ignoring a lot of differences between them.

Actually some people wondered if Buddhism was just another form of Daoism. Remember that some had thought when Laozi left China and went to the west, he must've gone to India where he became known as the Buddha, and now those ideas are coming back to them in a slightly different form. Actually by the way, in another example, in the standard translation of the Chinese Bible, the opening of the gospel of John, which you may remember is, "In the beginning was the word, and the word was with God, and the word was God." When the translators looked at that passage they had to make a choice as to whether they would translate the word "word," in Greek it's logos with a Chinese word that meant word, or whether they would pick a Chinese word that was philosophically loaded in a similar way to the word logos is in Greek. That's what they went with. As I said, the standard Chinese translation, John 1 starts with, "In the beginning was the Dao, and the Dao was with God, and the Dao was God." The influence goes both ways, religious Daoism when we talked about neo-Daoism is certainly influenced by Buddhist ideas and practices and then both of those religions are going to compete for State support.

The Buddhist conquest of China is a huge topic, with dozens of important figures ranging from monks and scholars, to missionaries and merchants, and kings. I'm going to focus, however, on one particular individual, a Chinese monk named Xuanzang. His dates are 600 to 664, so this is a time when all of China was once again unified under imperial rule. The Sui dynasty brings it all together in 581 and then that dynasty lasts for about 30 years is all and then that's followed by the Tang dynasty from 618 to 907 so about 300 years, one of the great glorious times of Chinese culture and art and poetry.

Xuanzang was raised in a Confucian family. His older brother was a monk and he became interested in Buddhism and eventually he became an initiate himself at the age of 13. He was a very bright boy. It said that he gave lectures to some of the older monks at that time, but when the Sui dynasty fell, he fled south with his older brother. Later on Xuanzang described his experiences to one of his disciples that would write a biography of Xuanzang. This is what he says. At that time, so this is the fall of the Sui dynasty and the turmoil between Sui and Tang. Xuanzang says the magistrates were destroyed and monks either perished or took to flight. The streets were filled with bleached bones and the burnt ruins of buildings. At this time, the books of Confucius and the sacred pages of Buddha were forgotten. Everyone was occupied with the arts of war.

At the age of 20, Xuanzang became a full monk and then he went with his brother to the capital of the new founded Tang dynasty. He started to learn Sanskrit, which is the language of some of these scriptures that are coming in from India, but the multitude of texts and the variety of schools was still very confusing. He came across a partial translation of a text by Vasubandhu's brother, Asanga on Yogacara Buddhism; remember the consciousness-only school. There were some missing parts and Xuanzang thought if only I could get the whole text then all of my questions and puzzles and doubts would be resolved.

He decided that he was going to leave China. In 629, so he was 29 years old, he doesn't have official permission, and because of border problems at the time it was illegal for people to leave, but he sneaks out. He makes his way across the Silk Road. He writes later an account of his travels where he talks about dangers on the road from the heat, the desert, from robbers. He finally arrives in India a year later, coming in from Afghanistan in the northwest. Nobody goes directly from China to India. They have to go around and then down to the northwest because the Himalayan Mountains are there.

When he gets to India, Xuanzang discovers that the problems were much bigger than just a few missing chapters for a text. He found that there was a huge tradition of Indian philosophy and lots of competing schools of Buddhism that the Chinese hadn't really heard so much about. During his years in India, he debated other Buddhists, and Jain monks, and Hindus. He talks about meeting Samkhya and Vaisheshika philosophers. He visited many of the holy sites associated with Buddhism. He spent two years studying at Nalanda University. You may remember that institution from Lecture 14. After 16 years abroad, during which time he traveled about 15,000 miles. Xuanzang returned to China with 657 texts, along with several dozen statues and relics.

The Emperor had heard that he was coming and wanted a personal interview with him. When he saw him the Emperor said so, "Why do you leave without permission?" But, he continued, "Since you're a monk, then I forgive you." Things are okay. Actually the Emperor did more than forgive him. The Emperor sponsored a translation project. He set up Xuanzang in a special monastery; this is the Big Wild Goose Pagoda in Xi'an. If you visit Xi'an today you can still see this place. Xuanzang was there along with 20 assistant translators and together they did very accurate translations of over seventy texts, some of them are quite long, and that took them about 20 years.

These translations aren't just going to use Daoist terms that don't quite fit. They're going to very carefully explain the Sanskrit terms; they sometimes invent some new terms to fit these Sanskrit concepts. Students came to study with Xuanzang, at this monastery, from all over China, and even from as far away as Korea and Japan.

This was perhaps the largest translation project in Chinese history. There were texts from the Madhyamaka School, texts about Indian logic and Buddhist metaphysics, even a Vaisheshika work, but especially they were interested in Yogācāra text. Now remember Yogācāra Buddhism, Vasubandhu is the newest, most advanced Buddhism at the time. Xuanzang did a translation and then an amalgamation, amalgam of ten Sanskrit commentaries on Vasubandhu's Thirty Verses. Incidentally, the Emperor also asked Xuanzang to translate the Dao De Jing from Chinese into Sanskrit, which he did, but apparently that didn't have a great effect in India, remember the Darshana Hotel is not all that interested in what's going on out in the Dao Hotel.

Xuanzang wrote a travelogue called the *Record of Western Lands*. One of his assistant translators wrote a biography of Xuanzang that's sort of an as told by, Xuanzang would tell stories about this and then later after he was dead his disciple wrote this biography of him based on his personal recollections. He tells this story of going to Bodh Gaya, which was the site of the Buddha's enlightenment under the Bodh tree.

This is how this biography explains that event,

> With the most sincere devotion [Xuanzang] cast himself down with his face to the ground, and with much grief and tears, he sighed, and said: "At the time when Buddha perfected himself in wisdom, I know not in what condition I was, in the troublous whirl of birth and death. But now, in this [lesser age], having come to this spot and reflecting on the depth and weight of the body of my evil deeds, I am grieved at heart, and my eyes filled with tears."

This is always the problem with pilgrimages is you end up at the right site, but you are several hundred years too late to see the event that had caught your attention in the first place. Xuanzang knows that at the time that Buddha was enlightened he was somewhere, maybe not in this world, maybe as an animal or something, but whatever it was his sins were such that he wasn't allowed to be right there where the action was really happening.

On his deathbed, Xuanzang recited the Heart Sutra, which is a one page synopsis of a Perfection of Wisdom Sutra and it has those famous lines "form is emptiness, emptiness is form." His translation of the Heart Sutra is still recited throughout East Asia to this day. Xuanzang is a great mind. He's a traveler, translator, a philosopher, and a monk, but the Yogācāra School wasn't all that appealing in China. They were interested in some different sorts of Buddhism.

There are four major schools of Buddhism that become prominent in China: Tiantai, Huayan; that means Flower Garland, Pure Land, and Chan or Meditation School or Zen. None of those four schools was particularly important in India. I'll describe each of them and try to keep them in mind because we'll see them again in Lecture 19 when we talk about Japanese Buddhism.

Two of the schools focus on doctrine, that's the Tiantai and Huayan and then two of the schools on practice, and that's Pure Land and Zen. All of them arise from the same problem. The Chinese didn't know much about the Indian background of Buddhism and its various schools. They just had translations of scriptures and some of those structures contradicted each other, even though each claimed to have come from the Buddha himself. Remember the definition of a Buddhist Sutra is a record of something that Buddha has said. They generally start with the words, "Thus have I heard" and it's thought that Ananda had memorized everything that the Buddha had said.

How are you going to resolve these contradictions? There's already a model at hand. It's the Mahayana explanation of Theravada. Theravada Buddhism was the original Buddhism that the Buddha taught to regular people, but there were these higher teachings, secret teachings that he reserved for his more advanced disciples. The Chinese have an ideal of harmony through syncretism, of bringing things together. Think about Dong Zhongshu and the Hundred Schools of Philosophy and how that comes into what Dong Zhongshu does in Han dynasty Confucianism bringing together Yin-yang in the Five Phases and the teachings of Confucius.

The Chinese idea is the Buddha must have said different things to different audiences depending on their capacity to understand. This is a concept called skillful means that he'll use whatever it takes to try to get people to the next level of spiritual progress. Of course, they were curious what's the last word, what's the Buddha's final truth?

We go to these four schools. The first is Tiantai, named for Tiantai Mountain near the hometown of its founder and in Japanese this school is called Tendai. Tendai Buddhists say that there are different levels of sutras and the Lotus Sutra is the highest. The Lotus Sutra is going to be the most important Buddhist scripture in East Asia. We'll talk more about that when we talk about Japanese Buddhism. According to Tiantai Buddhists, there are three truths, that all things are empty by products of causation with dependent origination. They have no independent nature. Number two; they do, however, have temporary existence, and then the third level of truth is there's a perspective that transcends both of these, sort of a middle way. Buddhists love anything about the middle way.

Tendai Buddhists say that all minds are the manifestations of one mind, of absolute reality, and that's the Buddha-nature that's in all people and in all things. There are 3,000 realms of existence and they're all interconnected so that each is present in each; all reality, they say, is "immanent in a single instance of thought."

We go to the Huanyan School; this is named for the Huanyan Sutra, the Flower Garland Sutra. It's similar to Tiantai, but it takes those ideas to another level, actually to the fifth level. The first level is Theravada, that people are products of causation, there's no-self. The second level is Mahayana, that everything is emptiness, and then the third level is the Higher Mahayana, that emptiness is not inconsistent with the illusion of phenomena. It's like Madhyamaka. Fourth is the level that's beyond words, and then the fifth and highest is going to be the Flower Garland Sutra, which brings everything together in one absolute reality in which everything has the nature of non-being. The Huayan Sutra, they said, was actually the first Sutra that the Buddha gave right after he became enlightened, but no one understood what he was talking about. Then, he started talking about the Four Nobel Truths and all of the things that Theravada Buddhists have preserved.

According to Huanyan Buddhists, every part of the universe reflects and incorporates every other part through interpenetration and through mutual identity of all things. It's sort of a form of monism. If you think that's hard to understand; it was hard for the Empress Wu to understand as well. Empress Wu is the only woman in Chinese history who actually rules as an emperor. There were other women who were dowager empresses or who ruled as regents, but Empress Wu in the Tang dynasty, just puts all that aside and says no I'm the Emperor.

There's a monk named Fazang who lives from 643 to 712. He's a prolific author, a great mind in Chinese thought and he tries to teach this Huanyan Buddhism to Empress Wu and he does so with a couple of object lessons. There was a Golden Lion at court and he gave a famous sermon on the Golden Lion. He said the parts of that lion, the hair and the claws and the eyes and so forth, they all exist in relationship to each other, but in the end, it's all gold. Gold is the unchanging, underlying principle of that statue. It's the Li; we'll talk more about that idea when we talk about neo-Confucianism that will be a really important principle.

He says that the lion, itself, is changing phenomena. The gold is all one substance, but then it can be made in lots of different shapes, including a lion shape. There was another demonstration he made with ten mirrors. He sat eight of them in an octagonal pattern about 10 feet across, plus one mirror above and one mirror below. Then he took a small statue of the Buddha and a torch for illumination and put it right in the middle so that you could see the statue of the Buddha in the mirrors, but in the mirrors you could also see the image of the Buddha in all of the other mirrors as well. This is a demonstration of how everything is interconnected and mutually identified.

Had Fazang come today, I think he would've liked the idea of holograms. You remember that those are 3D images so it's like looking through a window almost and you can sort of see everything behind there. If you cut up a 3D image or break it, if it's on a sheet of glass, each fragment contains the image of the whole thing. I mean you could still see the whole thing through it though it's a little blurry. He would've loved that; the idea that the Buddha nature is in everything and everyone and it's the same. There's a technical word called tathāgatagarbha–the womb of the Buddha. The idea is that everyone is a Buddha in embryo, even if you're not that close now in some future life, you will become a Buddha, you have that potential within you that will someday blossom and develop, maybe someday when you're reborn in India.

This is an attractive idea to the Chinese because it's rather optimistic. It's something like Mencius' belief that all people have within themselves the capacity to become sages. When Xuanzang went to India, he discovered that the concept of Buddha-nature was not part of Indian Buddhism. There are lots of arguments between Xuanzang's disciples and Fazang over this key issue, notion in Chinese Buddhism.

This brings us to the third form of Buddhism in China, Pure Land Buddhism. They say that the world is hopelessly corrupt; that Enlightenment in this life is impossible. You just can't learn the truth about it and you can't put Buddhism into practice the way that you would like to. Your best hope is to be reborn into Amitabha's Western Paradise, or the Pure Land. Amitabha is a Bodhisattva who created this land. You could be reborn there and then you could work on salvation at your own speed and it's sort of a more delightful circumstance. There's not a lot of evidence, but some scholars think that there may have been some Zoroastrianism influence in the formation of this type of Buddhism in India, ideas of heaven.

This becomes very popular because ordinary people can be Pure Land Buddhists and it becomes devotional. It's like Bhakti Yoga where you chant the name of the bodhisattva, Amitabha or sometimes known as Amida. You say Namu Amida Butsu, which means praise to Amida Buddha and hope that he will take you into his Pure Land after you die.

The fourth form of Buddhism is Chan Buddhism, a school that focuses on meditation. The word comes from the Sanskrit word dhyāna; which is transliterated as Chan in Chinese and then transformed into Zen. We'll just call it Zen since you may be familiar to that. These Buddhists are against ritual and scholasticism. They talk about a direct transmission of enlightenment from person to person, back to the Buddha. The story is that Buddha silently holds up a flower and Kasyapa, one of his disciples smiled at the time and Buddha realized that Kasyapa had understood that there was a transmission of true enlightenment, mind to mind without words. There's a famous poem attributed to Bodhidharma that describes Zen as "A special transmission outside the scriptures, no dependence on words and letters, direct pointing at the soul of man, seeing into one's own nature to attain Buddhahood."

According to legend, Zen was brought to China by the 28th patriarch Bodhidharma in the 5th century so his spiritual lineage goes all the way back to the Buddha, 28 jumps. The historical data for Zen Buddhism in China begins in the 7th century with a split over questions about the pace of enlightenment. The Northern School, led by Shenxiu said that it was gradual, and the Southern School, under Huineng, said that sudden enlightenment was possible. Huineng, he lives from 638 to 713 will win out; and he's probably the most important figure in Chinese Zen.

Here's the famous story, from the Platform Sutra. The fifth patriarch of Zen knew that he would soon die and decided to determine his successor through a poetry contest, of all things, because through some verse that someone had written, he could determine the level of the spiritual attainment of the writer. One of his foremost students, Shenxiu wrote the following poem: "The body is the Bodhi tree, remember that's the tree that the Buddha was enlightened under. The mind is like a clear mirror / At all times we must strive to polish it / And must not let the dust collect." He was pretty nervous about this so he wrote the poem anonymously on the wall one night. The master saw that and he said that's alright, but can you do another one. Let me see.

At about the same time, there was also a young man in the monastery who wasn't a monk, but he was a kitchen helper, sometimes described as a rice pounder. He had been an illiterate seller of firewood and then he'd heard of a wandering monk talk about the Diamond Sutra. He became interested in Buddhism, actually gained some spiritual progress and went to live in the monastery. He'd heard all of this talk about the success from this poem and read the poem to him; he's still illiterate, and he wrote a rejoinder and then he had someone write it on the wall at night anonymously. His poem said "Bodhi originally has no tree / The mirror has no stand / Buddha nature is always clean and pure / Where is there room for dust?" Alright so you don't have to polish anything, there's nothing to do; you just realize the Buddha nature within.

Huineng was summoned to a secret interview once the master had discovered who had written this poem or who had written the poem and had somebody else actually write it on the wall. Huineng was given a robe; that sort of is the mark of succession, and the master said, You're the one, but no one is going to accept the illiterate kitchen help as the next master of this temple so you probably should leave right now, so he fled. There's a contrast between Confucian-like self-cultivation and Daoist-like sudden transformation. Also, ideas of ineffability, of things can't be put into words, spontaneity, and unconventional teaching methods, sometimes Zen masters would shout at their students or tweak their nose, or use koans, which are these kind of riddles that are intended to jar you out of ordinary ways of thinking, like one is "If you meet the Buddha, kill the Buddha," whatever that might mean. We'll talk more about that when we come to Japanese Buddhism.

Meditation is the crucial method for both the northern and the southern schools. We'll come back to these ideas a little bit later. Before we leave, there's one more famous koan from Huineng. The story is that there were two monks watching a flag flapping in the wind and one monk said, "It's the flag that's moving," and the second monk said, "No, it's the wind," and Huineng came by at the time and he said, "Not the flag or the wind. It's your mind that's moving." Where to from here?

Buddhism was dominant in China in the early Tang dynasty, but eventually it faded somewhat due to political concerns about monasteries and their political power and the amount land that they control, and monks who didn't pay taxes and didn't provide labor service, and didn't serve in the army. There was some government persecution, particularly in the 9th century, and China's loss of control over the Silk Road sort of brought an end to the renewing flow of ideas and scriptures that had been coming in from India. Confucianism will shift to accommodate Buddhist insights. We'll see that in Neo-Confucianism. There's a decline among the elite, but Buddhism is still very popular among the common people.

As an example of its popularity or popular Buddhism, let's go back to the story of Xuanzang's journey to India. That eventually became one of China's most beloved novels. A writer named Wu Cheng'en published a book in 1529 called *Journey to the West* or sometimes the title is translated as *Monkey*, and in this book Xuanzang is a monk in search of scriptures. He goes to India, but he's joined by three divine companions, each of whom has been assigned to protect him as penance for past sins. The most famous of these companions is Monkey, who is mischievous, and impatient, and arrogant, but he's also strong and brave. He has a magical staff and can transform into many forms. Remember when we talked about the Ramayana and the Monkey King who helped out Rama, his name was Hanuman, they seem to be related here. Together, these four travelers fight demons and monsters, and they overcome all sorts of obstacles.

For example one adventure, after they finally get to India and they speak to the Buddha himself and they get scriptures from the Buddha, several pack loads worth. They're on their way back home as a big storm comes up and they start to blow around and then they see them some of these scrolls are blank, there's nothing on them. They quickly open up the rest and they're all blank. There is not a word on any of these scriptures and so they rush back to the Buddha, they say what have you done here, and the Buddha says oh the true scriptures are indeed wordless, they're beyond words, but if the Chinese are so foolish and unenlightened that they need scriptures with words, well I can give those to you as well, and he does. You probably recognize some connections right, Zen is a form of Buddhism beyond words; Madhyamaka, philosophy is everything it's emptiness.

Journey to the West and especially the exploits of the Monkey are still very popular in China. They're the subject of stories, and art, and plays, and films, and even a long-running TV series. The last time that I was in China, I was there with my 12-year-old son, and there was a cartoon version that we enjoyed together. It seemed like it was on TV all the time. In many ways, the subject of this lecture is transformation: an Indian religion becomes a Chinese faith; Sanskrit scriptures become Chinese texts; and a historical pilgrimage becomes a work of fiction. Let me give you two more quick transformations. The Bodhisattva Avalokiteśvara, who's known as Guanyin in the Lotus Sutra, goes from being male in India to being female in China. Remember gender is an internal thing.

The Maitreya Buddha, the Buddha who's going to come at the end of time and restore Buddhism and bring in a new age, he becomes the happy, fat Buddha, sometimes known as the laughing Buddha that you may have seen in Chinese restaurants or such; that form comes when he was incarnated as a Zen monk of the 10th century named Budhi, who was sort of round and cheerful and he had candy that he used to give out to children. That fat, happy monk may seem like the opposite of "all life is suffering." But, perhaps it's a better fit for Chinese culture. We'll see lots of transformations of all kind through the rest of the lectures in this series.

Prince Shotoku, Lady Murasaki, Sei Shonagon
Lecture 18

The earliest Japanese civilization was built on three gifts from the Chinese: Buddhism, a writing system, and the idea of a unified empire. Prince Shotoku, a 7th-century regent and devoted Buddhist, adapted Confucian principles to create a bureaucracy for the Japanese state. Lady Murasaki and Sei Shonagon were two of the first great writers in the Japanese language—contemporaries (and perhaps rivals) who produced two very different but nonetheless classic books.

People inhabited the Japanese islands for thousands of years, but it wasn't until the 6th century A.D. that they developed what we would call a civilization, inspired by contact with the Chinese mainland via Korea. The ruling clans of Japan adopted Chinese models of scholarship, religion, and governance, but they did so selectively, ignoring some aspects of Chinese culture and merging others with Japanese traditions.

One of the foremost advocates of Chinese-style political reform was Prince Shotoku, the nephew and regent of the Empress Suiko in the late 6th and early 7th centuries. Shotoku set up Chinese-style court ranks, adopted the Chinese calendar, and sent diplomatic missions to China, famously (and perhaps accidentally) insulting the Chinese emperor with the greeting "From the ruler of the land where the sun rises to the ruler of the land where the sun sets."

Shotoku is credited with composing the Seventeen-Article Constitution—

Prince Shotoku advocated Buddhist and Confucian ideals.

253

Sei Shonagon's witty, amusing observations in the *Pillow Book* exemplify the aesthetic ideal of *okashi*.

not a constitution in the democratic sense but a list of governing principles combining Confucianism, Buddhism, Daoism, and Legalism. Its central principle is harmony, or *wa*, from which right views will grow. Like a good Confucian, Shotoku said that rulers should lead by moral example and believed in clear hierarchies; like a good Daoist, he emphasized harmony and smooth conflict resolution. He was also a Buddhist and wrote an important commentary on the Lotus Sutra. His belief in collective decision making, consensus, teamwork, and community remain important in Japanese management practices today.

By the Heian period (794–1186), Chinese culture dominated Japanese politics and art. At court, male aristocrats were expected to learn Chinese well enough to compose Chinese-language poetry. Writing in Japanese was strictly for women. As a result, men wrote mediocre Chinese poetry, while a few women wrote spectacular Japanese-language literature. Two of the greatest are known as Murasaki Shikibu and Sei Shonagon. (Their real names are unknown.)

Murasaki Shikibu, commonly called Lady Murasaki, was a young widow and lady in waiting to Empress Shoshi at the turn of the 11th century. Her *Tale of Genji*, probably the first novel in world history, is a romance between the ideal gentleman Prince Genji and his true love, Murasaki. Murasaki belongs to a lower social station; he can only take her as a secondary wife. But Genji's other marriages, his dalliances, and his political intrigues take their toll on Murasaki. She dies young, and Genji is devastated. He comes to realize his own failings, the unhappiness he has caused others, and the inevitable passing of all things—a distinctly Buddhist message. This novel is still worth reading for its realistic, nuanced observations of emotion and psychology.

Men wrote mediocre Chinese poetry, while a few women wrote spectacular Japanese-language literature.

Sei Shonagon was a contemporary of Murasaki and lady in waiting to Empress Shoshi's co-wife, Empress Teishi. Her *Pillow Book* is a collection of wry observations, complaints, lists, and musings on court life and culture, often very humorous ones. (Appropriately, a pillow book is a notebook kept at one's bedside to capture stray thoughts.) Her work is a celebration of refinement and taste.

Aware and *okashi* are two of the key terms in Japanese aesthetics. *Aware* is "sensitivity to things" or "a capacity to be moved by things." It is a primary characteristic of the *Tale of Genji*. *Okashi* is something that brings a smile to one's face, either in delight or amusement. This is the mood of the *Pillow Book*. Although from the same time and place, the books are striking opposites, but each is a jewel of Japanese culture. ∎

Suggested Reading

De Bary et al., eds. *Sources of Japanese Tradition*.

Mitchell, *Buddhism*.

Morris, *The World of the Shining Prince*.

Varley, *Japanese Culture*.

Questions to Consider

1. How are cross-cultural borrowing and adaptations significant in the development of traditions?

2. Can literary works be judged by universal principles, or must they be assessed by the standards of their own culture? What is the role of beauty in an intellectual tradition?

3. How do later generations appropriate and reinterpret earlier thinkers and ideas for their own needs?

Prince Shotoku, Ladies Murasaki, Sei Shonagon
Lecture 18—Transcript

Hello again. We come to a lecture that we've all been waiting for now because the convention in the Dao Hotel in Japan is going to get started. Japanese Civilization comes quite a bit after India and China started their civilizations. There were people living in the Japanese islands for thousands of years, of course, but it wasn't until the 6th century A.D. that they developed the level of social and government organization that we usually associate with the term "civilization."

The transition seems to be connected with political developments on the Asian mainland. In the 6th century, some of the ruling clans of Japan adopted Chinese models of scholarship, of religion, and governance. The contact with Chinese culture most often came to Korea, which is the closest point of the Asian mainland to Japan, so, a quick historical recap of what's going on in East Asia in the 6th century. In China, they've becoming unified again after three centuries of competing kingdoms and civil war under the Sui and then the Tang dynasties. In Korea, this is the time of the Three Kingdoms, but Silla is on the move and is going to take over most of that. Silla has a connection with China and Buddhism is the official religion there. There was a loss of Japanese domains in Korea and now Japan is starting to see itself as being rather weak and decentralized. Something needs to change.

There were three great gifts that came from China to Japan through Korea. The first was a writing system, so the Japanese used Chinese characters to write their language, even though Chinese and Japanese are not related languages at all. When I talk about the Do Hotel that's the Japanese version of the Chinese pronunciation of Dao; that same character can also be read *michi*, which also means road or something, but it's in a more traditional Japanese pronunciation.

The second great gift that comes from China is Buddhism and there are monks and statues that are sent from one of the three Korean kingdoms into Japan. One of the prominent clans, the Soga clan adopts Buddhism and then when they become prominent Buddhism is going to flourish in Japan. The third gift is the ideal of a unified government under an emperor. Japan is going to have an emperor, even though it's a different sort of empire than we've seen before. In other places, these empires take in huge territories and multiple ethnicities and languages and customs. Japan is a much more homogenized place, but they do have an emperor.

The Japanese borrowed a great deal from China, but they borrowed selectively. They ignored some aspects of Chinese culture, like say eunuchs, that just didn't make any sense to them so there aren't eunuchs around the Japanese emperor. They took other cultural traditions from China and merged them with local traditions such as those that were associated with the native religion of Japan called Shinto, that has myths about the origins of the Japanese divinities and the islands, purification rituals, and a notion of *kami*, these beings with spiritual power, divinities, but also great mountains or sometimes old trees or even people might have some degree of kami to them, spiritual power.

An example of this sort of hybrid culture is the Japanese were wary of Mandate of Heaven theories, which after all justified rebellion in some circumstances. Remember we talked about that with Mencius. Consequently they have had only one dynasty through their entire history. The current emperor of Japan, Emperor Akihito, is a direct descendant of emperors in the 6th century and the royal clan traces its origins or lineage back to the Japanese sun goddess Amaterasu. Actually one reason for this institutional longevity is that Japanese Emperors have often reigned but not ruled, sometimes the most powerful person in Japan made himself Shogun and had his own government. In China, that person would just kick out the old family, start a new dynasty, but in Japan the royal family continues in a figurehead sort of role.

We're going to talk about one of the foremost advocates of Chinese style reform and that's Prince Shotoku. He lived from 573 to 621, which makes him about a contemporary of Muhammad. Shotoku was the nephew and also regent for the reigning Empress Suiko. She ascends the throne in 592 when her half brother was assassinated. She's about 40 years old and her nephew Shotoku is 20 and together they'll work together to bring order to China. She has a 36-year reign; it's the longest until the Meiji emperor in the 19th century.

Prince Shotoku set about bringing in Chinese-style court ranks. He adopted the Chinese calendar. He sent students and diplomatic missions to China. He is also remembered for one of Japan's most famous insults. He wrote a letter to the Chinese emperor and addressed it "From the ruler of the land where the sun rises to the ruler of the land where the sun sets," sort of a you're a declining power and we're a rising power. I don't know that he did that intentionally, he actually really respected China, but the Sui emperor was not impressed by that. He said those Japanese barbarians need to learn some manners.

Today, however; Shotoku is most famous for his Seventeen-Article Constitution that he put forward in 604. We're not sure that he's the author; there's some scholarly debate about that. There may've been some contributions from Korean refugees who knew Chinese and knew something about Chinese culture, but we'll give Shotoku credit for this since it does seem to fit the kind of ideas and the general pattern of his regency. This Seventeen-Article Constitution is not like the US Constitution, which specifies a particular government structure, and functions, and powers of different branches of government. Shotoku's Constitution is a list of basic principles or moral injunctions. There are 17 of them and perhaps that has to do with the Book of Changes since eight is the largest yin number and nine is the largest yang number. You put those together and you get 17.

Let me give you an example of how this sounds. When you listen to this I want you to think if you can identify aspects that are from Confucianism, Buddhism, Daoism or Legalism. It starts out in this way,

> Harmony is to be valued, and an avoidance of wanton opposition to be honored. All men are influenced by class feeling, and there are few who are intelligent. Hence there are some who disobey their lords and fathers, or who maintain feuds with the neighboring villages. But when those above are harmonious and those below are friendly, and there is concord in the discussion of business, right views of things spontaneously gain acceptance.

Notice this hierarchy, higher and lower, and then cooperation and harmony.

The second article of this constitution starts, "Sincerely reverence the three treasures … the Buddha, the Law, [that's going to be the Buddhist teachings,] and the Sangha." That's the community of monks and nuns; that's obviously Buddhist. Article number three,

> When you receive the Imperial commands, fail not scrupulously to obey them, be obedient to the Emperor. We're going to see that theme again so keep that one in mind. 'The lord is heaven, the vassal is earth. Heaven overspreads, the Earth up bears. When this is so, the four seasons follow their due course, and the powers of Nature obtain their efficacy.

So there maybe some Daoist notions of harmony with nature in there.

Other articles talk about rule by example, about avoiding covetous desires, about punishing the evil and rewarding the good, sounds sort of Legalist, making sure that the responsibilities of the ministers are clear, employing the people's labor in accordance with their seasons. Notice that there's not really anything from Shinto here. It's very much borrowing of Chinese culture. It's very eclectic. It's practical and they're borrowing, but also adapting. There's an emphasis on harmony and a smooth resolution of conflict.

Prince Shotoku also wrote a commentary on the Lotus Sutra, a Buddhist scripture that became the most important religious text in Japanese history. It's from the Mahayana tradition; remember the Tiantai Buddhists thought that the Lotus Sutra was the highest sutra, the highest level of sutra that the Buddha ever gave. It was translated from Sanskrit into Chinese in the 3rd century and then the Buddha taught the sermon; this is the way it starts, I'm setting the situation. He taught the sermons to 12,000 monks, 6000 nuns were listening along with 8000 bodhisattvas, and 60,000 gods were all tuning into this sermon. As the Buddhist spoke, a ray of light came from his forehead and illuminated 18,000 worlds, in each of which a Buddha was preaching.

The messages of the Lotus Sutra are that the Buddha is eternal, that salvation is universal, and the three vehicles are one. There's also a story, a famous parable of a burning house. There was a merchant, a well-off merchant, who had many sons, a large house, and his house caught on fire. As he saw the flames start to go up he wanted to get his sons, but he knew that he couldn't go around and grab them all individually so he needed to tempt them to come out.

He promised three sorts of things to different sons. To some sons he promised a goat-cart, just think of it like a big wheel tricycle maybe for the really young ones. To other sons, he promised deer-carts; that might be like a motorcycle, and to other sons, maybe the older ones, he promised ox-carts, the equivalent might be like a muscle car, like a mustang or something. They come out responding to those promises and he actually gives them all something much better, and all the same thing. He gives them a Maserati sports car, let's say. Then he asks the question is anybody going to be disappointed in that?

The idea is that the Buddha uses skillful means. He teaches different things to different people at different time depending on their spiritual receptivity or their level, but in the end he offers enlightenment to all of them, which is the same everyone gets the same, but it's much more wonderful than anything that they can imagine. This is a harmonious way of resolving the conflicts between different Buddhist schools.

Today, Prince Shotoku often heads the list of the most admired individuals in Japanese history. He's seen as a key figure in the development of the spirit of wa; that's harmony; remember the Constitution starts, "Harmony is to be valued ..." and then number 17 of that, the last article says, "Decisions on important matters should not be made by one person alone. They should be discussed with many." The idea of collective decision making, of consensus, of teamwork, a strong sense of community; those are very significant in Japanese business practices and in management techniques.

Actually they're important in Japanese baseball. There was a book written a few years ago called *You Gotta Have Wa*, which talked about the dilemma of American baseball players who went to play in Japanese leagues and then were sort of put off and felt very alien and they didn't quite fit into this Japanese notion of teamwork and consensus. The idea of wa, of harmony is part of the Japanese national character. This is the way they think of themselves.

That seems to be a post-WWII interpretation of Shotoku and his Constitution. In earlier ages, he was celebrated as a proponent of Buddhism, even in incarnation of the Buddha, and then when Neo-Confucianism came into Japan and became dominant then Shotoku was criticized for the same thing. He was the person who made Buddhism popular here and that sort of caused all of our problems. After the Meiji Restoration in 1868, when Japanese nationalism was growing, many people argued that the main message of the Constitution was Article 3, give loyalty and obedience to the Emperor.

Then there was a shift after World War II and it may be illustrated by a story about Japanese currency. The American Occupation authorities banned the publication of Shinto images that had been associated with emperor worship. They debated whether they should ban pictures of Prince Shotoku as well, because he had been a symbol of ultranationalist patriotism during the war. But the director of the Bank of Japan convinced them that the Prince was actually a symbol of pacifism, because he had taught that "it is noble to have wa; he made it a principle not to have conflicts." Something similar happens to Emperor Hirohito, who was the war Emperor, but then after the war he was thought of as a man of peace because he had encouraged his people to surrender peacefully after the atomic bombs were exploded, brought an end to World War II.

Shotoku's image was on various Japanese banknotes from 1946 to the mid-1980s. Nowadays on the Internet you can find claims that Shotoku invented sushi. That's not true, but it's an illustration of how the Japanese still want to give him credit for all sorts of cultural achievements. You may be asking so who replaced Prince Shotoku on the 10,000 yen bill? The answer is Fukuzawa Yukichi; we're going to talk about him in Lecture 32.

In the year 2000, a commemorative 2000 yen bill was released with the image from the Tale of Genji and a picture of its author, Murasaki Shikibu. She's going to be the next great mind in this lecture. Actually, there are two of them, Murasaki Shikibu and Sei Shonagon: both of them are Japanese, both of them are women; both of them are from the same time period. They even knew each other.

The Heian Period; this is from 794 to 1186. It is often thought of as the classic age of traditional Japanese culture—art, and architecture, and literature, and poetry; there're just wonderful things happening. By this time though, direct contact with China has come to an end, mostly because of political turmoil in the late Tang Dynasty, but there's still a strong influence of Chinese culture that continues in the Japanese court at Kyoto, then it was called Heian. That's where we get the name Heian period.

Chinese was still the official language of the Japanese government, and male aristocrats were expected to learn Chinese well enough to compose Chinese poetry. Writing in Japanese would have been much easier and consequently many people felt that that was a mode of expression that was better suited for women. The result of this rather sexist attitude was that Japanese men generally wrote sort of mediocre Chinese poetry, while a few Japanese court women were writing spectacular literature in their native language. These include two women who clearly belong among the great minds of the Eastern intellectual tradition.

In Japan, we'll focus more on literary figures that we did in India and China, though there's great literature in India and China as well. But aesthetics; the philosophy of beauty, and art, and taste, plays a central role in Japanese thought. We don't know much at all about the lives of Murasaki Shikibu and Sei Shonagon. We don't even know their real names. What we do have are titles: Murasaki is the name of one of her book's main characters, Shikibu is the name of a post that was once held by her father; while Sei Shonagon is a clan name, Shonagon means "minor counselor" and it was a position held by some male relative, maybe her father, we're not sure.

We'll start with Sei Shonagon. She lives from 966 to 1017. Her father was a minor official, a scholar, and a famous poet. She apparently married and had a child, and then served as a lady-in-waiting to Empress Teishi for seven years, from 993 until Teishi's death in childbirth, in 1000 A.D.

Murasaki Shikibu was slightly younger. She was born about 973 into the prominent Fujiwara clan. Her father was a provincial governor and a scholar of Chinese. She was married at the age of 25, which is rather late for this society, and then was widowed just two years later, at 27. A few years after that, she was summoned to be a lady-in-waiting to Empress Shôshi and she died around 1014, maybe at the age of 40 or so. Both women knew Chinese fairly well, but such knowledge was considered unladylike, so both of them wrote in Japanese. Murasaki learned Chinese from overhearing her brother's lessons. She was actually quite a bit better at Chinese than he was, which led her father to exclaim, "Just my luck! What a pity she was not born a man." The two women wrote books that are really the opposite of each other.

Lady Murasaki is the author of the *Tale of Genji*, which is probably the first great novel in world history. It's about Prince Genji, the son of the emperor and one of his minor wives, and his many love affairs. It's not, however, an erotic work. It focuses on the psychological and emotional aspects of love, rather than the physical aspects. I should mention here that the personal lives of aristocrats in 10th-century Japan were rather complicated. Marriages were arranged for sons and daughters in their early teens, and the wife generally continued to live with her parents.

Later, a man might also marry two or three secondary wives, but often husbands lived in separate households from their wives. Love was not generally connected to marriage, and affairs were accepted for both men and women. Genji cuts a striking figure in this world. He's the ideal gentleman. He's handsome, and elegant. He's a great lover, a talented dancer, a musician, and a poet. He's generous and thoughtful. Even after an amorous relationship has come to an end, he is still unfailingly gracious and kind to his former lovers. And the women, as described by Murasaki, are not at all interchangeable. Genji comes to know them as individuals, but he never seems to find exactly what he's looking for.

The great love of his life, a girl named Murasaki, the character we name the author for, she belonged to a lower social station, and though he eventually marries her as a secondary wife, the complications of his other marriages, and his dalliances, and political intrigues all take their toll. When Murasaki dies, this is the character in the novel, childless, in her 40s, Genji is devastated and he comes to realize his own failings, the unhappiness that he's brought to others, and the inevitable passing of things. You notice some Buddhist overtones here?

The Tale of Genji is a long novel, with 54 chapters and 1000 pages. The action takes place over the course of 70 years, and there are about 50 important characters. Lady Murasaki writes with elegance and delicacy. She also includes 795 poems in her novel. This is how Japanese aristocrats, at the time, fell in love. You don't catch a glimpse of a stranger across a crowded room, but instead you catch a glimpse of someone's calligraphy and you say my goodness such taste, such refinement, I really ought to get to know the writer of that better. But what makes this novel still very much worth reading today, are the realistic, nuanced observations of emotion and of psychology.

I'll give you just one quick example:

> The lady, when no answer came from Genji, thought that he had changed his mind, and though she would have been very angry if he had persisted in his suit, she was not quite prepared to lose him with so little ado. But this was a good opportunity once and for all to lock her heart against him. She thought that she had done so successfully, but found to her surprise that he still occupied an uncommonly large share of her thoughts.

This affair is cooling down, does she love him, does she not love him? Does she want to break up, or doesn't she? These are sort of common feelings, perhaps even among us a thousand years later.

The next book is the *Pillow Book*, by Sei Shonagon. This is a collection of wry observations, of complaints, lists, and musings on court life and on culture. Where the Tale of Genji is long and complex and filled with pathos, the contents of the *Pillow Book* are short, random, and often kind of funny.

The odd title comes from a conversation that Sei Shonagon had with the empress, who had just received a gift of paper and paper was a very valuable commodity at the time. The empress had said I'm not sure what to do with this; that similar gift had gone to her husband the emperor and she was having a copy of Sima Qian's *Records of the Scribes*, the *Shiji* copied onto his gift. That seemed like a noble thing to do. She said what should I do with my paper and Sei Shonagon said, "Let's make them into a pillow" by which she meant let's bind them into blank notebooks that we can place by our pillow when we go to sleep and then that'll give us a place where we can jot down stray thoughts or ideas that we might have. She said fine and so apparently she gave these notebooks to Sei Shonagon.

Sei Shonagon was obviously intelligent, and quick-witted. She's witty; she's observant, though she could also be dismissive of those she considered beneath her. But, her work is a celebration of refinement and taste.

She makes lots of observations here. For example, she says that preachers should be good looking so that we pay close attention to what they say. If we look away, we may forget to listen, so ugly preachers can often be the source of sin. The great translator Arthur Waley, once said that his favorite passage from the *Pillow Book* was this: "I love to cross a river in very bright moonlight and see the trampled water fly up in chips of crystal under the oxen's feet." It's just a very descriptive description.

Let me give you some more. In the *Pillow* Book she includes 164 lists, things that are regrettable, things that are admirable, embarrassing things, hateful things, elegant things, etc. Let me just share a few of these with you because they're just so much fun. So these are Things That Make You Feel Nostalgic and they include "Things children use in doll play. ... On a rainy day, when time hangs heavy, searching out an old letter that touched you deeply at the time you received it." Remember we're after nostalgia here, "last year's summer fan."

Another list: Things That Make One Uncomfortable—"Someone relays a bit of gossip without knowing that the subject is listening. Even if the person is only a servant, this makes one feel uncomfortable. ... The doting parents of an unattractive young child pet him, play with him, and repeat his sayings, imitating his voice." kind of irritating. "When someone is wide awake, chattering away, it is disconcerting if a companion simply lies there half-asleep." And then one more, something that makes you uncomfortable, "Someone performs complacently on an out-of-tune zither in front of an expert musician."

Here's a list about Things That Have Lost Their Power—"A large boat which is high and dry in a creek at ebb-tide. ... A large tree that has been blown down in a gale and lies on its side with its roots in the air." Remember Things That Have Lost Their Power, "the retreating figure of a sumo wrestler who has been defeated in a match." And then this last example, "A woman, who is angry with her husband about some trifling matter, leaves home and goes somewhere to hide. She is certain that he will rush about looking for her; but he does nothing of the kind and shows the most infuriating indifference. Since she cannot stay away forever, she swallows her pride and returns." Again, Things That Have Lost Their Power.

For some of the theory, I want to introduce two terms that are important to Japanese aesthetics. *Aware* and *okashi*, now *mono no aware*, which is sometimes just shortened to *aware* is a "sensitivity to things." It's "a capacity to be moved by things," especially those things that are tinged with sadness, such as the fall of a flower or the passage of time. *Aware* is a primary characteristic of the *Tale of Genji* as you follow Genji through many years and sort of see the impermanence of all things and you're moved by that.

Okashi is something quite different. It's something that brings a smile to one's face, either in delight or in amusement. It's much lighter and more charming than *aware*, and it's oftentimes associated with Sei Shonagon's *Pillow Book*. What striking opposites! Though they both came from the same time and the same place and the same culture, it's interesting that even though the court in Kyoto borrowed extensively from Chinese culture, what emerges in Japan is quite distinctive. There's nothing quite like *aware* and *okashi* in China.

Murasaki Shikibu and Sei Shonagon apparently knew each other, but I'm not sure that they were friends, they were more like rivals. In her diary, Lady Murasaki wrote this, a few years after Sei Shonagon had left the court. She said,

> Sei Shonagon ... was dreadfully conceited. She thought herself so clever and littered her writings with Chinese characters; but if you examined them closely, they left a great deal to be desired. Those who think of themselves as being superior to everyone else in this way will inevitably suffer and come to a bad end, and people who ... [try] to capture every moment of interest, however slight

267

[remember all those lists], they are bound to look ridiculous and superficial. How can the future turn out well for them?

That may seem a little bit snarky.

Murasaki is critical of pride and she's concerned with reputation, yet she also shows an awareness of how things can change, and there is perhaps a hint of compassion there. Perhaps! How can a person like that, things turn out well for a person like that. But remember, a refined culture, and Heian court culture is extremely refined. It needs sharp criticism to keep up standards, to keep everybody on their toes, but Murasaki takes the edge off that criticism by almost immediately criticizing herself, remember the Japanese ideals of harmony and humility that we saw in Shotoku's Constitution! She continues in her diary lamenting that she hasn't accomplished much herself and then says, "and when I play my [zither] rather badly to myself in the cool breeze of the evening, I worry that someone might hear me and recognize how I am just 'adding to the sadness of it all'; how vain and sad of me."

The last word, we'll leave to Prince Genji, who in a discussion of the varieties of Japanese literature observed that "to dismiss all these types of fiction as so much falsehood is surely to miss the point. For even in the Law that the Buddha in his great mercy bequeathed to us, there are parts known as skillful means." Remember the Parable of the Burning House in the Lotus Sutra, that he says different things to different people so that different people can respond to that. Continue with Genji's quote, "So when we regard these works of fiction in their proper light, we find that they contain nothing superfluous."

Here you have a fictional character commenting on the nature of fiction! It's almost post modern kind of, it's sort of an interesting situation. From a harmonizing Buddhist perspective, like that of Prince Shotoku, each type of literature has a role to play in bringing about a greater awareness and understanding of life. In this lecture, we've seen how Japanese thinkers borrowed ideas and institutions from China and then used them to create a distinct rich culture of their own. We'll see more of this in the next lecture when we talk about Buddhism in Japan. I'll see you then.

Timeline

Year	India	Tibet	China	Japan	Korea	The Middle East and the West
c. 3500 B.C.						Earliest civilizations in Mesopotamia
c. 2575–2465 B.C.						Construction of the Pyramids at Giza
c. 2500–1500 B.C.	Harrapan civilization in the Indus Valley					
c. 2350 B.C.						Rise of the Sumerian Empire
c. 2000 B.C.			Development of the Chinese writing system			Hebrew migration from Ur to Canaan
c. 2000–1500 B.C.						

Timeline

Year	India	Tibet	China	Japan	Korea	The Middle East and the West
c. 1760–1122			The Shang, China's first historical dynasty, rules the North China Plain			
c. 1500–1000 B.C.	The Vedas are composed					
1400–1000 B.C.						Zoroastrianism is founded
1045 B.C.			The Zhou dynasty is founded			
1020–721 B.C.						Kingdom of Israel
900–500 B.C.	The Upanishads are composed					
c. 800 B.C.	Life of Uddalaka, history's first known philosopher					
c. 680			The *Yijing* is composed			

270

Year	India	Tibet	China	Japan	Korea	The Middle East and the West
563–483 B.C.	Life of the Buddha					
c. 551–479 B.C.			Life of Confucius			
550 B.C.						Achaemenid Empire founded in Persia
540–468 B.C.	Life of Mahavira					
509 B.C.						Roman Republic founded
c. 500 B.C.			Life of Laozi; composition of the Daodejing			
480–390 B.C.			Life of Mozi			
470–399 B.C.						Life of Socrates
427–327 B.C.						Life of Plato

Timeline

Year	India	Tibet	China	Japan	Korea	The Middle East and the West
c. 400–200 B.C.	The Mahabharata, including the Bhagavad Gita, is composed					
4th century B.C.			Sunzi (Sun Wu) writes *The Art of War*		Choson civilization established	
384–322 B.C.						Life of Aristotle
380–305 B.C.			Life of Huizi			
372–289 B.C.			Life of Mencius			
369–286 B.C.			Life of Zhuangzi			
350–275 B.C.	Life of Kautilya					
330 B.C.						Alexander the Great conquers the Achaemenid Empire

Year	India	Tibet	China	Japan	Korea	The Middle East and the West
322–185 B.C.	The Mauryan Empire unites the Indian subcontinent					
300–c. 210 B.C.			Life of Xunzi			
2nd century B.C.?	Composition of the Yoga Sutra					
280–233 B.C.			Life of Han Feizi			
269–232 B.C.	Reign of the Mauryan emperor Ashoka; spread of Buddhism throughout India and Sri Lanka					
247 B.C.–224						Parthian Empire rules Persia

Timeline

Year	India	Tibet	China	Japan	Korea	The Middle East and the West
221 B.C.			China is united under the first Qin emperor			
200 B.C.–200			The Han dynasty			
c. 195–105 B.C.			Life of Dong Zhongshu			
c. 145–86 B.C.			Life of Sima Qian			
110 B.C.			Sima Qian begins writing the *Shiji*			
108 B.C.					China overthrows the Choson ruler	
57–18 B.C.					The Three Kingdoms (Koguryo, Paekche, and Silla) arise in the lower peninsula	

Year	India	Tibet	China	Japan	Korea	The Middle East and the West
27 B.C.						The Roman Republic becomes the Roman Empire
c. 4 B.C.–A.D. 30						Life of Jesus of Nazareth
1st century	Development of Mahayana Buddhism		Buddhism is introduced into China			
45–116			Life of Ban Zhao			
2nd century	Life of Nagarjuna; development of the Madhyamaka school of Buddhism					
105			Cai Lun invents paper			
132			Zhang Heng invents the seismograph			
216–276						Life of Mani

Timeline

Year	India	Tibet	China	Japan	Korea	The Middle East and the West
224–651						Sassanid Empire rules Persia
283–343			Life of Ge Hong			
4th century	Life of Vasubandhu; development of the Yogacara school of Buddhism					
4th–6th centuries	The Vedas are written down					
mid-4th century				First unified Japanese state founded		
c. 313					The Three Kingdoms break free of Chinese dominance	Edict of Milan legalizes Christianity in Rome
354–430						Life of Augustine of Hippo

Year	India	Tibet	China	Japan	Korea	The Middle East and the West
late 4th century	Life of Ishvara-krishna					
552				Korean monks bring Buddhism to Japan		
476						Fall of the Roman Empire in the West
c. 499	Aryabhata composes his treatise on mathematics					
570–632						Life of Muhammad
573–621				Life of Prince Shotoku		
597						Augustine of Canterbury reestablishes Christianity in England

Timeline

Year	India	Tibet	China	Japan	Korea	The Middle East and the West
600–664			Life of Xuanzang			
604				Shotoku issues the 17-Article Constitution		
610						Muhammad receives his first revelation; Islam founded
617–686					Life of Wonhyo	
622						The Hijirah (flight from Mecca); Muslim calendar begins
629		Songtsän Gampo crowned; beginning of Tibet's recorded history				

Year	India	Tibet	China	Japan	Korea	The Middle East and the West
c. 640s			Development of Chan (Zen) Buddhism			
661–750						Umayyad caliphs spread Islam throughout North Africa and into Spain
668					Silla overthrows Koguryo and Paekche and unifies the peninsula	
c. 670s						Development of Sufi Islam
711	Umayyad Muslim army conquers Sind (southwestern Pakistan)					
750–1258						Abbasid caliphate

Timeline

Year	India	Tibet	China	Japan	Korea	The Middle East and the West
755–763			An Lushan Rebellion			
763		King Khrisong Detsen invites Chinese and Indian monks into his kingdom; start of Tibet's conversion to Buddhism				
768–824			Life of Han Yu			
775		Padmasambhava (Guru Rinpoche) arrives from India to found Tibet's first monastery				
788				Mount Hiei Buddhist temple founded		

Year	India	Tibet	China	Japan	Korea	The Middle East and the West
788–822	Life of Shankara					
794–1186				Heian period		
9th century		Tibet and China agree to a peace treaty				
800						Charlemagne is crowned Holy Roman Emperor
804				Saicho and Kukai visit China to study Buddhist doctrine		
843–845			Daoist emperor Wuzong persecutes Chinese Buddhists, Christians, and Zoroastrians			

Timeline

Year	India	Tibet	China	Japan	Korea	The Middle East and the West
980–1052		Life of Atisha; second dissemination of Buddhism to Tibet				
918–1392					Koryo dynasty	
960–1279			Song dynasty; urban and commercial expansion throughout China			
966–1017				Life of Sei Shonagon		
973–1014				Life of Murasaki Shikibu		
973–1048						Life of Al-Biruni
997–1030	Mahmud's raids and Al-Biruni's visits to India					Reign of Mahmud in Ghazna (Afghanistan)

Year	India	Tibet	China	Japan	Korea	The Middle East and the West
c. 1000			Rise of Neo-Confucianism			
1012–1096		Life of Milarepa				
1017–1137?	Life of Ramajuna					
1030						Al-Biruni writes *Researches on India*
1095						Pope Urban II calls for the First Crusade
1130–1200			Life of Zhu Xi			
1058–1111						Life of Al-Ghazali
1066						Norman Conquest of England

283

Timeline

Year	India	Tibet	China	Japan	Korea	The Middle East and the West
1133–1212				Life of Honen; establishment of Pure Land Buddhism		
1158–1210					Life of Chinul; reform of Buddhist monasticism	
1160						The University of Paris is founded
1173–1263				Life of Shinran		
1191				Eisai brings Rinzai (sudden enlightenment) Zen to Japan		
1197–1276	Life of Madhva					
1222-1282				Life of Nichiren		
1225–1274						Life of Thomas Aquinas

Year	India	Tibet	China	Japan	Korea	The Middle East and the West
1227				Dogen brings Soto (gradual enlightenment) Zen to Japan		
1231						Pope Gregory IX establishes the Inquisition
1236–1251		Mongol conquest; Tibet is officially a province of Yuan dynasty China			Monks undertake the printing of the entire 1,512-volume Buddhist canon	
1274–1281				Failed Mongol invasions of Japan		

285

Timeline

Year	India	Tibet	China	Japan	Korea	The Middle East and the West
1292			Marco Polo arrives in Fuzhou, China			
1313			Zhu Xi's commentaries on the Four Books are added to the civil service exam curriculum			
1333–1573				Muromachi period		
1357–1419		Life of Tsongkhapa; Geluk school and the line of the Dalai Lama established				
1363–1443				Life of Zeami; Noh drama comes to maturity		

Year	India	Tibet	China	Japan	Korea	The Middle East and the West
1368		Mongol Yuan dynasty collapses; Tibet regains independence				
1392–1910					Choson (Yi) dynasty	
1418–1450					Reign of Sejong the Great; development of the Hangul writing system	
1449–1473				Shogunate of Ashikaga Yoshimasa; flowering of Japanese aesthetics, called the Higeshiyama period		

Timeline

Year	India	Tibet	China	Japan	Korea	The Middle East and the West
1453						Fall of the Byzantine Empire (the Roman Empire in the East)
1469–1492						Lorenzo de' Medici's patronage of the great artists of Europe sparks the High Renaissance
1469–1530	Life of Guru Nanak					
1472–1529			Life of Wang Yangming			

Year	India	Tibet	China	Japan	Korea	The Middle East and the West
1492						Spanish Christians complete the Reconquista, driving the Muslims from Spain; Christopher Colombus embarks on his Atlantic crossing
c. 1499	Guru Nanak founds Sikhism					
16th century					Lives of Yi Hwang (Yi T'oegye) and Yi I (Yi Yulgok); rise of the Four-Seven debate	

Timeline

Year	India	Tibet	China	Japan	Korea	The Middle East and the West
1517						Martin Luther issues the 95 Theses; Protestant Reformation begins
1522–1591				Life of Sen no Rikyu; refinement of *wabicha* (tea ceremony) as a Zen art form		
1542–1605	Life of Akbar the Great					
1564–1624	Life of Sirhindi					
1575	Akbar constructs the House of Worship as a center for open religious debate					

Year	India	Tibet	China	Japan	Korea	The Middle East and the West
1603				Tokugawa Ieyasu becomes shogun and unites Japan		
1603–1620						First permanent English colonies (Virginia and Plymouth) founded in the Americas
1609–1610						Johannes Kepler develops the laws of motion; Galileo Galilei discovers Jupiter's moons

Timeline

Year	India	Tibet	China	Japan	Korea	The Middle East and the West
1644		Treaty between the Dalai Lama and the Manchu emperor of China, establishing each other's spheres of authority				
1644–1911			Manchu (Quin) dynasty, the last Chinese dynasty, rules China, Tibet, and Mongolia			
1686–1769				Life of Hakuin		
1775–1783						American Revolution

Year	India	Tibet	China	Japan	Korea	The Middle East and the West
1785						Charles Wilkins creates the first English translation of the Bhagavad Gita
1787–1799						French Revolution
1816				Dogen's *Shobogenzo* is first published, almost 600 years after its composition		
1835–1901				Life of Fukuzawa Yukichi		
1848						Karl Marx publishes *The Communist Manifesto*.

Timeline

Year	India	Tibet	China	Japan	Korea	The Middle East and the West
1850–1864			Taiping Rebellion			
1853–1854				Commodore Matthew Perry forces Japan to open itself to European trade		
1858	British crown officially takes control of India					
1858–1927			Life of Kang Youwei			
1861–1865						American Civil War
1861–1941	Life of Rabindranath Tagore					
1866–1925			Life of Sun Yat-sen			

Year	India	Tibet	China	Japan	Korea	The Middle East and the West
1868				The Meiji Restoration begins		
1869–1948	Life of Mohandas (Mahatma) Gandhi					
1879–1944					Life of Han Yongun (Manhae)	
1873–1938	Life of Muhammad Iqbal					
1887–1975			Life of Chiang Kai-shek			
1891–1962			Life of Hu Shi			
1893						Parliament of World Religions; Vivekananda's plea for religious tolerance

Timeline

Year	India	Tibet	China	Japan	Korea	The Middle East and the West
1893–1976			Life of Mao Zedong			
1898			The Hundred Days' Reform			
1898–1901			Boxer Rebellion			
1905			Confucian civil service exams are discontinued		Japan claims Korea as a protectorate	
1912			China is declared a republic; Sun Yat-sen is elected provisional president but is overthrown two months later			

Year	India	Tibet	China	Japan	Korea	The Middle East and the West
1914–1918				---- World War I ----		
1917	Gandhi organizes the indigo workers' Satyagraha, the first of his five major Indian Satyagrahas		Sun Yat-sen and Chiang Kai-shek establish the Nationalist government and begin a military campaign to retake China			Russian Revolution establishes the Bolshevik government
1919			The May 4th Movement protests the Treaty of Versailles in Tiananmen Square		Korean declare independence from Japan, followed by massive but unsuccessful uprisings	
1920			Schools begin teaching colloquial, as well as classical, written Chinese			

Timeline

Year	India	Tibet	China	Japan	Korea	The Middle East and the West
1921			Chinese Communist Party founded			
1929–1939						The Great Depression
1935		Birth of Tenzin Gyatso, 14th Dalai Lama				
1937			Japan invades China,			
1939–1945				------- World War II -------		
1945			Nationalist-Communist civil war; Communists establish the People's Republic of China under Mao on the mainland, and the Nationalist government under Chiang retreats to Taiwan			

298

Year	India	Tibet	China	Japan	Korea	The Middle East and the West
1947	India and Pakistan are established as separate, independent states					
1950		Chinese invasion reestablishes China's rule				
1950–1953					Korean War; division of Korea into the communist North and republican South.	
1958–1961			The Great Leap Forward reorganizes Chinese agriculture, leading to massive famine			

Timeline

Year	India	Tibet	China	Japan	Korea	The Middle East and the West
1959		The Dalai Lama and his government flee to India				
1966–1976		Persecution of Buddhists during China's Cultural Revolution	The Cultural Revolution, ending with the death of Mao and the ascension of Deng Xiaoping			
1989			Student protests in Tiananmen Square on the anniversary of the May 4th Movement protests			The Dalai Lama is awarded the Nobel Peace Prize

Bibliography

Al-Biruni. *Alberuni's India*. Abridged ed. Translated by Edward C. Sachau. New York: Norton, 1993. This edition is a shortened version of Sachau's 1888 translation, and it is hard to overstate how much fun it is to look through, whether one is interested in science, history, comparative religion, or culture. Al-Biruni was obviously interested in all aspects of the medieval Indian world that he visited.

Aldiss, Stephen, ed. *Zen Sourcebook: Traditional Documents from China, Korea, and Japan*. Indianapolis: Hackett, 2008. This fine collection includes writings by Huineng, Chinul, Dogen, and Hakuin, among many others. Highly recommended.

Blacker, Carmen. *The Japanese Enlightenment: A Study of the Writings of Fukuzawa Yukichi*. Cambridge: Cambridge University Press, 1964. This is a classic work, which I think is still one of the best introductions to Japan's most famous Westernizer, a man who sometimes uneasily bridged two very different cultures.

Boyce, Mary. *Zoroastrians: Their Religious Beliefs and Practices*. 2nd ed. London: Routledge, 2001. The religion of Zarathustra can be a puzzling faith to outsiders, but Boyce provides clear explanations of its origins, scriptures, and later history.

Brown, Judith M. *Gandhi: Prisoner of Hope*. New Haven, CT: Yale University Press, 1991. There are many biographies of Gandhi, but Brown's work remains a towering achievement. Brown is especially good at connecting Gandhi to the broader context of Indian culture and thought.

Carr, Brian, and Indira Mahalingam, eds. *Companion Encyclopedia of Asian Philosophy*. New York: Routledge, 1997. A fine collection of essays dealing with most of the philosophical traditions in this course. Sometimes a bit detailed, but always worth consulting.

Chan, Wing-tsit, trans. *A Source Book in Chinese Philosophy*. Princeton, NJ: Princeton University Press, 1969. If you go with only one book of Chinese philosophy in translation, this should be it. Chan covers the entire range of Chinese thought from Confucius to Maoism. He includes the entire Daodejing and is particularly thorough with the texts of Chinese Buddhism. His introductions alone make this a classic in the field.

Chin, Ann-ping. *The Authentic Confucius: A Life of Thought and Politics*. New York: Scribner, 2007. A biography that attempts to sort the legendary from the historical Confucius and in the process provides a good introduction to his ideas in their original context.

Chung, Edward Y. J. *The Korean Neo-Confucianism of Yi T'oegye and Yi Yulgok: A Reappraisal of the "Four-Seven Thesis" and Its Practical Implications for Self-Cultivation*. Albany: State University of New York Press, 1995. This is an authoritative account of the most famous philosophical controversy in Korean history as conducted by two of Korea's most esteemed thinkers (who are also known as Yi Hwang and Yu I). It is also an example of how Neo-Confucianism spread from China throughout East Asia.

Cohen, H. Floris. *The Scientific Revolution: A Historiographical Inquiry*. Chicago, IL: The University of Chicago Press, 1994. A comprehensive study of one of the most significant events in world history, with a whole chapter devoted to a review of various explanations that have been put forward for why modern science did not emerge from the technologically sophisticated civilizations of China and Islam.

Collinson, Diané, Kathryn Plant, and Robert Wilkinson. *Fifty Eastern Thinkers*. NewYork: Routledge, 2000. Brief synopses of the major ideas of the great Asian philosophers. Very useful for beginners.

Confucius. *The Analects of Confucius*. Translation and notes by Simon Leys. New York: W. W. Norton, 1997. This is one of my favorite translations, It renders Confucius' words into modern, colloquial English, then provides notes to explain the original cultural details.

De Bary, William Theodore, and Irene Bloom, eds. *Sources of Chinese Tradition, Vol. 1: From Earliest Times to 1600*. 2nd ed. New York: Columbia University Press, 2000. This is one of the most comprehensive collections of excerpts from Chinese intellectual history available. It was a classic when it was first published in 1960, and it has since been updated with the most recent archaeologically recovered texts. The translations and introductions set the standard for Chinese studies.

De Bary, William Theodore, and Richard Lufrano, eds. *Sources of Chinese Tradition, Vol. 2: From 1600 through the Twentieth Century*. 2nd ed. New York: Columbia University Press, 2001. The second volume of de Bary's updated 1960 tour de force. Remarkable in the breadth of the sources that it includes.

De Bary, William Theodore, Donald Keene, George Tanabe, and Paul Varley, eds. *Sources of Japanese Tradition*. 2nd ed. 2 vols. New York: Columbia University Press, 2001–2005. In similar manner to their sister volumes in the Sources series, these two books provide a comprehensive overview of Japanese history as recorded in primary sources. The Japanese great minds in this course are all well represented, along with dozens and dozens or additional thinkers.

Dogen. *Moon in a Dewdrop: Writings of Zen Master Dogen*. Translated and edited by Kazuaki Tanahashi. New York: North Point Press, 1995. Dogen's writings are both philosophically and religiously rich. This book offers translations of a wide variety of his works, including poetry.

Dundas, Paul. *The Jains*. 2nd ed. New York: Routledge, 2002. An authoritative yet accessible introduction to the thought of Mahavira and the religion he founded.

Durrant, Stephen W. *The Cloudy Mirror: Tension and Conflict in the Writings of Sima Qian*. Albany: State University of New York Press, 1995. Durrant draws connections between Sima Qian's history and the story of his life, in particular Sima's relationship with the Confucian tradition.

Earhart, H. Byron. *Japanese Religion: Unity and Diversity*. 4th ed. Belmont, CA: Wadsworth, 2003. Much of the history of Japanese thought is focused on religion, and Earhart's textbook covers many great Japanese minds in relationship to each other and also in their historical contexts.

Embree, Ainsley T., ed. *Sources of Indian Tradition, Vol. 1: From the Beginning to 1800*. 2nd ed. New York: Columbia University Press, 1988. This is an anthology of fairly short excerpts (with wonderful introductions) of primary sources in Indian philosophy. Along with the other volumes in the series, this collection offers an excellent introduction to the actual writings of Asian thinkers.

Gandhi, Mohandas K. *The Penguin Gandhi Reader*. 2nd ed. Edited by Rudrangshu Mukherjee. New York: Penguin, 1995. I have found this to be the most accessible and engaging of the many anthologies of Gandhi's writings.

Graham, A. C. *Disputers of the Tao: Philosophical Argument in Ancient China*. La Salle, IL: Open Court, 1989. Of the many introductions to classical Chinese philosophy, this is the best, written by an acknowledged master in the field. The scope of his insights and eloquence of his translations are breathtaking.

Hakuin. *Wild Ivy: The Spiritual Autobiography of Zen Master Hakuin*. Translated by Norman Waddell. Boston: Shambhala, 1999. A masterpiece of both Zen Buddhism and Asian autobiography, Hakuin's work is a psychologically astute approach to spirituality and enlightenment.

Han Yongun. *Everything Yearned For: Manhae's Poems of Love and Longing*. Translated by Francisca Cho. Somerville, MA: Wisdom, 2005. This is a marvelous translation of Han Yongun's most famous book, a work of Buddhist verse that is often read as political allegory or love poetry. Han is also known by his Buddhist name Manhae.

———. *Selected Writings of Han Yongun: From Social Darwinism to Socialism with a Buddhist Face*. Translated by Vladimir Tikhonov and Owen Miller. Honolulu: University of Hawaii Press, 2008. The best anthology of Han Yongun's prose available.

Hardy, Grant. *Worlds of Bronze and Bamboo: Sima Qian's Conquest of History*. New York: Columbia University Press, 1999. A study of Sima Qian's *Shiji* that finds meaning in the unusual, fragmented structure of that early Chinese history.

Harvey, Peter. *An Introduction to Buddhism: Teachings, History, and Practices*. Cambridge, Cambridge University Press, 1990. This text will guide you through all three of the major Buddhist traditions: Theravada, Mahayana, and Vajrayana (basically, Southeast Asia, East Asia, and Tibet).

Hay, Stephen N., ed. *Sources of Indian Tradition, Vol 2: Modern India and Pakistan*. 2nd ed. New York: Columbia University Press, 1988. Along with the other volumes in the Columbia Introduction to Oriental Civilizations series (Sources of India, China, and Japan), this collection offers an excellent introduction to the actual writings of Asian thinkers.

Ivanhoe, Philip J., and Bryan W. Van Norden, eds. *Readings in Classical Chinese Philosophy*. 2nd ed. Indianapolis, IN: Hackett, 2001. New translations of most of the key early Chinese thinkers. A great place to start reading the philosophers themselves.

Juniper, Andrew. *Wabi Sabi: The Japanese Art of Impermanence*. Boston: Tuttle, 2003. This exploration of a key concept in Japanese aesthetics includes material on Zen, design, the tea ceremony, and Sen no Rikyu.

Kasulls, T. P. *Zen Action, Zen Person*. Honolulu: University of Hawaii Press, 1985. An engaging philosophical treatise that brings together Nagarjuna, Daoism, Dogen, and Hakuin.

Keene, Donald. *Yoshimasa and the Silver Pavilion: The Creation of the Soul of Japan*. New York: Columbia University Press, 2005. Donald Keene, one of the eminent scholars of Japan, introduces readers to the artistic flowering in the medieval court of the Shogun Yoshimasa and then demonstrates how those sensibilities have informed Japanese culture ever since. The topics he covers include theater, painting, architecture, sand gardens, poetry, the tea ceremony, and Zen.

Kohn, Livia. *Daoism and Chinese Culture*. Cambridge, MA: Three Pines Press, 2001. Kohn offers not just an introduction to Laozi and Zhuangzi but also an exploration of how their ideas were adopted by and adapted to later generations of Chinese thinkers, including people like Ge Hong.

Kupperman, Joel. *Classic Asian Philosophy: A Guide to the Essential Texts*. 2nd ed. New York: Oxford, 2006. Kupperman offers essays that are philosophically accurate but also accessible, insightful, and useful for those seeking for practical applications in their own lives. His chapters include discussions of the Upanishads, the Dhammapada (an early Buddhist text), the Bhagavad Gita, Confucius, Mencius, Laozi, Zhuangzi, and Zen.

Laozi. *Daodejing*. More than any other text mentioned in this course, students will benefit from reading multiple versions of the Daodejing. Fortunately, Laozi's book is quite short, and there are many reputable translations. I recommend four: D. C. Lau, *Lao Tzu: Tao Te Ching* (Penguin, 1964), Victor Mair, *Tao Te Ching: The Classic Book of Integrity and the Way* (Bantam, 1990), Robert G. Hendricks, *Lao-Tzu: Te-Tao Ching* (Ballantine, 1992), and Philip J. Ivanhoe, *The Daodejing of Laozi* (Hackett, 2003).

Lee, Peter, ed. *Sourcebook of Korean Civilization*. 2 vols. New York: Columbia University Press, 1993–1996. A groundbreaking collection of primary sources in translation from throughout Korean history.

Lieberthal, Kenneth. *Governing China: From Revolution to Reform*. 2nd ed. New York: Norton, 2003. A masterful survey of political thought and practice in China, from the Confucian ideology of the early empire to Mao Zedong's influence in the modern era.

McGreal, Ian P., ed. *Great Thinkers of the Eastern World*. New York: HarperCollins, 1995. This is probably the book that best mirrors the contents of this course. Highly recommended.

McLeod, W. H. *The Sikhs: History, Religion, and Society*. New York: Columbia University Press, 1989. An excellent introduction to the religion founded by Guru Nanak, with a focus on Nanak's own life and thought.

Mencius. *Mencius*. Translated by Irene Bloom. Edited by Philip J. Ivanhoe. New York: Columbia University Press, 2009. A recent, readable translation of the second greatest Confucian thinker after Confucius himself.

Miller, Barbara Stoller, trans. *The Bhagavad-gita: Krishna's Counsel in Time of War*. New York: Bantam Books, 1986. A lovely translation with a lucid introduction that will help readers make sense of the concepts behind the poetry.

———. *Yoga: Discipline of Freedom*. New York: Bantam, 1998. This is a full translation, with commentary, of Patanjali's Yoga Sutra. It's hard to imagine a more lucid, engaging rendition, particularly given the sometimes cryptic nature of the sutra genre in Indian philosophy.

Mir, Mustansir. *Iqbal*. London: I. B. Tauris, 2006. The best concise introduction to Iqbal's life and thought, with equal attention given to his prose and poetry.

Mitchell, Donald W. *Buddhism: Introducing the Buddhist Experience*. 2nd ed. New York: Oxford, 2007. If you want an overview of Buddhism in India, China, Japan, Korea, and the modern world, and if you're still not sure about the differences between Theravada, Mahayana, and Vajrayana Buddhism, this is the book for you. Mitchell puts the major thinkers into their historical contexts and shows the connections between them.

Moeller, Hans-Georg. *The Philosophy of the Daodejing*. New York: Columbia University Press, 2006. This brief work features all sorts of wise insights about a text that has puzzled readers for millennia. Moeller is particularly good at suggesting what Laozi's book might mean for modern readers.

Morris, Ivan. *The World of the Shining Prince: Court Life in Ancient Japan*. New York: Kodansha, 1994. Originally published in 1964, this classic study offers a fascinating glimpse into the unique historical setting that made possible both Murasaki Shikibu's *Tale of Genji* and Sei Shonagon's *Pillow Book*. In fact, those two works are primary sources for Morris's historical reconstruction of the era.

Nagarjuna. *The Fundamental Wisdom of the Middle Way: Nagarjuna's Mulamadhyamakakarika*. Translation and commentary by Jay L. Garfield. New York: Oxford University Press, 1995. There's no getting around it; this is a difficult text. But it is worth taking a look at to get a sense of the philosophical sophistication of the Buddhist tradition. This translation, from Tibetan sources, is in some ways easier to follow than earlier renditions from the original Sanskrit.

Powers, John. *Introduction to Tibetan Buddhism*. Rev. ed. Ithaca, New York: Snow Lion Publications, 2007. The subject of Tibetan Buddhism can be frustratingly complex and confusing. Powers does a fine job in identifying major themes and figures in a comprehensive, yet accessible manner.

Puligandla, Ramakrishna. *Fundamentals of Indian Philosophy*. Fremont, CA: Jain Publishing, 2007. This is one of the best overviews available of the entire range of Indian intellectual history, and Puligandla's explanations of sometimes rather difficult concepts are remarkably clear.

Radhakrishnan, Sarvepalli, and Charles Moore, eds. *A Source Book in Indian Philosophy*. Princeton, NJ: Princeton University Press, 1957. It might seem strange to recommend a book that is more than 50 years old, but this classic anthology is still in print, and for good reason. Radhakrishnan was one of the great Indian philosophers of the 20th century, and his collection of primary sources in Indian thought—particularly the six orthodox schools—is still a great place to begin an in-depth study of the subject.

Rahula, Walpola. *What the Buddha Taught*, Rev. and exp. ed. New York: Grove Press, 1974. A classic introduction to the ideas of the Buddha, with translations from major sutras (or suttas, as they are known in Pali).

Reid, T. R. *Confucius Lives Next Door: What Living in the East Teaches Us about Living in the West*. New York: Vintage, 1999. A humorous, intriguing investigation of the continuing influence of Confucianism in modern East Asia and how that social system compares with Western culture.

Schram, Stuart. *The Thought of Mao Tse-Tung*. Cambridge: Cambridge University Press, 1989. A detailed analysis of the ins and outs of Mao's ever-changing ideology, which continues to be prominent in contemporary China, at least in theory.

Selin, Helaine. *Encyclopaedia of the History of Science, Technology, and Medicine in Non-Western Cultures*. 2nd ed. 2 vols. New York: Springer, 2008. You will probably need access to a university library to find this reference work, but it is phenomenal in its coverage and insight.

Sen, Amartya. *The Argumentative Indian: Writings on Indian History, Culture, and Identity*. New York: Farrar, Straus and Giroux, 2005. Sen is a Nobel Prize winner in economics, and this collection of essays offers a great deal of insight into Indian civilization, but chapter 5, "Tagore and His India," is particularly useful. It is an ideal introduction to Tagore and Gandhi.

Sima Qian. *The First Emperor: Selections from the Historical Records*. Translated by Raymond Dawson. New York: Oxford University Press, 2009. If you are new to Sima Qian, or even to Chinese history, these engaging chapters concerning the unification of the China under the first emperor in 221 B.C. are a great place to begin.

Swann, Nancy Lee. *Pan Chao: Foremost Woman Scholar of China*. Ann Arbor, MI: Center for Chinese Studies, 2001. This biography of Ban Zhao (formerly spelled Pan Chao) was first published in 1932, but it is still the best study available, in part because it includes an annotated translation of all her extant works.

Sunzi. *Sun Tzu: The Art of War*. Translated by Samuel B. Griffith. London: Oxford, 1963. This is the classic version of the text, though Ralph D. Sawyer's translation, *The Complete Art of War* (Boulder, CO: Westview, 1996) includes a related, recently discovered manuscript as well.

Tagore, Rabindranath. *Rabindranath Tagore: An Anthology*. Edited by Krishna Dutta and Andrew Robinson. New York: St. Martin's Press, 1997. This collection offers a wide sampling of Tagore's extensive literary output from drama to fiction, letters to essays, and poetry to songs.

Terrill, Ross. *Mao: A Biography*. Rev. and exp. ed. Stanford: Stanford University Press, 2000. Mao remains a very controversial figure, but Terrill offers one of the more balanced and readable biographies available. For a shorter introduction, see Jonathan Spence's 1999 book *Mao Zedong*, in the Penguin Lives series.

Thapar, Romila. *Asoka and the Decline of the Mauryas*. Rev. ed. New York: Oxford University Press, 1998. This study, by one of India's most prominent historians, places Emperor Ashoka's rule and ideas into their original historical contexts. A classic work updated.

Varley, Paul. *Japanese Culture*. 4th ed. Honolulu: University of Hawaii Press, 2000. More than just a series of essays, this is a comprehensive history of Japan with a focus on culture, art, and thought. It is an ideal introduction to a unique civilization.

Williams, Paul. *Mahayana Buddhism: The Doctrinal Foundations*. New York: Routledge, 1989. This overview will help place the achievements of Nagarjuna, Vasubandhu, and Fazang into their proper intellectual context, so that readers can trace the development of the schools represented by those thinkers. Williams offers clear explanations of sometimes difficult concepts.

Wriggins, Sally. *The Silk Road Journey with Xuanzang*. New York: Basic Books, 2003. This is a fun example of popular history that still takes care to get the facts straight. Xuanzang's was an amazing pilgrimage that took him from China to India, and Wriggins (who actually retraces his steps) tells his story in an engaging fashion.

Zhuangzi. *The Complete Works of Chuang Tzu*. Translated by Burton Watson. New York: Columbia University Press, 1968. One of the most entertaining philosophical works ever written, translated with verve by one of the greatest translators of the 20th century.

Series

For those looking for brief overviews, the Very Short Introductions series published by Oxford University Press has volumes devoted to Buddhism, Hinduism, Gandhi, Buddha, Indian Philosophy, Buddhist Ethics, Sikhism, Modern China, and Modern Japan.

In addition, there are several short biographies in the Library of World Biography series (Pearson/Longman; edited by Peter N. Stearns) that are useful for this course, including those of Fukuzawa Yukichi, Sun Yat-sen, and Zheng He (the Ming dynasty admiral who commanded Chinese fleets that sailed to Southeast Asia, India, and even Africa).

The Penguin Classics series offers excellent translations (often with insightful introductions) to many of the texts that are discussed in the course, including Kautilya's *Arthashastra*, Sunzi's *Art of War*, the Bhagavad Gita, Buddhist Scriptures, the *Analects*, Laozi's *Daodejing* (or Tao Te Ching), Japanese No Dramas, the Mahabharata, *Mencius*, Sei Shonagon's *Pillow Book*, the Rig Veda, Murasaki Shikibu's *Tale of Genji*, the Upanishads, and *Zhuangzi* (they spell it Chuang Tzu).

Internet Sources

Diamond Sutra Recitation Group. *King Sejong the Great*. http://www.koreanhero.net/kingsejong/index.html. A 112-page pamphlet, this is not a critical biography by any means, but it provides a quick overview of the achievements of one the most admired figures in Korean history.

Internet Encyclopedia of Philosophy. http://www.iep.utm.edu. An online collection of articles on philosophers and philosophical movements, with special attention given to Chinese and Indian thought.

Sivin, Nathan. "Why the Scientific Revolution Did Not Take Place in China—Or Didn't It?" University of Pennsylvania. http://ccat.sas.upenn.edu/~nsivin/scirev.pdf. This is a 2005 revision of an article first published in 1982. It's a classic in the field.

Stanford Encyclopedia of Philosophy. http://plato.stanford.edu/contents.html. A massive database of philosophical essays written by experts. Many of the great minds in this course have articles devoted to them.

Credits

Text permissions

© Francisca Cho, 2004. Reprinted from *Everything Yearned For* with permission from Wisdom Publications, 199 Elm Street, Somerville, MA 02144 USA. www.wisdompubs.org

Chan, Wing-Tsit. *A Source Book in Chinese Philosophy.* Princeton: Princeton University Press, 1963. © Princeton University Press. Used by permission.

Music provided by

Digital Juice

Notes